*Our
Tempestuous
Day*

Also by Carolly Erickson

The Records of Medieval Europe
Civilization and Society in the West
The Medieval Vision
Bloody Mary
Great Harry
The First Elizabeth
Mistress Anne

Our Tempestuous Day

A History of Regency England

*Carolly
Erickson*

Quill

William Morrow

New York

Library of Congress Cataloging-in-Publication Data

Erickson, Carolly, 1943–
Our tempestuous day.

Bibliography: p.
Includes index.
1. Great Britain—History—1789–1820.
2. England—Social life and customs—
19th century.   I. Title.
[DA521.E75   1987]   942   86-30460
ISBN 0-688-07292-5

Printed in the United States of America

First Quill Edition

1 2 3 4 5 6 7 8 9 10

BOOK DESIGN BY JAYE ZIMET

To Marty

Preface

An old, mad, blind, despised, and dying King;
Princes, the dregs of their dull race, who flow
Through public scorn,—mud from a muddy spring;
Rulers who neither see nor feel nor know,
But leechlike to their fainting country cling
Till they drop, blind in blood, without a blow.
A people starved and stabbed in th'untilled field;
An army, whom liberticide and prey
Makes as a two-edged sword to all who wield;
Golden and sanguine laws which tempt and slay;
Religion Christless, Godless—a book sealed;
A senate, Time's worst statute, unrepealed—
Are graves from which a glorious Phantom may
Burst, to illumine our tempestuous day.

A few years ago I reread Shelley's familiar lines on England in 1819, and they set me to wondering. Shelley wrote of a diseased and violent society, yet Regency England is synonymous with gaiety and vigor, swagger and style—a style set, to a large extent, by the flamboyantly hedonistic Prince Regent.

The more I read about the decade of George IV's Regency—roughly the years between 1810 and 1820—the more I began to perceive its layers and complexities, and to understand how it could give rise to two such different images. For beneath the surface glitter of Regency life—the opulent interiors, the elegant dress, the grand, scenic architecture— was an underlying malaise, a pervasive emptiness and sense of loss that afflicted a wide spectrum of the populace. Equally powerful was a shift in the moral tone, an urge to uplift, improve and spiritually regenerate the realm—and the world, if possible. These forces, along with the explosive undercurrents of popular unrest and political radicalism, gave the decade its tensions, which worked themselves through amid war, recurrent economic crises and brutally rapid social change.

What follows is a portrait of that tempestuous, quicksilver age, written without any view to comprehensiveness but with an eye to recounting its events as they unfolded for those who lived through them. A great many well-known personalities—Shelley among them—are not mentioned here, but quite a few lesser-known and unknown characters are. What emerges, I hope, is what Regency audiences would have called a series of "transformation scenes," a kaleidoscopic sequence of views which, taken as a whole, circumscribe an age.

Through the months of research and writing this account I have been heartened and nurtured by Martin, Gabrielle and Tiffany Scolnick, Elizabeth Fishel, Jeremy Joan Hewes, Janet Peoples, and Linda Williams; by my editor, Lisa Drew; and by Alan Williams, whose encouragement and comments on the manuscript meant a great deal to me. My able assistant, Susan Svensson, provided essential help that eased the everyday tasks of writing. And my peerless agent, Lynn Nesbit, contributed not only expert professional advice but time and valued support. I am very grateful to all of them.

Albany, California
February 5, 1985

·

*F*irecrackers exploded in the Strand, frightening the horses in the street and attracting a crowd of cheering boys. An illuminated display rigged atop a tall building showed a huge anchor outlined in lights, and under it an immense likeness of King George in his royal robes. In the grand saloon of the City of London tavern an array of distinguished guests sat down to a lavish banquet in honor of the king, who looked down on them benignly from a large painting inscribed "By a grateful people to their King and Father, on completing the 50th year of his reign, October 25, 1810."

London was celebrating George III's Golden Jubilee. At seventy-two the king, who had reigned over England throughout his adult life, was still vigorous, still attentive to the everyday affairs of government. He was still able to force his large, fleshy body up onto a horse and ride for

.

hours with his sons and daughters in Windsor Great Park; he went sea bathing at his favorite resort of Weymouth, plunging into the icy water in the cold of early morning; he reviewed his troops and held court and lectured his thirteen children with as much energy as ever.

The immense crowds that came out into the streets to cheer the old king on his Royal Jubilee thought of him as a beloved father, or grandfather, an abiding presence in their lives. Few could remember when he had not been king. Many, perhaps the majority, could not remember the years of his prolonged unpopularity, when his subjects had hated him and called him a tyrant and made his life so bitter that he wanted to give up the throne. The very qualities his people had once ridiculed in him were now cherished—his unbending morality, his liking for plain dress, plain food and plain living, his saurian manner and stolid personality.

And his steady, old-fashioned courage. It was the quality the king himself admired most in others, and hoped for in his sons. He had it in abundance, and had displayed it when, ten years earlier, a would-be assassin shot at him at close range as he entered his box at the Drury Lane Theatre. The shots narrowly missed the king who, "on hearing the report of the pistol, retired a pace or two, stopped, and stood firmly for an instant; then came forward to the front of the box, put his opera-glass to his eye, and looked round the house without the smallest appearance of alarm or discomposure." The assailant was identified and taken out, and when the uproar had subsided in the theater, the patrons insisted on singing the national anthem three times over in honor of their stalwart monarch.[1]

The king's courage had heartened his people in their long war against the French. When Bonaparte prepared a vast invasion fleet to carry his soldiers across the Channel, the king declared himself ready, old as he was, to lead England's defending soldiers, and made plans to carry his proposal into effect. It was no wonder the people cheered him and erected statues of him, and wrote Jubilee odes in commemoration of his anniversary on the throne. One of these odes, "by an old midshipman," was printed in the *Morning Post*:

.

But, let what will come up—or rising stocks, or falling,
We Navy-lads, and th'Army too, on shore, in grand
    procession,
To Church will all repair—blessings from Heaven calling,
That health and glory George may hail, on many a blest
    accession!
      Then dine, and see who boasts,
      While "on both top-ropes swaying,"
      The most appropriate toasts,
      And loyal songs essaying;
      But, first and last, be sure we'll sing
      That glorious one—God save the King!
      And then next morning rise
To beat our foes, and bring home peace, that long-desired
    prize!
      HUZZA![2]

There were many who cried "Huzza!" on Jubilee night, yet the celebrations were muted, for the king was known to be laboring under great anguish of mind, and rejoicings seemed inappropriate. His youngest and most beloved daughter, Amelia, was dying. The family was gathered at Windsor, in sad anticipation of the princess's death, and the reports of her physicians left no hope that she might recover. She had given her father a keepsake, a ring into which were set one of her jewels and a lock of her hair. The inscription read "Remember Me." She had put it on his finger as he sat by her bedside, and the king, heartbroken at the thought of losing her, had burst into tears.

Now, however, the princess was nearly insensible, and could neither sleep nor eat. Her death was hours, at most days, away. She was thin and wasted, her face and features altered. At twenty-seven she was still girlish, more a child than a woman; though she had fallen in love with one of the king's equerries, Charles Fitzroy, she had not been allowed to marry him, and so she contented herself with leaving him everything she owned in her will.

Fitzroy was with King George on the morning of his Jubilee, as were Princes Frederick, Edward, and Adolphus and Princesses Augusta and Sophia. They took their morning exercise together, riding through the castle grounds with

.

11

several of the royal equerries for escort. Afterward the princes and princesses went to see their sister Amelia, but the king did not join them. He had been accustomed to visiting her very often, but now that her death was imminent he could not bear to see her, knowing that it might be for the last time. Twice before he had suffered the loss of a child. His son Alfred had died in infancy, and his son Octavius as a small boy. "There will be no heaven for me," he had said sadly at the time, "if Octavius is not there."

Waiting for Amelia to die put the king under great strain, a strain he found all the harder to bear as it came at a time of national and family crisis.

The war was going badly for England. Bonaparte was master of the continent, and the French fleet, though weaker than the British, was growing stronger month by month. Three years earlier, in 1807, Tsar Alexander I of Russia had made an alliance with the French; Bonaparte had recently taken an Austrian bride, Maria Louisa, cementing his Austrian alliance; the French occupied Prussia and, with the exception of a few rebellious regions, controlled or held in subordination the remaining European states.

Nor did there seem to be much hope that either Britain's government or her army could stand up against the invasion fleet Bonaparte continued to prepare on the Normandy coast. A personal feud within the Duke of Portland's government resulted in its collapse in 1809, and the one that succeeded it, under the lackluster leadership of Spencer Perceval, was indecisive and inept. England's one opportunity to strike a blow against the French on the battlefield, by supporting Spain, ended in disaster when the commander, Sir John Moore, was killed at Coruña and the British embarked for home.

Soon after this defeat, early in 1809, came the forced resignation of the Commander-in-Chief of the Army, Prince Frederick, Duke of York, the king's second son and his favorite. The duke was dishonored by a scandal in which it was alleged that he, with his mistress, Mary Ann Clarke, had profited from the sale of army promotions. After two long months of investigations in the House of Commons, the duke was

.

declared not guilty of corrupt practices, but his evident indiscretion in disclosing secrets to his mistress led to his dismissal. Besides being a loss to the army, the duke's disgrace saddened his father, who had always been proud of him.

Of all George III's sons, Frederick seemed to show most promise. He was a man's man, bluff and physical, resolute and practical. What he lacked in imagination he made up for in family loyalty, and if he matched his dissolute elder brother the Prince of Wales in gambling, drunkenness and womanizing, he did not let these pastimes incapacitate him. He was a good son, an obedient son, the kind of son a father could lean on in his old age—and in fact the king liked to put his weary head on Frederick's broad shoulder from time to time.

Frederick had been bred to be a soldier. By the age of seventeen, a colonel, he was sent to Hanover for further military training, returning six years later more handsome and self-confident than ever. Everyone spoke highly of him, praising his brotherly concern for the Crown Prince and talking of how he had fought a duel partly in his brother's defense. One of the queen's ladies had insulted the duke and his elder brother. Frederick replied in kind, whereupon the woman's son challenged him to a duel. In the ensuing contest the duke came within an inch of losing his life when his opponent's pistol ball grazed his head, cutting off a curl from his wig. But like his father, Frederick stood resolute in the face of danger, and preserved both his honor and his life.

The promotion scandal, however, showed him in a very bad light, and destroyed what credit he had won in public opinion as a reasonably able commander.[3] The rather sordid details of his liaison with Mary Ann Clarke came out in the parliamentary inquiry. Mrs. Clarke, a courtesan who lived grandly in a mansion where she employed twenty servants, had come to an agreement with the duke in which he promised to pay her a thousand pounds a month. The extravagance of this bargain compounded its immorality, but there was worse to come. The duke stopped paying Mary Ann, and to satisfy her creditors she had been reduced to taking bribes from officers wanting to move up in rank, promising them that she would use her influence with her royal lover on their behalf. The fact that Mrs. Clarke was "a very pretty woman," with a sweet voice and feminine manner, and that she gave "spirited and well applied answers" when questioned in the House only made the duke look worse. By the time the inquiry ended it was clear to nearly everyone that, while technically innocent, Frederick was responsible for everything that had happened. If only he had stayed at home, content with his wife, Princess Frederica, the whole unsavory chain of events would have been avoided.

Scandal was endemic in the royal family, yet the king refused to resign himself to it. He wanted to believe, in the face of overwhelming evidence to the contrary, that his wayward sons were not beyond redemption and that his adored daughters—"all Cordelias," as he called them—lived unblemished lives. (Knowing the effect it would have on him, the rest of the family left him in ignorance of the fact that Princess Sophia had borne an illegitimate child, the father an ugly, dwarfish little man thirty-three years her senior.) The king himself was upright and moral, the soul of propriety. Why should his children be so eager to depart from his model? Yet they did, repeatedly and, it often seemed to him, with a vengeance.

Most recently, the fifth son, Ernest, Duke of Cumberland, had managed to come under suspicion of murder.

Ernest was the least wholesome of George III's seven sons. Proud, vain and ill-humored, he took offense easily and was quick to imagine that he was being deprived of his rights or due rewards. A battle injury had scarred him, making him monstrous. ("His left eye," the Prince of Wales wrote, "is shockingly sunk, and has an amazing film grown over it.") Ernest had a propensity for making cruel mischief within the family, spreading rumors about his siblings and in-laws and poisoning their already precarious reputations with his "lies and malice," though he was capable of generous behavior toward them as well. He was intermittently fond of his eldest brother and quite fond too—some said overly fond—of his sister Sophia. It was the erotic side of his nature, in fact, that was alluded to in hushed tones. There were hints

.

(but no proof) that he had made sexual advances to Sophia—certainly the Prince of Wales thought him capable of this—and he may have been bisexual or homosexual.

This was what people said, at any rate, when the duke's valet was found lying on his bed in the ducal apartments with his throat cut. They conjectured that Ernest had seduced the valet, Joseph Sellis, who had then blackmailed him; the duke had murdered his blackmailer.

The circumstances of Sellis's death gave rise to suspicion. Though the jury at the inquest determined that Sellis had killed himself after attacking his master (who did receive a number of serious wounds), at least one expert witness noted that in order for Sellis's wound to have been self-inflicted the dead man would have had to be right-handed, but in fact he was left-handed. Furthermore, there had been bad feeling between the duke and his servant, with the former taunting Sellis "in his violent, coarse manner" and provoking his fury.

Murderer or not, Ernest was infamous. People would remember how for several days it was the fashion to go and visit his apartments at St. James's Palace, and to see the bloodstained walls and point out where the body and the razor had been found.[4] The incident gave them one more outrageous impropriety to lay at the door of the royal dukes, to their father's increasing dismay.

All this was on the king's mind as he prepared to meet his children on the night of his Jubilee. The war, his dying daughter and shameful sons, the state of his Electorate of Hanover which, thanks to Bonaparte's recent division of its territories between France and Westphalia, had ceased to exist. And most troubling of all, his dream.

It was a horrifying dream that always came to him the night before he fell ill, and he had dreamed it the previous night. He had been so alarmed that he told one of his confidants, "I am sure I am going to be ill—for I had the same dream last night that I have had every time the night before my illness."[5] It was no ordinary sickness that he feared, but a nameless affliction that in the past had gone on for months and whose symptoms resembled lunacy. It was hellish for

.

15

the king, nearly as bad for those around him and perilous for the nation.

And as King George entered the room, his wife, Queen Charlotte, on his arm, to greet his children the "dreadful excitement" in his countenance told them that their father was once again in the grip of his singular malady.

It had come upon him four times before, first when he was in his mid-twenties, then again at the age of fifty, and again at sixty-three and sixty-six. The symptoms were invariably the same—agitation, "hurry of spirits and an excessive love of talking," insomnia and severe abdominal spasms. Put simply, the king appeared to take leave of his senses.[6] He talked on and on, hour after hour, his words coming so rapidly at times as to be incoherent. He could not seem to stop talking. He contradicted himself, he repeated himself, he addressed the empty air, becoming more and more insistent the longer he went on until his voice grew hoarse and his veins stood out purple and swollen.

The king's "dreadful excitement" was fearsome to see, for he was out of control, desperately nervous, and his eyes, which bulged "like black currants," were the eyes of a madman. It was impossible to predict what he would say or do. He would suddenly jerk his bulky body up out of bed, dash from room to room in a frenzy, and roar off on some impossible errand. He imagined that London was sinking beneath the waves of a huge flood, and that he had to save the state papers before they were destroyed. He ranted on against the queen, and evoked the seductive shade of a woman he had once admired, Lady Pembroke. He mounted his horse and tried to ride it into a church. He dropped his breeches and displayed his backside. He embarked on a frenetic parody of kingliness, knighting his pages, sending dispatches to nonexistent courts abroad, discoursing incessantly on any and all subjects until speech gave way to a pitiable wailing that his wife and children found unbearable to listen to.

During the king's second attack, in 1788, the royal doctors announced that he was suffering from "biliary Concretions in the Gall Duct," and tried to agree on a treatment. More doctors were called in. They conjectured that the symptoms resulted from "the force of a humor which was beginning to show itself in the legs, when the king's imprudence drove it from thence into the bowels." The "humor" threatened his life, but the medicines they gave him to cure it "repelled it upon the brain," causing his erratic behavior. To draw it down into his legs again they forced the patient into hot baths, smothered him in blankets, and burned the soles of his feet with plasters of cantharides and mustard. Blisters erupted, and when in his pain the king tried to tear off his bandages the doctors shook their heads over his worsening violence and applied leeches to his temples to see if they couldn't draw off the humor that way.

The physical symptoms came and went, but the strange loquacity and odd imaginings persisted. It was whispered that the king was insane, and in time a doctor was brought in—some questioned his medical qualifications—who specialized in the treatment of lunatics. This man, Francis Willis, with his sons John and Robert initiated a mode of treatment that was little short of torture. Announcing that he "broke in" patients "as horses in a menage," Dr. Willis and his muscular "keepers" proceeded to treat the king like a crazed animal, immobilizing him by wrapping him in a winding sheet or fastening him into a straitjacket, his legs tied firmly to the bed. If his language became offensive, as it often did, a handkerchief was stuffed into his mouth. The Willises insisted on keeping control over their royal patient, determining when and how often he could have visitors and claiming precedence over his other doctors. Their medical philosophy was simple and, for its time, enlightened; other "mad doctors" treated their patients by repeatedly beating them into insensibility. The threat of forcible restraint put the patient into a state of "salutary fear," the Willises said, which tended both to encourage self-control and to bring his wandering wits back to reality.

Such was the intention of the straitjacket and the "restraining chair," into which the king was fastened for hours on end. Such was the intent, too, of the tartar emetic put into his food and drink, which made him so agonizingly nauseated that he wanted to die. The doctors meant well, but succeeded

.

only in enraging their suffering victim until he escalated his violence—which, naturally, led them to treat him with even greater severity.

Each time the disease appeared the king had in the end always recovered, suddenly and spontaneously, after, typically, a few months of incapacity. The mysterious malady vanished, the king regained his customary ponderous lucidity. There was always fear of a relapse, though, and for months following his recovery everyone around him watched him nervously, fearful that his slightest fever or stomach pain might be the indicator of a new attack. The queen was particularly apprehensive, having been terrorized by her raving husband when at the peak of his mania and refusing, after his last period of illness in 1804, to live with him any longer as his wife. She kept up appearances, she fulfilled her duties as queen and as mother to their children. But she locked her bedchamber door to the king, and would not go near him without a chaperone.

Tonight, though, she held his arm as he entered the room where his children were gathered to celebrate his anniversary, and continued to stay with him, as if trying to manage him, while he circled the room greeting each of his sons and daughters in turn.[7] They were all present but Amelia, and the eldest daughter, the queen's namesake Princess Charlotte, who was married to the King of Württemberg and lived abroad. The remaining four princesses were all still unmarried and living at home, a fact which made them increasingly irritable as they approached middle age and their heaviness and plainness became more pronounced. There was extroverted Augusta, and Elizabeth, practical and intelligent, warmhearted Mary, who had been tending her youngest sister during her long illness, and Sophia, mercurial and moody. The princesses adored their father, forgiving him his overprotectiveness. "My father," Princess Elizabeth would write later, "was the finest, purest, and most perfect of all characters. He was a man after God's own heart."[8] Their concern for him was at its height this evening, for it was clear that he was not himself. The queen, who "dragged him away" quickly from each person he talked to, was not

.

herself either, and it would be up to her daughters to soothe her once the evening was over.

Having greeted his daughters, King George turned to his sons, taking more time with them and speaking to each in turn individually. He squinted at each of them as they approached him—for he was nearly blind—and then, having determined which son it was, addressed him so loudly and uninhibitedly that the other guests were embarrassed. Though they differed widely in personality the seven royal dukes resembled one another strongly. Round-faced, with prominent, widely spaced eyes, large noses and full, sensuous lips, they had all grown portly with age and carried something of their father's leaden, porcine dullness in their expressions. Ernest had a malevolent gleam in his one good eye, and George, Prince of Wales, was capable of showing animation, but as a group the princes were fleshy and unimpassioned, the offspring of their stolid father and exceptionally ill-favored mother.

There was responsible, reliable Adolphus, Duke of Cambridge, sickly Augustus, Duke of Sussex, and the infamous Duke of Cumberland, still recovering from his wounds and staying temporarily with the Prince of Wales at his London residence, Carlton House. William, Duke of Clarence, came next, blunt and outspoken. Last of all the king talked with his two eldest sons, Frederick and George, leaving no one in doubt as to which one he preferred.

It galled him that the heir to the throne was not the manly Frederick but the womanish George, and his dislike of his heir had caused dissension in the family for decades. The king was seventy-two, the Prince of Wales nearly fifty. Their enmity had long ago congealed; they were at best incomprehensible to one another. The thought of the prince, hugely fat, elegantly attired and nervously unsettled, presiding in his stead made King George shudder. As for the prince, for years he had been wishing his father dead.

As he spoke to his sons the king acted strangely. His words were "sublime and instructive," but oddly chosen. The old familiar symptoms of his illness were recurring, the overly rapid speech, the compulsive loquacity, the vehemence and

.

agitation that always signaled the onset of his dreaded malady. Frederick had seen it coming the day before, when his father had rambled on to him about a scriptural quotation. "If the thing I tell you be true," the king had said accusingly to his son, "why will you not believe me and let me go my own way?" He went on without stopping to tell the duke of a parson who "preached me one of the best sermons upon that I ever heard upon that text. He preached that sermon in the morning, and then in the evening he preached the damnedest sermon that ever was heard."[9] The contradicting, the blasphemy were not characteristic of King George except when ill. Clearly he was on the verge of another relapse.

In London the trappings of the Golden Jubilee were taken down one by one. The fireworks went out, the crowds dispersed. The odes written for the occasion were recited and forgotten, and the huge paintings of the king and the banners saluting him were furled and stored away for another year. In her private lodge at Windsor Princess Amelia remained insensible, but alive; she would linger on for another week. But King George, already past grieving for her, was not to be aware of her death when it came. For by then he was himself dead to the world, dreaming that Amelia had gone to live happily in Hanover.

The doctors were summoned, but they found their patient lost in imaginings no one else could fathom. The family temporarily drew together in their time of crisis, the Prince of Wales now at their head. "The truth is," wrote George Canning, who was privy to affairs at court, "that poor old Knobbs is just as mad as ever he was in his life."

*A*n American businessman, Louis Simond, landed at Falmouth on the Cornish coast in the last days of 1809, curious to see England and the English at first hand. For the next twenty-one months he traveled the coach roads that linked the major cities and the cart tracks that wound into the rural hinterland, leading past fields and through hamlets seldom visited by outsiders. Simond was cosmopolitan, perceptive and articulate; born in France, he had emigrated to America and done well there. Worldly without being cynical, and without marked prejudice, he was uniquely suited to describe the England of the early Regency. As he traveled he kept a journal, and recorded in it with great sharpness and immediacy what he saw and heard in the course of his wanderings.[1]

The customs officers at Falmouth swarmed over the ship Simond arrived in, ransacking every cabin, spilling out the

.

contents of every barrel and chest and box searching for contraband and confiscating surplus stores, especially liquor. Their rigor in seizing as many of the ship's goods as they could was characteristic of what Simond called "this warlike and commercial country." So was the treatment he received. Because he had been born in France, England's enemy, he was not able to obtain a passport in Falmouth—as his fellow passengers were—but had to write to London for one. There were days of confusion and inconvenience, but no ill treatment. "Twenty-two years of absence have not expiated the original sin of being born in France," he wrote, "but I have no right to complain—an Englishman would be worse off in France."

The little port of Falmouth Simond judged to be "old and ugly"—as indeed it must have been by American standards. But its setting, in a peaceful, green harbor surrounded by gentle hills, was lovely. The tide washed at the foundations of the houses crowded along the shoreline, their steps were overgrown with seaweed. The people in the streets were ruddy-cheeked and well fed. Many of the men were wearing the uniforms of the volunteer regiments to which they belonged, while the women were "highly dressed, or rather highly undressed, in extremely thin draperies," their shoes clattering on the pavement as they passed.

Everyone in Falmouth, it seemed, was talking about the government's latest military fiasco, the Walcheren expedition. British troops had landed a few months earlier at the mouth of the Scheldt, with the aim of taking Antwerp and so launching an assault on Bonaparte from the west. But Antwerp proved to be too heavily defended, and most of the men were withdrawn, save one division occupying the marshy, windswept island of Walcheren. Miserable winter weather and an epidemic of "Walcheren fever" had killed some four thousand officers and men by the time the remnant force was ignominiously withdrawn, and of the men who returned alive, eleven thousand were disabled with the fever. Everyone was clamoring against the expedition and the ministers responsible for it, Simond wrote, and the dissatisfaction

.

was so widespread and so severe that the government was not expected to survive.

Simond set out for London early in the new year, 1810. His way led through open moorlands, which revealed "distances of great beauty; hills behind hills, clothed in brown and green, in an endless undulating line." The inns he rested in were comfortable and clean, staffed by courteous and obliging servants, and the farmhouses and outbuildings he passed, though old and poor, were "remarkably neat, and in great order." Their good state of repair impressed Simond; even the windows were kept clean and unbroken, with "no old hats or bundles of rags stuck in, as in America, where people build, but do not repair."

Inside, the cottages were meagerly furnished, with no rugs to cover the bare stone floors and only a few benches, a table or two, some shelves, and perhaps a spinning wheel. As it was the Christmas season, green boughs were hung around the walls. These were the dwellings of the laboring poor, yet despite their starkness they seemed comfortable. "The poor do not look so poor here as in other countries." In England, "poverty does not intrude on your sight," the American remarked. "It is necessary to seek it." To be sure, there were a few beggars on the roads, but many more soldiers, hurrying on foot and in carriages toward Plymouth, where they were to embark for the continent.

The congestion on the roads began to increase a good deal by the time Simond reached the outskirts of the capital. The overladen coach seemed to take forever to cover the last ten or fifteen miles. It stopped every half-mile or less to crowd in more and more passengers, most of whom sat outside, clinging to the top of the swaying vehicle which threatened to overturn each time it gathered speed. With each stop there were fresh quarrels over fares, over seating space, "the getting up, and the getting down, and damsels showing their legs in the operation, and tearing and muddying their petticoats— complaining and swearing."

As they entered the great metropolis a smoky haze engulfed them, and the coach was soon lost in a maze of busy,

.

dirty streets. "A sort of uniform dinginess seemed to pervade every thing," Simond wrote. Even the people wore dark, dull clothes, "harmonizing with mud and smoke." The shop windows were bright with color, and a delicious aroma of fresh buns and tarts floated out into the streets from the pastrycook shops. But the overall impression of the city was uninviting, as of a monstrous thing swollen out of recognition. "This palpable immensity has something in it very heavy and stupefying," the visitor remarked, and he felt uneasy and helpless in its midst.

From a smallish medieval town London had grown, in the reign of Queen Elizabeth I, to a city whose two focal points were the Tower and the mercantile City in the east and Westminster Abbey and St. James's in the west, the two regions connected by the riverside highway of the Strand with its palaces and gardens. Over the hundred years that followed Queen Elizabeth's death new streets and squares came into being to fill in the open fields and marshlands between the commercial east and political west of the city, and the areas around Lincoln's Inn, Covent Garden and adjacent neighborhoods became crowded with emigrants from the countryside.

The growth of London accelerated throughout the eighteenth century, the red brick of Tudor and Stuart buildings yielding to the gray and brown brick of the Georgian city. An orderly grid of pavements spread out from the crooked medieval lanes of the old town, reaching ever farther north and westward and southward into Southwark and Lambeth. Along the river, wharves and piers increased in number, and eastward beyond the Tower the ring of unhealthy, overcrowded slums widened.

Simond arrived in London at a turning point in her history, as she was on the threshold of renewal and aesthetic reinvigoration. But of course he had no hint of this as he settled into lodgings near Portman Square in the fashionable West End, and began gradually to get his bearings and to accustom himself to the rhythm of the city's life.

Nothing and no one stirred before ten o'clock in the morning, he noted, when the shops began to open. The daily parade of the Horse Guards from the barracks to Hyde Park, cymbals crashing and drums pounding, punctuated the morning's idleness, but it was not until three or four o'clock in the afternoon that fashionable people went abroad to pay visits, shop or attend the crowded assembly rooms. Midafternoon was the beginning of the fashionable day, which went on until the early hours of the morning.

At dusk the streetlights were lit—the new technological marvel of gaslight—which gave the effect, Simond thought, of "two long lines of little brightish dots," yielding little illumination, as there were no reflectors. While this went on people were dressing for dinner, and from six to eight o'clock carriages rolled noisily past in ever-increasing numbers, delivering well-turned-out passengers to their hosts' and hostesses' doorsteps. The guests did not knock on the doors themselves; instead a footman jumped down from the box, lifted the heavy door knocker, and rapped out a tattoo "with an art, and an air, and a delicacy of touch, which denoted the quality, the rank, and the fortune of his master."

For the next two hours the streets were quiet, but at ten o'clock the noise of passing carriages began again, louder than ever, as loud, Simond thought, as the thundering of Niagara Falls. It was "a universal hubbub," "a sort of uniform grinding and shaking, like that experienced in a great mill with fifty pair of stones." Not until midnight did the terrible hubbub begin to abate, and at one o'clock it was still difficult to sleep for all the commotion. Gradually, though, the number of carriages diminished until, as the sky began to grow light, only a single carriage was heard now and then at a great distance. The fashionable world went to sleep, not to be roused until long after noon.

Such was the rhythm of London west of Soho Square; of the regions to the east and south the American wrote little or nothing, though it was here that the vast majority of people lived. With all its vanities, Simond preferred the fashionable world, though its amusements, he found, did not always repay the effort and inconvenience it took to pursue them.

He described the style of party-giving that prevailed in

.

the great squares. Invitations were issued weeks in advance, advising guests that the host and hostess would be "at home" on a certain day. The guests presented themselves, often delayed by a long line of waiting carriages clogging the street. After perhaps half an hour they were admitted. The hostess greeted them, and then came the tedium and discomfort of milling through the well-dressed crowd. "Nobody sits," Simond wrote, "there is no conversation, no cards, no music; only elbowing, turning, and winding from room to room; then, at the end of a quarter of an hour, escaping to the hall door to wait for the carriage, spending more time upon the threshold among footmen than you had done above stairs with their masters."

Then it was on to the next "at home," and so on throughout the evening. A party or, to use the current term, a "rout," was a highly public affair, no matter how exclusive the guest list might be. The mass of carriages in the street gave its location away, and the blaze of light from the unshuttered, uncurtained windows showed a display of well-coiffed heads that left no doubt as to what was going on inside. To be seen to entertain, as well as to be entertained by others, was essential to high society, as was, Simond reckoned, a fortune of at least three thousand pounds a year, preferably six.

What struck the American most about London were its vast extent, its smoky, sooty atmosphere ("like a great round cloud attached to the earth") and its political climate. Everyone discussed politics, vehemently and constantly, the women growing even more heated than the men. The government was not only criticized, it was ridiculed; ministers were depicted in outrageous caricatures, and people eagerly bought the prints and hung them in their houses. Political issues were thoroughly aired, and so were the politicians' marriages, family conflicts and love affairs, their duels, and their winnings and losses at the gaming table. Parliament was nearby—the Lords and Commons met in a group of old buildings near Westminster Hall—and anyone respectably dressed who handed the doorkeeper five shillings could listen to the debates. The air was electric with controversy. Conversation was haunted by a "plaintive mania": the government was about to fall, taxes were destroying the country, the City faced financial ruin, a dreadful crisis was upon England.

Yet having delivered themselves of these pronouncements of doom, Simond noted, Londoners went about living their lives "just as if they had nothing to fear." It was their habit to be in a constant state of alarm; they were sincere, but their anxiety did not paralyze them, and business, government, and amusement went on as usual.

Outside the capital the intensity of political debate was much tempered, Simond found, as he set off on the next stage of his tour of the country. Opinions were more moderate, people spoke less often about revolution and crisis. The newspapers and political journals Londoners devoured were not always available in provincial towns, and criticism of the government was balanced by a sense of stability and permanence that arose from the immemorial pattern of rural life. For hundreds of years that pattern had remained the same: the master in his great house and the tenants in their cottages. No matter what was said or done in the capital, the social order in the rest of England seemed secure.

Early in July of 1810 Simond left for the West Country, then traveled through Wales—"nothing wild, or properly speaking, picturesque, but all highly beautiful"—which struck him as more densely populated than other regions he had passed through. All the buildings were resplendent with whitewash, even the roofs and chimneys, and there were roses and honeysuckle in the cottage gardens, and neat stone paths leading to their doors. The language the people spoke to one another was unintelligible to outsiders, but they addressed visitors in English at the inns. Northward, near Aberystwyth, the cottages became fewer and the terrain hilly and remote. Here the inns were few and far between, and the people Simond encountered seemed to him to lead narrower lives than their fellow countrymen to the south. "The farmer knows nothing beyond the plough," he noticed, "and the post-boy only that part of the road to the next stage." The solitude closed in, there were no post-horses to be had, only plow horses taken from the fields and made to pull the coach.

.

27

Early in August Simond crossed the border into Scotland, and right away the scenery changed. "We passed this afternoon a tract of country very different from England," he wrote. "It is a succession of steep hills, with intervening valleys, all uniformly covered with a fine green turf, smooth, and unbroken by a single tree, bush, weed, or stone; sheep hanging along the sides of the acclivities, and here and there a shepherd-boy wrapped up in his plaid—nothing to interrupt the sameness and stillness, but the little stream bustling along each valley, over a bed of round pebbles."

Fields of potatoes and oats filled the cultivable areas, and as it was August haymaking went on from dawn to dusk. Yet Scotland was nothing like so fertile and productive as Wales, and the people lived in poverty. Crude dwellings sheltered beasts along with their masters; heaps of dung were piled against the outside walls along with the stacks of peat used for fuel. The families Simond saw were dressed in ragged plaids, the dirty children climbing on the dunghills, the men looking faintly like ancient Romans in their kilts.

He did not venture far into the Highlands, but spent some three months in Edinburgh, a city as far behind London in sanitation as it was in population. (Simond estimated that London was ten times more populous.) Every sort of filth was thrown into the streets, to the peril of pedestrians. "Passing through the narrow streets, morning and evening, you scarcely know where to tread, and your head is as much in danger as your feet." A cry of "gardy loo!" (a corruption of "*Gardez l'eau!*") gave warning that refuse from an upper story was on its way down, but there was not always time to get out of the way. Fortunately it rained nearly every day; the showers must have cleansed the pavements a little.

Edinburgh society imitated that of London, with assemblies and "at homes," fine houses and fine clothes. But because everything was on a much smaller scale, the entertainments were less crowded, and consequently—to Simond's pleasure—it was possible to converse, play cards or chess, or read the books and pamphlets left in a careless heap on a corner table.

The veneer of social refinement in the northern city was

.

noticeably thin. Well-dressed, highly respectable women, turned out in gown, gloves, hat and umbrella, were in the habit of walking through the streets barefooted. And as often as not they walked among laborers recently arrived from country villages, reeking of the animals they lived with, and the shabby poor of the town. Simond described the Edinburgh fishwives, carrying enormous loads of fish strapped across their chests, singing as they tramped along on their way to market. "They look strong, healthy, and very cheerful," he wrote, "but in general remarkably ugly."

Simond liked Edinburgh's mild climate, the beauty of its setting, and the relative unpretentiousness of its people. The constant juxtaposition of gentility and raw country manners charmed him. "Taken altogether," he concluded, "I do not know any town where it would be pleasanter to live. It is, to a great degree, the Geneva of Britain."

For the next month, in the late winter of 1811, Simond toured the north of England and the Midlands. The contrast between barren Scotland and the relatively cultivated North Country was unmistakable. Though not beautiful the land was productive, the farms with their innumerable haystacks and windmills were orderly and their inhabitants cleaner and plumper than the Scots. At Newcastle the American toured a coal mine and made notes on the immense quantities of coal sent to London—five hundred coal ships, each loaded with two hundred tons of coal, made the trip to the capital twelve times a year.

Farther south, approaching Leeds, the coach passed vast flocks of sheep, grazing in turnip fields. Plowing was under way, and the black earth of the plowed fields stood out amid the vivid green of the meadows. Though it was early March the weather was warm and springlike, and the trees were budding.

Night had fallen when Simond reached Leeds, "and from a height, north of the town," he wrote, "we saw a multitude of fires issuing, no doubt from furnaces, and constellations of illuminated windows (manufactories) spread over the dark plain." The commercial nerve center of the town was the clothiers' hall, for Leeds was a cloth town. But the industry

.

was severely depressed, and the weavers, whose wages had been falling steadily for years, were lucky now to find employment at all, as exports of finished cloth dropped by half. Simond heard about the discontented workers, desperate and wretchedly poor, "brutified, vicious, and troublesome to their employers," chafing under their enforced idleness and looking "with an evil eye" on the machines they feared would replace them.

Sheffield was "another steam-engine town, all iron, and steel, and smoke," but Birmingham was the manufacturing center par excellence, and there a local merchant led Simond on an extensive tour of the factories.

"The manufactories are mostly of hardware and glass, and are less unhealthy, although more dirty, than those of Manchester and Glasgow, which require heat and confined air, and clog the lungs with floating particles of cotton." A technique had been discovered of keeping much of the coal smoke out of the air—a technique which could be put to great use in London, Simond thought—and the factories were lit by burning hydrogen gas, which made them "absolutely as light as day."

One factory employed three hundred workers who produced ten thousand gun barrels a month. Here iron was pounded flat by huge steam-powered hammers, then molded into shape. Large millstones used to polish the metal turned so rapidly that they splintered under the strain, sending fragments hurtling through the walls or the roof and causing accidents. The power of the giant machines was awesome: immense mechanical scissors cut bars of iron as easily as if they had been paper; metal was melted and poured like butter, or rolled flat like pastry.

Elsewhere Simond thought "much ingenuity was miserably wasted" in the manufacture of such unnecessary if intriguing things as "extraordinary cheese-toasters," toys, walking sticks that folded out into chairs, pocket umbrellas, and similar gadgets.

A book Simond had read described the horrors to which Birmingham workers were exposed. Their complexions were clogged with dust and oil and smoke, the author claimed,

.

their eyes were perpetually bloodshot and their hair was tinged with green from their nearness to the brass works. Simond could find no trace of these telltale blemishes. To him the workers looked healthy, and were not only polite but generous with their time, stopping work (and losing money, for they were paid by the piece) to answer questions and explain what they were doing.

From Birmingham Simond went via Warwick to Oxford, which to him looked "old, dusty, and worm-eaten, the streets silent and deserted." He stopped too at Windsor, whose terraces and towers, with banners floating in the wind, pleased him. The king was walking on the North Terrace, and Simond got as close as he could to catch a glimpse of him. He was wearing his customary plain blue coat and a hat that flapped over his eyes. General Manners, an aide, walked beside him, holding him under the arm while he strode rapidly up and down, talking all the time "with an appearance of earnestness" and so loudly that he could be heard twenty yards away. He looked thin and stooped, though energetic. "This does not look like recovery," Simond recorded, and went on to complete the final leg of his journey back to London.

By the time Simond left England early in the fall of 1811, having spent nearly two years observing the country and its people, he was convinced of its prosperity and of the underlying soundness of its political system. "There is really, notwithstanding the loud complaints, an inundation of wealth in the country," he wrote. Despite the drastic decline in trade, the wave of bankruptcies, the falling wages and rising prices that hurt workers so cruelly and the bare lives of the country poor, there were riches abundant, and with them a sense of comfort in everyday life that ought to be the envy of other countries. However corrupt and badly administered, the political system was robust, built as it was on a sound and venerable social system.

And there was something else unique to England. The sophistication, opinions and manners of the capital leavened the entire country. "There are no retired places in England," Simond remarked when staying at Windermere far to the

.

north of London, "no place where you see only the country and countrymen; you meet, on the contrary, everywhere town-people elegantly dressed and lodged." England, he thought, was "the country-house of London." "Here we are, in a remote corner of the country, among mountains, 278 miles from the capital—a place without commerce or manufactures, not on any high road; yet everything is much the same as in the neighborhood of London." Everything but the scenery, of course; that was picturesque. The Londoners who went to Windermere in such numbers went there for the vistas of cloud and lake and mist-enshrouded mountains. But they had trouble finding servants. "It is plain that there are too few poor for the rich."

Other travelers who visited England in the early years of the Regency came to the same conclusions Simond did— that neither the country's appalling government nor the appalling outspokenness of the opposition presented any real threat to England's stability and prosperity, or to the generally enviable life of her citizens. But they, like Simond, recorded another dimension of English life, one that might have disturbed them more had it not been so commonplace. This was the omnipresence of the military, the reminders visitors met with at every turn that England was a nation at war.

There were soldiers everywhere, on the high roads, marching in their columns, in the streets, in the taverns and inns. Martial music accompanied many public functions, recruiting went on in the open air. Military monuments were raised in village and town squares—"How many monuments to Nelson we have met in England!" Simond exclaimed—and it was a rare Englishman or woman who had no relative or friend wounded or killed in the war.

At Bristol Simond could see, from his hotel room, the five regiments quartered in the town exercising on the square before the cathedral. At Ormskirk, thirteen miles from Liverpool, the local militia was assembled, "and looked full as well as troops of the line, performing their exercise with great precision." There was a grand review held on Wimble-

don Common in June of 1811, and the American went to
see it, as he had heard the Prince Regent was to take part.
He ordered his driver to wedge his carriage in among the
hundreds of others that ringed the immense parade ground,
and watched as the troops were drawn up in two parallel
lines, each line some two miles long. The Regent appeared,
an hour late, looking "fat and fair" and mounted on a magnificent horse. The crowd had grown impatient waiting for him,
as the day was very hot and there were thunderclouds on
the horizon. But the review was impressive enough once it
began, with the men firing in sequence from one end of
the long line to the other and back again in a continuous
ripple of movement and sound.

Some 200,000 people, by Simond's estimate, turned out
to watch the review on Wimbledon Common, arriving in
carriages or on foot—the pedestrians renting space, once they
arrived, on carts and wagons provided by enterprising farmers. The crowd was so large and so unruly that squads of
light horsemen had to ride the bounds of the field to keep
order. The people watched the spectacle, cheered for the
soldiers, ran in every direction when the volley of gunfire
made the horses rear, damaging the wagons.

After nearly twenty years of war Londoners were so habituated to its violence and pomp that they thirsted for the
sight of soldiers standing smartly in unbroken lines, their
uniforms bright with color, flourishing their arms with precision and aplomb. The pageantry of war, its dazzling ritual
thrilled them; never mind that England's wartime fortunes
had never been bleaker than in this year of 1811.

A few months after the disastrous Walcheren expedition
ended a new popular panorama was presented in the capital.
It re-created the British bombardment of Flushing, which
had gone on for two days and nights while the greater part
of the town was burned and some six hundred civilians were
killed. "The spectator is placed in the middle of the town,
on top of some high building," wrote Simond, who witnessed
it. "Bombs and rockets pierce the roofs of the houses, which
are instantly in flames, or burst in the middle of the streets,

.

full of the dismayed inhabitants, flying from their burning dwellings with their effects, and carrying away the sick and wounded."

It was a devastating scene, though not as devastating as the actual bombardment. (A British soldier who watched the destruction of Flushing from a vantage point while on sentry duty wrote about it immediately afterward. "The roaring of guns and mortars, the hissing of rockets, shot and shells, the chiming of the church bells, the French sentries calling at intervals 'All's well,' the noise of the people trying to extinguish the fires, but above all, the heart rending cries of the poor women and children, beggars description."[2])

The panorama the Londoners experienced was very real—yet unreal. The houses they saw burning were not real houses, full of helpless people; the bursting rockets and leaping flames were all artifice, a stage set. It was not horror but the phantasm of horror that people flocked in such numbers to see. Simond found it abhorrent. "At the sight of so much misery, all the commonplaces about war become again original, and the sentimental lamentations on suffering humanity oppress and sicken the soul, as if they were uttered for the first time." But his was the reaction of a foreigner. To Londoners the exhibition was cathartic, it gave them a pleasurable frisson of danger even as it horrified them. They lived, as the American had noted, in a constant state of alarm, of heightened excitement. In such a state a vision of catastrophe was oddly soothing.

.

3

*T*he incapacity of the king in late October of 1810 triggered a political crisis of the first magnitude. No one could say when, or if, he would recover. Meanwhile the ordinary course of public business was halted. Parliament was temporarily adjourned. Politicians met in worried knots to speculate and argue over who would gain power and who would lose it. There was uncertainty every-where, and it affected the stock market, the timbre of social life, even the literary world. ("The present momentous state of public affairs is arresting the attention of every one," wrote the novelist Walter Scott, "and I have seldom seen a more dull publishing season.")

If King George did not recover soon, there would have to be a caretaker government, a Regency, with the Prince of Wales as Regent. But the government was Tory, and the prince had been a lifelong Whig; a Regency would therefore

·

mean the fall of the government. Moreover, it would mean a new government plagued by confusion and lack of direction, for the Whigs, having been (save for one brief period) long out of office, were unused to power and had been without clear leadership since the death of their longtime head, Charles James Fox, four years earlier.

As the weeks went by, the Tories insisted that the king's recovery was imminent, while the Whigs vociferously asserted that they knew him to be "very bad—at the last gasp," and celebrated their approaching return to power in advance by giving parties and congratulatory dinners. Their joy at their sovereign's debility was thought to be indecent by some, premature by others. Nothing at all could be done, of course, until after the doctors had given their opinion. Parliament reconvened, with both parties rounding up their supporters so energetically that the roads were "covered with messengers, official and unofficial, to bring up Lords and Commons, ministerial and opposition of all kinds and sects." The doctors made their appearance, and discussed their patient's condition, but succeeded only in deepening the general uncertainty.

The king was definitely not insane, said Dr. Robert Willis, merely deranged, or delirious. True, when in his delirious state he had no idea who he was, or who anyone else was, and imagined himself now "hunting and halloing with hounds, now commanding an army and leading it to battle, now talking with visionary objects." But even so, these "waking dreams" were quite unlike the cunningly plausible reasoning of the madman. In fact, said Willis's colleague, Dr. Reynolds, the king's memory was good, his acuteness of mind considerable. It was only his judgment that was hopelessly askew. Furthermore—and here all the doctors concurred—there was a good chance of his recovery.

That King George's derangement fell short of lunacy comforted no one, particularly as those who had seen him reported that he had grown terribly thin and kept up his old habit of incessant talking ("a sort of wailing, most horrible and heartrending to hear").[1] Unless he improved very considerably, and very rapidly, a Regency bill would have to be proposed. There was no alternative.

Toward the end of December the Prime Minister, Spencer Perceval, introduced a bill establishing a restricted Regency for twelve months, and debate over it began. Prolonged debate was unwise, given the urgent issues facing the government. The war danger had never been greater, yet it seemed likely that, barring a financial miracle, there would be little or no money in the Treasury to continue it. There was a trade crisis. Firms were being forced into bankruptcy, and those that managed to avoid it were having to cut their workers' wages and working hours drastically. Less obvious but much more insidious was the increasing depreciation of the pound, with war payments draining gold from the Treasury in alarming amounts. These dangers called for immediate attention, yet through January debate continued over the Regency and its precise form. Meanwhile the king, to the exasperation of everyone save his Tory ministers, became lucid for longer and longer stretches of time and threatened to throw the whole mechanism of government into confusion again.

No one was more agitated by the prevailing uncertainty than the Prince of Wales, whose excitable nerves were constantly on edge, even at the calmest of times. He was not an entirely well man—probably he suffered from his father's malady in a milder form—and it took very little to send him into a state of extreme anxiety, triggering a host of physical symptoms from high fever and galloping pulse to abdominal spasms and, ultimately, complete collapse.

With his unique capacity for self-dramatization Prince George saw himself rather than his father at the center of the political maelstrom, and the realization that he might soon have to face the burdensome tasks of kingship left him tense and drained. There would be factions, the ministers would squabble and intrigue among themselves. He would have to confront them, control them. The image of himself as Regent was immensely flattering to the prince's vanity, even though it made his knees weak and sent him running to the liquor cabinet. But as the weeks of indecision went by and he began to imagine himself in the Regent's role, he found the waiting harder and harder to bear. One minute he blustered about how he would show the world his courage, when the time came; the next he was complaining of illness, dosing himself with laudanum and canceling appointments he said he was not well enough to keep.

At forty-eight the prince was still boyish. There was something puckish in his face, an air of mischief and even of innocence that went oddly with his almost indecently corpulent body. His features had always been more pretty than handsome, round and cherubic, set off by a fine head of light brown hair that had not yet begun to thin. When at his best his grace of manner was extraordinary, though he was often not at his best, or even civil. His boyishness had its petulant side; he sulked, he was capable of malice. He could be cruel. But when in the company of a carefully chosen group of guests, enjoying an excellent dinner, he blossomed into conviviality and showed his rare charm.

"I had the honor last Tuesday of dining with the Prince of Wales at Lord Melbourne's," Charles Burney, an eminent historian of music, wrote in a letter to his daughter Fanny in 1805. "He is so good-humored and gracious to those against whom he has no party prejudice, that it is impossible not to be flattered by his politeness and condescension."[2]

Lord Melbourne kept a very good table, and a fine wine cellar, and the prince drank heavily all evening long. "I was astonished to find him, amidst such constant dissipation, possessed of so much learning, wit, knowledge of books in general, discrimination of character, as well as original humor," Dr. Burney continued. "He quoted Homer in Greek to my son as readily as if the beauties of Dryden or Pope had been under consideration. And as to music, he is an excellent critic."

The party was still going on at one in the morning, when Lady Melbourne and her daughters came home from the theater. Coffee was served, and the conversation flowed on, with Prince George living up to his reputation as a matchless raconteur and entertaining the company with his accom-

.

plished mimicry. Hours later, he wished them a princely good night, leaving Burney with the impression that for depth of culture and refinement of breeding he had no equal. "Besides being possessed of a great fund of original humor, and good humor, he may with truth be said to have as much wit as Charles II, with much more learning," he concluded.

Burney had seen Prince George at his most relaxed and comfortable. On other occasions he turned on his guests, becoming nasty and ugly, or else embarrassed them by becoming so drunk that he was violently sick on the floor. He was capricious and unpredictable, a victim of his moods and of a constitution that fluctuated according to the condition of his nerves. As he approached fifty he was beginning to show signs of age and strain. He had recently put on much more weight, and was said to be "grown enormously large." An acquaintance who saw him at Weymouth in 1809 thought that he had changed for the worse, the lines deepening around his mouth and eyes, his complexion sallow.[3] He was walking with his younger brother Adolphus along the Esplanade, taking large quantities of snuff from a snuffbox he carried in his coat pocket, and it was impossible not to notice the contrast between Prince Adolphus's "elastic vigor" and his elder brother's tired gait. "He has a shattered look," the observer remarked, and was amazed at how much his appearance had altered.

The prince had been shattered, as he himself might have said, by love.

He was an obsessively amorous man, and leaving aside his wife—for whom he felt only aversion and hatred—he had been infatuated with a succession of mistresses virtually all of his adult life. One of these women, Maria Fitzherbert, stood out as something more than a mistress.

She had been twenty-eight when he met her, he twenty-two, and within hours of their meeting the prince had fallen utterly in love with her; within months he had sworn to renounce the throne, if need be, in order to make Maria his wife. Fearful of losing her, he resorted to the desperately romantic gesture of attempting suicide, and she, deeply affected by the sight of his wounded body, limp and blood-

·

stained, agreed to allow him to place a ring on her finger in token of marriage.

To the extent that this informal ceremony was in any way binding, it offended legality several times over, for not only was the prince too young to marry without his father's consent, but in marrying a twice-widowed Roman Catholic he excluded himself from succession to the throne. However, Prince George and Maria Fitzherbert lived very much as man and wife for the following two decades, with interruptions for the prince's marriage of state to Princess Caroline of Brunswick and for his intermittent infidelities. But with the prince in his early forties and Maria nearly fifty, their long attachment had cooled. Lady Hertford, a handsome, haughty and rather imperious woman, quickened a new infatuation in him, and he began to "fret himself into a fever" over her with his customary nervous ardor.

He wrote letters to Lady Hertford day and night, imploring her to leave her husband and come to live with him, and when she refused, he panicked. In need of a substitute— in need, in fact, of anything womanly and warm—he threw himself on Henrietta, Lady Bessborough, who afterward described their nearly indescribable encounter.

"He has killed me—such a scene I never went through!" she wrote to her lover, Lord Granville Leveson Gower, in December of 1809. He "threw himself on his knees, and clasping me round, kissed my neck before I was aware of what he was doing. I screamed with vexation and fright; he continued sometimes struggling with me, sometimes sobbing and crying."

The display of hysterics went on for hours, and gradually, as Lady Bessborough realized that Prince George was driven more by insecurity than lust, she began to see the humor in the situation. Vows of eternal love, entreaties, despair, promises succeeded one another, all emanating from "that immense, grotesque figure flouncing about half on the couch, half on the ground." Had not her heart been breaking, she wrote, she would have laughed out loud. Finally she succeeded in convincing her elephantine suitor that she could

.

never consent to be his mistress, after which they "came to a tolerably friendly making up," and the prince tried her patience for two more hours, gossiping about other people's love affairs.

Lady Bessborough was very much a woman of the world, and knew a good deal about love and the strange things it made people do, but even so the prince's behavior was repellent to her. "I really felt revolted and indignant at his disgusting folly," she told Lord Granville, and no wonder.[4]

Without Maria to steady him, and lacking any other woman to fully take her place—though Lady Hertford came as close as any—Prince George languished. Then came his father's illness, and the months of indecision over the Regency issue, months that were at the same time a period of mourning for Princess Amelia. Her death demoralized her eldest brother, who had always been tenderly affectionate toward her. She had called him "dearest Eau de miel" (dearest Honeywater) and had trusted him as her executor, and when she died he was said to be "deeply affected." He engaged an artist to make a death mask of her face, only to be deterred by the opposition of some of the princess's servants, who disliked the idea. Her illness had ravaged her features too much, they said, and the project was dropped.

The new year of 1811 began, and debate over the Regency bill continued. The merits of Prince George, and his fitness to be Regent, were endlessly discussed. And there was another issue that called for discussion, though it was a very awkward and delicate one: the issue of the Princess of Wales.

Prince George had married Princess Caroline in 1795—no one, except the pope and Maria Fitzherbert herself, had ever taken Maria's pseudo-marriage to the prince seriously—and had regretted it ever since. Caroline of Brunswick was his first cousin, the daughter of his father's sister. Their close relationship would in itself have made her unsuitable as his wife, especially as there was a strong taint of mental instability in the immediate family which any children she had would be likely to inherit. But Caroline had further disadvantages. She was short and heavy, graceless, unattractively

·

buxom and with "jutting hips." She dressed very badly, was slovenly and, inexcusably, smelly, since she was careless about bathing and changing her underwear.

Astonishing as such lapses were in a future Princess of Wales and Queen of England, there was worse. Caroline was notoriously loose in her morals, and her promiscuity and lack of self-control were common knowledge. She liked men, she enjoyed making love, and enjoyed it, quite simply, as often as possible. She was, by any standard, the wrong choice, even for a prince who professed not to care whom he married as he had no intention of loving her as a wife. He was forced to marry, to ensure the succession and because, once he married, Parliament would not be so intransigent about settling his disgracefully large debts. But as to whom he married, one German princess was as good as another. It was said that the prince's then current favorite, Lady Jersey, goaded him into marrying the ill-famed and ill-favored Caroline deliberately to vex her own rival, Maria Fitzherbert. Whatever the truth of this, the folly of Prince George's choice blighted his life for a quarter of a century.

By 1811 the Prince and Princess of Wales were as estranged as a couple could be, and this, people said, was likely to prove a serious drawback once he became Regent and to wreak havoc with court etiquette. For years the prince had wanted a formal separation, but his father refused to allow one (though even the king, who always liked Caroline, was troubled by reports that since coming to England she had had many lovers and had borne an illegitimate child). Instead the grievances between husband and wife were allowed to fester, with the prince refusing to enter any room where his wife was and claiming that he would rather see toads and vipers crawling on his food than sit at the same table with her.

There was no end to the rancor between them. He claimed that her erratic behavior was meant to provoke him and drive him out of his mind. "There is no end to her wickedness, her falsity, and her designs," he wrote in exasperation. She was "the most unprincipled and unfeeling person of her sex."[5] Caroline, for her part, complained that her dissolute

husband had humiliated her for years by his infidelities, insisting that she was unjustly victimized for having become
the wife of "Mrs. Fitzherbert's husband." The prince spied
on her, slandered her, and tormented her by not allowing
her to see their daughter, Princess Charlotte, who was her
only earthly consolation.[6]

All in all it was a sorry situation, made worse by Caroline's
total lack of discretion and cheerful blowsiness. Though
dumpy and middle-aged, at her dinner parties she flirted
seductively in gowns far too low-cut to flatter her overflowing
bosom. Her heavy coquetry was vulgar enough in her own
drawing room; to imagine her at court—where the prince
had utterly forbidden her to show herself—was unthinkable.
Yet if Prince George became Regent, there would be no
hiding Caroline. She would be sure to embarrass him—and
the realm.

On February 5 the Regency bill finally passed and with
elaborate ceremony the Prince of Wales spoke the words
and signed the documents making him Regent for his father
George III. As the prince sat, dignified and regal, at the
head of a long velvet-covered table in Carlton House the
principal dignitaries of the government came into the room
one by one and made their obeisances to him. He was flanked
by his brothers, the royal dukes, and by an attendant guard
of servants in livery and uniformed guardsmen. The ritual
was heartening to those who were apprehensive for England
and its monarchy, but it brought no satisfaction to the Whigs,
who had just learned, to their amazement, that the Regent
did not after all intend to change the government.

Prince George had been subjected to considerable pressure
to keep the Tory ministers, from his brothers Frederick and
Ernest (who was particularly adroit at playing on his fears),
from the queen, and from the king's doctors. Much as he
disliked the Tories as individuals, he found himself inclined
to agree with their views, while the combative Whigs on
the whole made him uneasy. Besides, there was no point
in making a sweeping change as long as King George continued to improve. If he were to recover, the doctors cautioned,
and if on recovering he found that his Tory ministers had

.

been turned out and replaced by men he detested, the shock might set him back and make his condition worse.

Besides this, Prince George's abandonment of his longtime Whig allies was one of several signs that in taking on the role of Regent he had begun to undergo a change. Weak and foolish though he often was, and would remain, the prince had a capacity for kingliness. The Tories, with their staunch loyalty to the monarchy and their sense of history and continuity, flattered that kingliness, while the Whigs, traditional enemies of the court and all it stood for, threatened to undermine it. Moreover, though he would have hated to admit it, the Regent was aware that he stood in his father's shadow, and owed it to King George to consider his preferences. As Regent the prince's manner subtly altered. He was said to be noticeably more gracious, more aware of a responsibility to exude regality.[7] He was exceptionally good at this, and he knew it, and drew strength from it as he struggled to accustom himself for the first time in his life to the hard work and long hours public business required.

It was a challenge for him at first, putting in seven or eight hours a day at his desk, reading and answering state correspondence, conferring with ministers, holding levées during which anyone and everyone begged favors from him and subjected him to persuasion and pressure. The strain led to "agitation in the blood," but he kept at it doggedly, as if to prove to his critics that he could do anything his father had done. Some of the work was tediously mechanical. Stacks of documents needed the Regent's signature. He sat at a table with his Assistant Private Secretary, General Turner, on one side of him and his Private Secretary, Colonel MacMahon, on the other, "the one placing a paper before him for his signature, and the other drawing it away."[8] It was estimated that he had signed his name some fourteen thousand times, remarking wryly afterward that "playing at king is no sinecure."

George III had been an extremely diligent ruler with an exceptional command of a wide range of topics. He kept detailed memoranda on the voting record of each Member of Parliament, with annotations indicating approval or dissatisfaction; he made notes on such things as "Artillery in North America" and "Reflections on the present state of the Navy"; when convicted criminals wrote to him to plead for mercy he took the trouble to investigate the evidence against them and study the judicial reports. Troop movements, battalion strengths, officers' records were carefully filed away in his memory, to be brought to mind later.

The Regent could not hope to match this level of omnicompetence, though he was quick-witted and had a grasp of essentials. And where his father had been habitually conscientious, the Regent was hopelessly self-indulgent, so that despite his good intentions he overslept, missed appointments and often kept his ministers waiting for hours. Still, overall, the political transition was a smooth one. It would not matter greatly, people began to say, if the king's illness were to be prolonged.

But the king was improving, steadily and dramatically. "It is true I have had a hard shake—a very hard shake," he said toward the end of February, "but I am now going on well, and the prince's conduct will give me time to recover quite, before I take to business again."[9] He slipped occasionally into unreality, but returned to his senses for most of the time. He was able to visit with his sons and daughters, walking up and down the terrace at Windsor with them, and even the queen conceded when she saw him that he looked better than she had expected and "seemed not to be so much fallen away." The king was strong enough to take a good deal of exercise, and mentally alert enough to play backgammon and to discuss politics. Perceval came to see him and explained to him the provisions of the Regency bill. How had the government been kept running, the king asked the Prime Minister, without his signature on Treasury warrants?

Though he professed to trust the opinion of his doctors that he was still too ill to think of resuming his responsibilities, King George was restless in his enforced idleness. He wanted something to do. While he tolerated it, he disliked

.

hearing about how his son was exercising his powers, and assured Perceval that "he should always be at hand to come forward if he was wanted."

In March the war news began to improve considerably. First, the French Armée du Portugal under Marshal Masséna retreated from Portugal, daunted by Wellington's defensive works, the Lines of Torres Vedras. Then in May Marshal Soult was defeated at Albuera, and for the first time there was a sense that the tide might be turning against the French. King George felt more than ever Father of his People as flags were flown and celebrations held to mark the victory. On one of his good days he rode in Windsor Park, and when the townspeople caught sight of him they cheered and thought for certain he would soon go back to being king in deed as well as in name.

He continued to receive visitors, and to follow the progress of the Regent's government, but when anyone spoke to him of retirement, of his need for rest, he showed his irritation. "Aye, aye, my Lord Chancellor," he burst out to Lord Eldon, "it's all very pretty talking, but if you had been kept out of your place for six months you would have been glad enough to get into it again!"[10]

It was a reminder, and the Lord Chancellor needed none, that the Regency was a fragile thing, resting on nothing more substantial than the opinions of a handful of doctors that the king temporarily lacked the capacity to rule. Doctors could be bribed, influence brought to bear. "The unsettled and feeble domination of a Regency," Walter Scott had written a few months earlier, "will not fail to have its usual effects in setting the worst principles of faction afloat and dividing the country between those who profess to stand up for the father and those who adhere to the son." By retaining his father's ministers the Regent had so far prevented this prophecy from coming true. But he might not prove so adroit as time went on.

·

*W*ord went out toward the middle of May, 1811, that the Regent would soon be giving a ball at Carlton House. Immediately opinion about it was divided. He ought not to be celebrating his father's misfortune so blatantly, some said—and besides, given Prince George's tastes and his supremely grand style of entertaining, his ball would be sure to cost a fortune, and the nation could ill afford it. But even as they criticized the coming fête people admitted to being curious to see the highly praised interior of Carlton House, and before long they were speculating about who would be invited and who wouldn't, and about what they would wear if they were lucky enough to be among the favored few.

The prince let it be known that he would invite fifteen hundred people, a large proportion of whom would be Members of Parliament. Among those to be excluded were all

·

women lower in rank than the daughter of an earl. The latter rule, though it followed Hanoverian court custom, led to such "lamentations and complaints" that exceptions began to be made, however, and before long it was clear that there would be many more than fifteen hundred names on the guest list.

By the end of May "the one subject of conversation was the fête," wrote George Jackson, a diplomat recently returned from Spain who had received his invitation to the Regent's ball some days earlier.[1] Not even the news of Wellington's victory at Albuera, or the sad announcements of the English who had died in the battle, deflected attention from the ball for long. It was to cost ten thousand pounds, insiders reported; the decorations were to be unimaginably lavish. So lavish, in fact, that the date for the grand event had to be advanced twelve days, to June 19, "because of the necessary preparations for it not being finished." This gave more time, of course, for those who had been left off the guest list to apply every pressure available to them, including bribery and blackmail, to acquire invitations. The choice of guests appeared to be somewhat haphazard: "husbands invited without their wives, mothers without their daughters; daughters who are not yet out; in some cases, people who are dead and buried." Amid such a random assortment of people, a few more or less would never be noticed.

June 19 arrived, and the ball guests, after spending all morning and afternoon at their toilettes, set off in their coaches an hour before the gates of Carlton House were to be opened. By eight o'clock the string of carriages reached to the top of St. James's Street, by nine to the top of Bond Street. As the carriages inched forward their overdressed, overpainted occupants were forced to submit to the scrutiny of a huge crowd that had gathered in the street to watch them pass. "The jostling and pushing to get a sight of the women, especially when accompanied by a star or a riband, was something extraordinary," Jackson wrote, "and the remarks of the people on the occupants of the carriages, as the latter crawled or jolted on at a snail's pace, were sometimes very droll and apt, though not always complimentary."[2]

.

Carlton House was at its most resplendent that evening. The prince and his architects had been renovating the mansion for years and many pronounced it the equal of Versailles. From the torchlit portico guests were ushered into the grand, high-ceilinged entrance hall lined with columns of porphyry marble. As they made their way, slowly and admiringly, through the suite of rooms beyond, the impression of grandeur and spaciousness grew. The Blue Velvet Room, the Regent's audience room, was bathed in a tender gray-blue from its thick carpet to its elegant velvet settees to its painted ceiling. A three-tiered crystal chandelier fringed in gold reflected the same hue in its sparkling depths. The Throne Room with its curtained Romanesque bays flanked by gilded Corinthian columns was rich with red brocade and carved, painted furnishings. The Circular Dining-Room was all mirrors and silver walls, the Rose-Satin Drawing Room glowed a warm pink touched with gold. Each room brought new wonders, the ceilings works of art in themselves, framed with gilded cornices, the doors ornately painted, the splendid furnishings in exquisite harmony with their settings. There were Gobelins tapestries and Aubusson carpets, Sèvres vases in colored porcelain, tables, cabinets and armchairs in wood with inlaid designs. The Regent had assembled one of the finest collections of French artworks in Europe, and one of the finest collections of paintings as well. Some two hundred Dutch and Flemish pictures, the majority of them masterworks, adorned Carlton House, and on the night of the ball the guests were shown his latest acquisition, Rembrandt's "The Shipbuilder and His Wife," which had cost him five thousand guineas.

Throughout the earlier part of the evening the guests continued to arrive, crowding into the assembly rooms in their hundreds and trying to make their way to the hot, stuffy ballroom where the Regent, his sister-in-law, the Duchess of York, and the guests of honor, the exiled royal family of France, were to be found. Louis XVIII—who asked to be called simply the Comte de Lisle, despite the prince's gracious insistence that *"Ici Votre Majesté est Roi de France"*—had been escorted to Carlton House by a detachment of Hussars, and was shown every kingly honor by his host. The Regent exulted in regality, and the presence of the rightful King of France, however remote his chances of ever being crowned might seem, glorified the fête for him. The king's presence mattered far more than the conspicuous absence of Queen Charlotte and the princesses, who disapproved of the ball. It certainly mattered more than the fact that the Duchess of York, and not the Princess of Wales, was serving as official hostess.

Dressed in a rich scarlet uniform, a magnificent star on his chest and a saber at his waist, the Regent presided happily over his brilliant array of guests. The women shone with diamonds, the men in their finely cut evening suits glittered with decorations. The ballroom was too crowded for dancing, but the musicians continued to play all evening, until at half-past two in the morning supper was announced and the entire assembly went down the long circular double staircase to the prince's apartments on the lower floor.

Here fresh wonders met their eyes: the Library, where elegantly bound volumes were encased in ornate bookcases flanked by golden columns, the Gothic Dining-Room and Golden Drawing Room, and the fairylike Gothic Conservatory. Chinese lanterns were hung at intervals down the length of this immensely long, narrow room, whose doors opened, at one end, onto a verdant garden. A colonnade of carved pillars supported a ceiling whose intricate traceries fanned outward in spider-web patterns. Stained glass filtered the subdued light to create the effect of a cathedral with nave and aisles, mysterious and otherworldly, and on the night of the ball, small colored glass lamps placed in the cornices and niches of the stonework turned the Conservatory into a fairy palace.

Supper was served under a large tent erected in the garden, held in place by gilded ropes and festooned with flowers. The interior of the tent was illuminated by glass lustres, which shone down on tables heaped with silver tureens, dishes and plates; hot roasts and soups were served along with cold meats and an abundance of fruit, all, according to Jackson, "of excellent and fresh cookery." Besides a variety

.

of superb wines, there was iced champagne at every three
or four places, and in all some two thousand people were
served with "no crowding, hurry or bustle in waiting."
Everything went as smoothly as in a private house.

The Regent and his principal guests were served in the
Conservatory, at his special table, some two hundred feet
long, set with his costly table service of gold and silver gilt.
Besides his sister-in-law, the Duchess of York, Lady Hertford
and Lady Charlotte Campbell, the latter a celebrated beauty,
sat with him, wearing gowns he ordered made for the occasion. (Maria Fitzherbert, though invited to the ball, chose
not to attend when she discovered that she was not to be
seated at the Regent's table.) Flowing down the middle of
the table, meandering between the heavy serving dishes, was
an artificial stream, complete with sand, moss, rocks, and
aquatic plants and spanned by miniature bridges. Live gold
and silver fish—roach, dace and gudgeons—swam among the
rocks, "exhibiting the brightness of their scales, reflecting
the light of five hundred flambeaux, to the infinite delight
of the guests."[3] This "serpentine river" was the talk of the
evening (though some called it "a paltry thing of bad taste"),
until the fish began to die, no doubt of oxygen starvation,
and took away everybody's appetite.

Dawn was breaking by the time the guests rose from the
supper table and began to call for their carriages. The ball
had been a success. Jackson judged it to be "the hand-
somest thing I have ever seen in this country, or, of its kind,
in any other"—and he had seen the splendors of most of
the European courts. The brilliance of dress, the evident
wealth ("the value of the diamonds," Jackson wrote, "I have
no doubt greatly exceeded what was ever before seen in any
assembly"), the cultivated conversation and appreciation of
art—all these marked the Regent's guests as eminently civi-
lized, members of England's inner circle of privilege and
culture.

But though the ball was for members of the inner circle,
the lesser orders were not to be excluded. The guests went
home, but the trappings of the fête—the festoons of flowers,
the displays of gold plate, even the dining table with its ser-

pentine river—were not dismantled. Instead, over the next several days Carlton House was left with its splendors intact for anyone who could afford a ticket to come and see.

They came by the thousands, gathering in front of the outer gates, swarming into the inner courtyard to press for admission at the great front door. Swept along by the pressure of the crowd, their gowns torn and their coiffures disheveled, some of the women were pulled in through the windows while the men continued to wait outside, fighting for space and air. Good manners were forgotten entirely. People were "thrown down and trodden under foot," their arms and legs fractured, their ribs forced in, all for a glimpse of the Regent's mansion.[4] "Curiosity was extreme," wrote Simond, "quite as much so as it might have been at Paris. The people, and not the low people," turned out in far greater numbers than anyone had foreseen, until on the last day, with a vast sea of bodies amassed in Pall Mall, each one clutching an entrance ticket, severe measures had to be taken.

The Duke of Clarence climbed up onto the outer wall of Carlton House and, facing the immense crowd, bowed and waved his hat in the air to attract their attention. It was the desire of the Prince Regent, his brother, he shouted, "to afford to the public a view of Carlton House." But because "the pressure of people had become so great and in proportion the danger . . . no more persons would on any account be admitted."[5] Still, by this time a great many Londoners had gone through the Throne Room and Rose-Satin Drawing Room and Gothic Conservatory, wondering at the paintings and art objects and at the luxury of the prince's private apartments, herded along by Yeomen of the Guard who urged them to "go on, go on" if they slackened their pace. For once, what the fashionable world had seen, they had seen too; instead of merely reading about the fête in the *Morning Post*, they had witnessed its glories at first hand.

Successful as the Regent's ball had been, the host had not been completely at ease. For one thing, he had had to exclude from the guest list a good many of his friends and preferred companions who did not measure up to the standards set by court etiquette. Queen Charlotte had advised her son not

.

to invite to his fête any woman "who had been notorious by any act of infidelity," and this stricture, had he observed it rigorously, would have led to the exclusion of most of the women he knew.

The society in which the prince had always moved, and still moved, was worldly. His friends, both men and women, tended to be profligate, informal and sexually broadminded. They lived irregular lives; husbands ignored their wives and lived with their mistresses, wives bore their lovers' children, everyone involved behaving toward everyone else with sophisticated civility. But while the Prince of Wales might associate with such people—much to the disapproval of his rigidly moral parents—the Regent could not. The dignity of the crown had to be preserved, appearances had to be kept up to some degree. Friends he had once welcomed at Carlton House could be welcome there no longer. He would have to invite them to his exclusive inner sanctum, the Marine Pavilion at Brighton, instead.

Brighton had always been the prince's town, a sort of private kingdom by the sea where he was the center of things and where he could live entirely as he chose. People understood him there, they welcomed him by ringing all the town bells whenever he arrived in his carriage from London. In the capital he hardly dared show himself in the street; in Brighton when he walked along the central thoroughfare, the Steine, people bowed respectfully to him and were honored when he inclined his head to them in return. In Brighton no one cared whom he entertained, or how he behaved. All rules were suspended, he could indulge himself to his heart's content.

The town owed its growth and prosperity to Prince George. In the years since his first visit there, in 1783, it had doubled and redoubled in size with new streets laid out every year and hundreds of new houses—some of them built solely of bricks in the Whig colors (then the prince's colors) of buff and blue—springing up along them. The houses were rented out, at exorbitant rates, to those who flocked to Brighton whenever the prince was in residence there.

He came at Christmastime, and in the summer when his

.

birthday, August 12, was the occasion for an annual town celebration. The navy put on a mock seabattle each August 12, followed by a military review with thousands of soldiers, bright in their scarlet, marching and forming on Race Hill two miles from the center of town. A local fraternal order made up of tradesmen, the "javelin men" of Lewes, marched in procession wearing the prince's colors, and the entire population wore buff and blue cockades. In the evening there was a birthday ball at the Castle Inn, and an ox was roasted in the open air and served, along with plenty of ale, to all and sundry.

In 1802 the town had erected a plaster statue of the prince, dressed in his regimental uniform, towering eighteen feet in the air. But the effect was spoiled when "some wanton persons" broke off the fingers of one hand, and then the whole of an arm, and finally part of the prince's flowing military cloak. The mutilated statue was an insult to the patron saint of the town, and the whole thing, pedestal and all, had to be taken down.[6]

Besides the sea bathing and the medicinal vapor baths ("a sort of stewing alive by steam"), visitors to Brighton were offered amusements of many sorts. Plays, concerts, horse racing, even cockfights and bull baiting were offered, besides the customary round of card parties and balls. The place to be seen, in the evening, was on the Steine. Everyone who mattered gathered there, even on nights when the heavy dew dampened their clothes and the high wind left them, as one contemporary wrote, "crusted with salt like Dutch herrings." But no entertainment could compare with the ongoing pageant of the prince when encamped at his Marine Pavilion, and as soon as he left, the rented houses emptied and trade dried up.

"Scarce a person of fashion remains," one Brighton resident complained after the departure of the prince. "The whole company now consists of antiquated virgins, emaciated beaux, and wealthy citizens with their wives and daughters." Beyond these, he added, there were only "a few needy adventurers, who are as watchful as lynxes for an opportunity of carrying off the golden prizes."[7] The tradesmen who opened

·

their expensive shops in North Street, nicknamed the "Prince's Place" whenever Prince George was in town, shut them again and returned to London. A few invalids patronized the medicinal baths, a maidservant or two kept up patronage at the library. But the Steine was deserted, save for an occasional flock of screaming seagulls, and the fishermen spread out their nets along it to dry in the sun.

If the prince brought prosperity to Brighton, it was often pointed out, he also brought an unsavory population in his wake. Pickpockets, cardsharps and social impostors plagued society. The *bon vivants* and voluptuaries in the prince's entourage attracted the London demimonde to Brighton. Low life flourished. Prostitutes increased in number; "we have now little French milliners in every part of town," a local satirist wrote. The presence of the 10th Light Dragoons so near the resort kept the French milliners busy in season and out, and helped to give Brighton a rakish, slightly sour atmosphere that the goings-on at the Marine Pavilion did nothing to dispel.

Physically and in every other way, the Pavilion dominated Brighton. The huge dome of the stables, rising sixty-five feet high at its center, floated serenely above the houses and shops, while the Pavilion itself with its outbuildings spread themselves out over several acres. In 1811 the Pavilion was still a neoclassical mansion, though plans existed for an audacious new exterior inspired by Mughal architecture. Inside, however, it was an exotic Chinese dream, dreamed by an imaginative escapist.

To Prince George China represented all the magic of the remote and faraway, combined with Oriental luxury and Oriental despotism. China to him was a land where celestial harmony reigned, eternal and unchanging, with contented peasants obeying their autocratic emperor without question. It was at the same time a land in the grip of enchantment, scenic and full of marvels, where in the heavens fearsome gods held sway.

This fantasy nourished him, flattering his regality while it both reflected and lulled his personal terrors. Beginning in 1802 he brought his fantasy to life in the Marine Pavilion,

·

ordering the rooms transformed by the installation of Chinese wallpaper and paintings, Chinese lanterns, Chinese dragons, pagodas, lotus leaves and serpents. The ceilings were painted to simulate blue sky with clouds, bamboo furnishings were introduced, along with lacquered cabinets, porcelain and imitation palm trees. The colors were dazzling in their intensity—vivid crimson and scarlet alongside peach and green, vermilion with lilac, blue set beside dark maroon and bright yellow. The walls of the entrance hall were brilliant green, the corridors French blue. "All is Chinese," a visitor to the Pavilion wrote in 1811, "quite overloaded with china of all possible sorts and of all possible forms, many beautiful in themselves, but so overloaded one upon the other, that the effect is more like a china shop baroquement arranged than the abode of a prince."

The fashion for chinoiserie, at its peak a half-century earlier, had long passed. Prince George attempted to revive it, but to many who saw his efforts the effect was gaudy and cluttered. There was too much richness of color and detail, too many outsize artworks, not to mention the costumes, models of junks, birds' nests and other curiosities that littered the galleries and drawing rooms. The prince nearly always went overboard in whatever he undertook, and craved strong sensual stimuli; his guests found the Pavilion almost stifling.

Yet the new décor was designed in part to accommodate large numbers of guests. There were several spacious rooms for giving parties, and apartments for houseguests who were invited to stay from two or three days to a week. Once arrived, they quickly discovered that, while their every wish was catered to and they were given every opportunity to enjoy themselves, still the prince was very much master in his own house. He was like a grand puppeteer, assembling his chosen puppets, controlling their movements, watching them react to the unique environment of the Pavilion and enjoying their reactions. He set the limits of their behavior, insisting on formal manners at dinner ("a sort of tiresome good behavior," as one guest put it) and then, as the evening wore on, encouraging them to put formality aside—up to a point.

·

The accounts left by those who were the Regent's guests at Brighton convey the impression that he alone was truly at ease there. Everyone else was kept in a constant state of mild anxiety, alert to their host's labile moods, always having to guess when he wanted them to be convivial and familiar and when he needed more deference.

It was awkward for them, having now to indulge his clownishness, now to treat him like the royalty he was. His manners were exquisitely correct, yet the jokes he told were earthy and coarse. A Frenchwoman recalled that "he had a marvelous knowledge of all the stories of gallantry at the court of Louis XVI," and told them, night after night, while the men laughed and the women either joined in the laughter or were faintly sickened. At his musical evenings, when he sang or played the cello, his captive audience was expected to applaud his quite tolerable dilettantism, but they were also expected to enjoy it—or at least to refrain from wincing—when in an infantile way he beat time to the music on the dinner gong.

The entertainment provided by the grand puppeteer was diverse. His band of wind musicians played, very loudly, a variety of his favorite works, with a heavy emphasis on Italian rococo. There was also the band of the 10th Light Dragoons, which played less often but more loudly. Prominent soloists performed, as did the gifted amateurs present. Sometimes the prince would order his newest works of art brought in for the company to admire. One evening he offered them a "phantasmagoria," or colored light show. Another time he took them by surprise during dinner. The room suddenly became dark, and a scrim dropped, lit from behind, to illuminate the headlines BRIGHTON—EARTHQUAKE—SWALLOW-UP ALIVE.

When he worked at it, the prince could be the most attentive and well-organized of hosts, but there were times when his entertainments had a more *ad hoc* flavor. Mrs. Creevey, who with her politician husband was often invited to the Pavilion, left a description of one evening's entertainment.

Having been invited to join an after supper party given by the prince, she dressed in great haste—for the invitation

·

arrived only an hour before she was due at the Pavilion—
and set off, with her daughters, in her carriage. Her host
was still dining, with a select company of friends, when she
arrived, and when he finally made his appearance in the room
where the rest of the guests awaited him it was eleven o'clock
and he was quite drunk. He greeted them, lurching from
one to another, and then led them all over "to see him shoot
with an air-gun at a target placed at the end of the room."
Despite his advanced state of intoxication his aim proved
true, and he shot skillfully, "and wanted all the ladies to
attempt it." Mrs. Creevey excused herself and her daughters,
saying they were all nearsighted, "but Lady Downshire hit
a fiddler in the dining room, Miss Johnstone a door, and
Bloomfield the ceiling."

The target shooting over, the prince called for his band
to play a waltz, and taking a partner, began whirling her
around the room. Almost immediately he became too dizzy
to stand, and dropping his poor partner, who fell over onto
another guest, he scrambled for his own footing in a most
undignified way. By this time Mrs. Creevey had had enough,
she wrote, and retired to the fire. "Oh, this wicked Pavilion!"
she concluded. "We were there until half past one this morning, and it has kept me in bed with the headache till twelve
today."[8]

Mrs. Creevey was not alone in her exasperation with the
prince's antics. Lord Grenville commented that the Pavilion
was "not furnished for society," and that he and others suffered from ennui. The host had a tendency to take center
stage and hold it for hours, boasting about how he had once
beaten "the bully of all Brighton" in a fistfight, rambling
on about his champion racehorses, telling stories of his war
experiences which everyone knew were invented, for Prince
George had never been anywhere near a battlefield. The wea-
ried visitors listened, and reacted politely, trying hard to
stay awake in the stuffy, overheated rooms.

"What with heat and emotion," a weekend visitor complained, the Pavilion was "overpowering," especially during
the summer when Brighton was "crowded, dusty and burnt
up, not a green blade to be seen." At such times the discom-

.

fort outweighed the honor of an invitation to the royal pleasure palace. The dazzling chinoiserie began to look tawdry,
the prince himself to resemble an aging, oily roué. But such
disillusionment was as a rule short-lived. A particularly gracious bow, a little special attention, and the most cynical
of the Regent's acquaintances was won back.

For his charm was all-conquering, and the glory of his
surroundings, whether at Carlton House or the Marine Pavilion, could not be surpassed.

.

*I*n November of 1811 a series
of violent incidents terrorized Nottinghamshire. Organized
bands of men, wearing masks and armed with muskets, pistols
and hatchets, appeared suddenly in the dead of night and
broke into the small hosiery workshops that were scattered
throughout the country villages. Hammermen carrying huge
heavy iron sledgehammers smashed open the doors of the
workshops, and once inside, beat at the wide stocking frames
until they were completely destroyed.

The attacks were as swift as they were sudden. The work
of destruction over, the men slipped back into the darkness
of the forest, leaving behind heaps of shattered glass and
splintered timber, broken looms and torn fabric.

Six frames were broken at the village of Bulwell on November 4, a dozen more at Kimberley a few nights later,
then on November 13 upwards of seventy frames were

.

smashed in a single attack at Sutton-in-Ashfield.

There was little the local authorities could do to stop the attacks. Magistrates could not police the whole of their sprawling rural jurisdictions. The military forces brought in—a squadron of dragoons, the Mansfield Volunteers, two troops of Yeomanry—were ineffective against mobile bands operating in familiar country under cover of night. The attackers were anonymous, faceless and nameless, save that they claimed allegiance to "General Ludd."

Week by week General Ludd's army grew, the scope of the attacks widening to take in Derbyshire and Leicestershire villages as well as the area around Nottingham. Shots were fired, at least one Luddite was killed. Nearly every night brought fresh destruction, with the Luddites burning workshops to the ground and setting fire to hayricks and barns as well. Emboldened by their success, the frame-breakers began occasionally to carry out their raids in full daylight, sometimes within earshot of the military, and to boast of their invincibility in letters signed "Ned Ludd" or "General Ludd." Employers, threatened with death and destruction by hordes of "Sworn Heroes bound in a Bond of Necessity," as one of the letters read, tried to protect themselves by destroying their own frames or storing them away, but the Luddite chaos continued to spread.[1]

> And by night when all is still,
> And the moon is hid behind the hill,
> We forward march to do our will
>   With hatchet, pike, and gun! . . .
>
> Great Enoch still shall lead the van
> Stop him who dare! Stop him who can!
> Press forward every gallant man
>   With hatchet, pike, and gun!

The Luddite song captures the chill menace of the midnight assaults. The secrecy, the anonymity, the felt power of the hammer-wielding bands spread fear throughout the Midlands. Newspaper reports exaggerated the scale of their activities, helping to lend their protest a mythic dimension.

The breaking of machinery was a symptom of a deeper destructive urge; something immemorial had been roused.

The Midland Luddites were laborers driven to violence by unprecedented economic crisis in their craft of framework knitting. Framework knitting was a skilled craft in which the workers, called stockingers, operated simple looms by hand. Master stockingers rented their looms from their employers, called hosiers, for a fee, and the work was done in the upper rooms of the master stockingers' homes by apprentices and journeymen.

During the course of the war with France and consequent trade restrictions the demand for stockings had fluctuated alarmingly, with a few boom years and many more depressed ones. Wages had gone steadily down, and many workers' hours were cut by half or more. Beyond this, the value of their labor was debased when hosiers shifted from producing elaborate designs—which required considerable skill to make—to turning out mostly plain stockings, for which the stockingers were paid much less.

All this was bad enough, but when hosiers began to compromise with quality the stockingers foresaw disaster. Poor-quality goods would ultimately undermine the market still further, they argued; they would be the ones to suffer. Inferior goods were made in a variety of ways, by using weak thread, by knotting the thread so loosely that it unraveled easily—and by making what were called "cut-up" stockings on wide frames, the frames destined to be the target of Luddite attack.

These wide frames, once used to make pantaloons, had recently superseded the traditional narrow frames stockingers were accustomed to. Shapes were cut out of large pieces of knitted fabric and then sewn, clumsily, with a seam instead of being knitted in one piece. Stockings made in this way soon fell apart, but the method was inexpensive and quick, and in the short run they sold well.

All the stockingers' grievances were brought to a head early in 1811 when exports of Midlands cotton goods fell by a third and, at the same time, the failed harvest drove food prices so high that fully half the population of Nottingham had to rely on public relief. Workers earning seven shillings a week—and these were the fortunate ones—had to pay more than a shilling for a single loaf of bread. The unemployed were desperate; laborers and farmers alike were in extreme distress. The government was repeatedly petitioned, but as the months went by conditions worsened. Stockingers were in an ugly mood, for in addition to their immediate hardships they had recently been disappointed in their efforts to win higher wages from the hosiers. Demonstrations were held, demands made. Finally, with the onset of winter, they turned to the only remedy left, and took up their muskets and sledgehammers.

The Luddites smashed and burned and threatened throughout a wide area of the Midlands in November and December, 1811, evading capture and making the nine troops of cavalry and two infantry regiments that had been sent to put a stop to their daring raids look foolish. "The insurrectional state to which this country has been reduced for the last month," wrote the Nottingham correspondent of the *Leeds Mercury*, "has no parallel in history, since the troubled days of Charles I." The paper hinted at a political conspiracy, and when the disorder raged on in January, all but shutting down the industry and in some areas giving rise to wanton criminality that had nothing directly to do with the desperation of the stockingers, the government finally acted.

Frame-breaking was already punishable by transportation for fourteen years—the law a result of earlier outbreaks of violence by the framework knitters. Now a bill was put forward making it a capital offense.

The bill was passed, but not without opposition. One of those who spoke against it in the House of Lords was a pale, handsome young lord who walked with a limp and spoke with exceptional eloquence and force of mind. He was George Gordon, Lord Byron, then twenty-three and on the threshold of his literary reputation.

"I have traversed the seat of war in the Peninsula; I have been in some of the most oppressed provinces of Turkey; but never, under the most despotic of infidel governments, did I behold such squalid wretchedness as I have seen since

.

my return, in the very heart of a Christian country."

Byron had returned only a few months earlier from an extended trip to the Middle East, and the poverty of Greece and Turkey was fresh in his mind. He went on to excoriate the Tories for attempting to cure the Luddite disease by force. "Are there not capital punishments sufficient on your statutes? Is there not blood enough upon your penal code, that more must be poured forth to ascend to heaven and testify against you?"[2]

The speech was long on rhetoric, short on specific recommendations. "I spoke very violent sentences," Byron told his friend Francis Hodgson after making his speech, "with a sort of modest impudence, abused every thing and every body, ... As to my delivery, loud and fluent enough, perhaps a little theatrical."[3] Theatrical or not, the speech was very well received by the Whig leaders Grenville, Grey and Holland. Grenville told the young man his rhetoric resembled that of the great Parliamentarian Edmund Burke, and the others paid him similar compliments.

The workers of the Midlands, Byron argued, were being sacrificed to enrich the hosiers. But surely the well-being of the poor ought to matter more than "the enrichment of a few monopolists." Byron had seen the framework knitters at first hand; he had stayed at his estate at Newstead in Nottinghamshire in December and had witnessed the effect of the Luddite destruction. His speech was impassioned, and frankly partisan, yet he was no zealot. In a letter to Holland stating his views and asking, with appropriate deference, for the older man's advice Byron added a self-deprecating postscript. "I am a little apprehensive that your lordship will think me too lenient toward these men, and half a frame-breaker myself."

By this time the Midlands were becoming calmer, but the Luddite fervor had spread to Yorkshire and Lancashire, where there was a much larger and more volatile population. Workers in the North were worse off than those of the Midlands; unemployment was even more widespread, the prospects for improvement in the woolen and cotton-spinning trades bleaker. In the dreary towns and wool villages people lived on potatoes and oatmeal, unable to supplement their low wages and meager diet by farming as the soil was too poor. In March and April of 1812 they began to organize themselves to attack the shearing frames and power looms that threatened their livelihoods. The pattern was the same as it had been in the Midlands: armed bands of men, their faces blackened or covered by masks, met in secret on the moors and then dispersed to predetermined sites to throw down the hated frames and looms and burn the workshops where they were kept.

The Luddites were becoming an underground army. Men were recruited to their ranks, "twisted in" with oaths, given the passwords and told the secret signs. Members of the brotherhood learned to recognize one another by mysterious gestures and cryptic messages. Luddites were instructed that to raise one's right hand over one's right eye was to invite a response from any other Luddite in the room, who would then raise his left hand over his left eye in response. Next the first signaler would raise the forefinger of his right hand to the right side of his mouth, after which his respondent would raise the little finger of his left hand to the left side of his mouth and ask, "What are you?" The correct answer was, "Determined." Then the questioner was to say, "What for?" and the answer was to be, "Free Liberty."[4]

There were rumors of thousands of men "twisted in," eight thousand at Sheffield, seven thousand at Leeds. Every community, it seemed, was permeated by them; nearly every family had one or more sworn men in General Ludd's forces. The militia was riddled with Luddites, they could not be counted on, as they were more likely to join the lawbreakers than to resist them. The militia, people said, was a training ground for rebels, who joined its ranks in order to learn how to use weapons, then turned the weapons against the forces of order.

The communities of the North closed ranks to protect the Luddites. Investigators found "a shyness in speaking of the subject" which baffled and frustrated them, and led them to make more and more use of spies and informers. These in turn sent to Westminster reports which made the Luddites

.

sound like revolutionaries—and in fact their protest had its political dimension.

A letter from "General Ludd" in "Shirewood Camp" to the Prime Minister, Spencer Perceval, informed the latter that "in consequence of the great sufferings of the poor whose grievances seem not to be taken into the least consideration by government," the General would be forced to call out his "brave Sons of Shirewood, who are determined and sworn to be true and faithful avengers of their country's wrongs." Perceval was told to warn his colleagues, and the Regent, that unless the distress in the Midlands and the North was alleviated, the Luddites would take strong measures, shedding "blood for blood."[5] Another letter threatened that "We will go and blow Parliament house up," and damned the "rogues" in power. "We will soon bring about the great Revolution," the letter concluded, "then all these great men's heads goes off."[6]

To a society barely twenty years away from the rampant carnage of the Terror in France, the Luddites' warnings were fearsome. The angry laborers seemed indistinguishable from Jacobins, intent on overturning the social order and unrestrained by convictions of loyalty or patriotism. In truth Luddism was, primarily, a vengeful outcry for bearable living conditions on the part of a wretchedly poor population of laborers, but it had overtones of something broader. It recalled past social upheavals with bloody outcomes: the great peasants' revolt of the fourteenth century, the rebellions under Henry VIII and Edward VI, the Civil War. The Luddites appropriated to themselves the archaic language of divine retribution. They were the scourge of a corrupt society, avenging angels sent by God to punish sinful England. Particularly to those who had never seen the Yorkshire dales or the Midland forests, Luddism loomed as an inchoate, apocalyptic force that threatened to engulf the realm.

The Luddite violence could hardly have come at a worse time for the Regent, who as the end of his restricted Regency approached was ill and tense. The Whigs, whom he had disappointed when he assumed power, looked for him to bring them into the government once the restrictions on his authority were lifted early in February, and they had some grounds for their hopes. The prince had designed a new court uniform in the Whig colors of buff and blue—surely an indication of changes to come. He was said to be tiring of his Prime Minister, and to have sorely tried the patience of the cabinet by paying no attention whatever to punctuality and repeatedly arriving at meetings hours late or missing them entirely.

Late in November, while the Regent was staying at Brighton, it became necessary to call a cabinet meeting, and he set the time and place for noon the following day at the Treasury in London. All the ministers, who were scattered around the environs of the capital, roused themselves at daybreak in order to arrive at the Treasury by noon. They assembled, they prepared themselves for business, they waited for Prince George. They waited an hour, then two. Impatient, they sent to Carlton House to find out what detained him. Word came back that he had arrived from Brighton in good time, but was "shut up with tailors examining different patterns of uniforms." The ministers fumed and fretted, concerned about the lawlessness in the Midlands—for at just this time the papers were full of news of Luddite raids—and conscious that each hour's delay could be significant. Sometime after three o'clock the Regent at last joined his ministers, apologizing for having kept them waiting. Unfortunately he would be unable to meet with them after all, he told them, as the queen had sent for him. With these words he left them again and drove off to Windsor.[7]

The prince treated his Tory ministers shabbily, yet he was decidedly ambivalent about the Whigs. Grey he vehemently disliked, though that did not prevent him from approaching the earl, through an intermediary, to see whether a reconciliation was possible; it was not. Grenville made him uneasy. Meanwhile Perceval's cabinet was losing what cohesiveness it possessed. The Regent was "nervous and fluctuating," limping on a sprained ankle and taking huge doses of laudanum—250 drops at a time—to help him sleep.

The state of the country, the condition of the government agitated him. Lady Hertford was much more demanding than comforting, while his brother Ernest, Duke of Cumberland,

.

infuriated him by mocking his illness behind his back, telling people that "a blister on the head might be more efficacious than a poultice on the ankle."[8] Whatever Ernest said, the prince knew himself to be ill. Beginning at the swollen ankle, the inflammation spread throughout his body, producing, in the words of one of his doctors, "a degree of irritation on his nerves nearly approaching to delirium." The family affliction came inevitably to mind. "What will become of us if, as well as our king, our Regent goes mad?" Lady Bessborough remarked. "It will be a new case in the annals of history." Lying motionless on his distended stomach, his head swimming from the effects of laudanum, in irritating pain the prince imagined that he had lost partial use of his right hand. In a panic he announced that he had palsy, his fingers were completely numb and useless. Nonsense, said Dr. Halford. It was just that his chubby hands were cumbered with so many rings and bracelets that they cut off the circulation.[9]

It was a gloomy Christmas. The Regent had "high words" with Ernest, the whole of Carlton House rang with their angry voices. Frightened, like most of the householders in the capital, by recent mass murders in the Thames dockside district of Wapping, Prince George gave orders that no strangers were to be admitted to Carlton House after eight at night, which prevented his servants from entertaining their relatives in the customary way and spoiled their holiday.

With the first of the year, the political decisions Prince George had to make were becoming very pressing, and before he could bring himself to act decisively, they were upon him. Unable to reconcile himself to the Whigs, he left the Tories in power, despite the severe ministerial quarrels that divided them.

The Whigs began immediately to take their revenge, turning on the Regent the weapon they knew would torment him most: his wife Caroline.

The Princess of Wales had been left in a sort of courtly purgatory ever since the Regency began. Excluded from the heaven of the court, she had not been consigned to the hell of divorce or exile. She lived in her modest rented house at Blackheath, behaving as outlandishly as ever, continually

.

going out of her way to shock the staid, well-bred ladies who were appointed to serve her. Now the Whigs raised the issue of Caroline's ill-defined status. Why was she not given a royal establishment befitting a Princess of Wales? If she were guilty of some crime, let her be charged or punished. But if not, she ought to share her husband's honors. Anything else was unseemly.

Caroline herself, who had many an old score to settle with her husband, played her part in the controversy to the hilt, driving all over London in her carriage, putting herself in the public eye, saying outrageous things about the Regent. "Oh, my God!" she burst out when his name was mentioned, "let them let out the poor, dear old king and shut up my husband!" Her remarks were widely repeated, as she knew they would be, and when the Regent heard them he was beside himself with fury. Carlton House was in an uproar. The most private of the ruler's private matters was being publicly aired.

The furor over the Princess of Wales arose as the Luddite agitation spread into Yorkshire and Lancashire. At the same time, there were food riots in many parts of the country. At Bristol a crowd gathered in the market to protest rising food prices and ended by seizing all the available food for themselves. Supplies of corn en route from the countryside to the towns were waylaid by angry mobs, provision shops were broken into and ransacked, food was thrown into the gutter by rioters who refused to pay the high prices being asked for it. At Truro, Plymouth, Falmouth, Chester and a dozen other towns the story was the same. Luddism, it seemed, had set off a chain of disturbances that might ultimately end in a mass rising throughout England and Wales.

Then on May 11 occurred the most alarming event of all. Spencer Perceval was standing in the lobby of the House of Commons, talking to a colleague, when a stranger approached him, pointed a pistol at his chest, and pulled the trigger. Perceval staggered and fell, gasping "I am murdered," or so witnesses thought. At the sound of the shot the M.P.s came rushing out of the chamber into the lobby. Someone sent for a surgeon as confusion grew amid shouts

.

of "Mr. Perceval is shot! Mr. Perceval is shot!" Many Members immediately assumed that the assassin was not alone, that there must be other armed men in the building, bent on killing all the ministers, or even all the M.P.s. There were cries of "Search all strangers!" but no one got around to doing this. Instead attention narrowed to the assassin, John Bellingham.

Bellingham announced that he had acted alone, and that he had decided to shoot the Prime Minister—who quickly died of his wound—out of frustration. He had been a businessman, but the war had driven him out of business, and for this he blamed the government. Like a good many others in that violent spring, he determined to take direct action, and "rejoiced in it," as he exultantly told his captors.[10]

A crowd had collected outside the House. When Bellingham was taken out under guard, to be imprisoned at Newgate, he was greeted with cheers. The crowd surrounded his coach, the police could not keep them off. They clung to the wheels, mounted the box, even forced open the doors to thrust their hands inside to shake Bellingham's. The numbers of police increased, but before the coach could move forward the crowd had to be beaten back with whips. Still they shouted and applauded, cheering and whistling, until the Horse Guards had to be called out to disperse them.

That same afternoon Samuel Taylor Coleridge was in Fleet Street, feeling faint from the heat and upset over the news of Perceval's death. "I was turned numb, and then sick, and then into a convulsive state of weeping on the first tidings," he confided in a letter to his friend the poet Robert Southey, "just as if Perceval had been my near and personal friend."[11] He went into a large public house, "frequented about one o'clock by the lower orders," and was shocked to find that, far from grieving, everyone there was celebrating. Some fifty men and women were drinking toasts, with a noisy clatter of pots, to the downfall of the government and the political success of their hero, the Radical politician Francis Burdett. As it happened, the assassin Bellingham bore a strong resemblance to Burdett, and the healths of both men were drunk repeatedly.

•

"God is above the devil, I say," Coleridge heard one of the revelers shout, "and down to Hell with him and all his brood, the ministers, men of Parliament fellows."

"More of these damned scoundrels must go the same way," came another voice, "and then poor people may live."

Coleridge was alarmed. Here was proof, he wrote Southey, of the enormity of lower-class hatred of the men in power. This was English Jacobinism, pure and simple, frightening in its pervasiveness and magnitude. Fearful of mass demonstrations, the city authorities did not give the late Prime Minister a public funeral, and hurried through the trial and execution of Bellingham. He was hanged on May 18, in front of Newgate prison, and as expected the execution was turned into a popular spectacle. Places were rented in houses which overlooked the site—Byron rented a choice one—and the criminal was sent to his death with cries of "God bless him!" and applause.

Perceval's death had precipitated another political emergency, and on May 22 the government fell. Prince George, who was said to be drinking very heavily and taking increasingly high doses of laudanum, gave the situation fitful, and exceedingly fretful, attention.

Heartened in their protest by Bellingham's daring act and by the continued inefficacy of the constables and militia, the Luddites went about their destructive work with more determination than ever, drilling their members, arming them with stolen weapons, marching on their midnight raids in bands many dozens strong. Their grievances, once local, had widened. They sent letters to the Regent calling him a "Damned Unfeeling Scoundrel" and threatening "Bread or Blood." Like Bellingham, they did not stop short of murder. In Yorkshire a hated manufacturer was assassinated, and others received death threats. All over the West Riding, messages were chalked on doors and walls, offering a hundred guineas for the Regent's head.

.

6

*F*ashionable London was distracted, while the Luddite violence was gathering strength in the spring of 1812, by the advent of a new literary lion. Lord Byron published the first two cantos of his long imaginative poem *Childe Harold's Pilgrimage* early in March, and within days the poem and its young author—he was then twenty-four—were the talk of every dinner table.

"Byr'n—Byr'n—Byr'n—" became a familiar sound at society parties, the low murmured hum of the celebrated poet's name. Hostesses competed for his attendance at their soirées, ladies of fashion contrived to have him placed beside them at supper. Girls swooned over the passionate, agonized hero of *Childe Harold*, the errant prodigal who "through Sin's long labyrinth had run," believing him to be none other than Byron himself.

The poem, with its breathless, pent-up emotion, its groans

.

and exclamations, its glooms and invocations of solacing Nature, showed great imagination and impressive verbal facility; beyond that, it created an exotic, melancholy ambience for the poet, a kind of dramatic stage set for his powerful, though bewilderingly complex, personality.

Its central character, a debauched young nobleman, was the weary survivor of many a love affair and many a night of riotous living. Childe Harold brooded endlessly on his waywardness, but remained unrepentant, and wandered restlessly through Spain, Portugal, Albania and Greece, suffering inner torment yet proud and aloof in his doomed isolation. He inspired pity mixed in delicious proportion with erotic infatuation. *Childe Harold* beckoned the women who read it toward a fantasy of dark rapture; in its strength and vividness it also had a marked appeal to men. At the heart of the poem was a message that struck true in 1812: the message that there was a canker at the root of things, that the times, like Childe Harold himself, were tragically fissured.

"And now Childe Harold was sore sick at heart," Byron wrote,

> And from his fellow bacchanals would flee;
> 'Tis said, at times the sullen tear would start,
> But Pride congealed the drop within his ee:
> Apart he stalked in joyless reverie,
> And from his native land resolved to go,
> And visit scorching climes beyond the sea;
> With pleasure drugged, he almost longed for woe.
> And e'en for change of scene would seek the shades below.[1]

Sullen, proud, joyless, drugged with pleasure, hell-bent on self-destruction—that was the young nobleman of the poem, and his creator. But at the same time the sinner knew his sin, and saw (though he could not follow) the way of redemption. A visionary, he was as capable of envisioning heaven as hell. His soul hung in the balance. He was poised over the edge of the abyss. His spiritual condition evoked the same pleasurable frisson of danger as the artificial spectacles of war Londoners turned out in such numbers to see. Such was the literary Byron—hopelessly confused with his fictional hero Childe Harold. The other Byron, the one his friends knew, was a convivial, vain, dissipated young lord who bit his nails and paid a great deal of attention to his pale complexion and flattering brown ringlets. He had been "a fat, bashful boy." He was no longer fat, but the bashfulness was still there, concealed behind a pose of misanthropic contempt and affectation. With his intimates he was often high-spirited. Thomas Moore, Byron's biographer and friend, referred to "his usual frolicksome gaiety," and both Byron's letters and his poems show that he had a highly developed sense of the absurd.[2] He had, in addition, great bravado, which showed itself in the boldness and originality of his work and in the way he crafted the persona he presented to the public once he became celebrated. And if he suffered from ennui at times, he was also athletic, which counteracted his languor.

It was in his outlook on himself and his fellow creatures that Byron was most like his fictional offspring Childe Harold. Good and evil, belief and unbelief preoccupied him. "I will have nothing to do with your immortality," he wrote to his friend Francis Hodgson, who was about to enter the clergy. "We are miserable enough in this life, without the absurdity of speculating upon another."[3] Yet he read theology, and his letters are full of flippant paraphrases of biblical texts—hardly a rare thing in that age, admittedly—and he never lost the Scottish Calvinism taught him as a child. At the same time, however, he felt that he had inherited from violent ancestors an ingrained tendency toward vice. "There is something Pagan in me that I cannot shake off," he mused. "I deny nothing, but doubt everything."

Byron was like Childe Harold in preferring other places to his native land. "I dislike England," he announced, "and the farther I go the less [I] regret leaving it." Shortly before the publication of his poem he resolved to "leave England for ever," and continued to talk in the same vein once society embraced him.[4] He suffered from what Simond, during his tour of the island, referred to as the English *"maladie du pays."* This illness was peculiar, according to Simond, in that it attacked travelers wherever they were. "It is not

.

merely the result of extreme regrets when they have left their country, and of that perpetual longing to return, felt by other people, but an equal longing to leave it," he explained, "and a sense of weariness and satiety all the time they are at home."[5] Byron's world-weariness, he was convinced, had left him prematurely aged. He was "as old at twenty-three as many men at seventy," he claimed, though the women who hung around him whenever he appeared in the spring of 1812 would hardly have agreed.

In their eyes he was a youthful demigod, exceedingly handsome, with a sexual charisma so overpowering that it disarmed and disturbed them. Women spoke of his smoldering "under-look," which struck them like a bolt of lightning and made them feel faint. His penetrating eyes, his pale, fine complexion offset by dark clothes and fringe of soft curls made a devastating impression.

"How very pale you are," Caroline Lamb wrote to Byron, as pale as "a statue of white marble, so colourless, and the dark brow and hair such a contrast. I never see you without wishing to cry." His ethereal and poignant beauty was such that no painter had been able to capture it, Caroline wrote. His impact had to be felt as well as seen.[6]

But the play of expression across his features had something dangerous and malevolent about it. The arresting, penetrating eyes were set too close together, the broad forehead was too often furrowed in a frown. "He had a great deal of vice in his looks," one lady wrote, and others shied away from him out of fear. Byron's mouth, according to the painter Thomas Lawrence, was "well-formed, but wide, and contemptuous even in its smile, falling singularly at the corners, and its vindictive and disdainful expression heightened by the massive firmness of the chin."[7]

One of the young women who saw him at a social gathering noted that he often hid his mouth with his hand while speaking. It was a way of hiding his natural sarcasm, she thought, which his mouth betrayed. He was trying not to be offensive, but she was too observant not to notice how "at times his lips thickened with disdain, and his eyes rolled impatiently."[8]

The young woman, Anna Isabella (called Annabella) Mil-

.

75

banke, was a well-connected twenty-year-old heiress from Durham, in London to hear lectures on mnemonics, geology and poetry. She read *Childe Harold's Pilgrimage*, judged it to be mannered but admired the author's capacity to describe deep feeling. Like everyone else in good society, she was curious about Byron, and found the rift in his nature particularly fascinating. The gossip she heard about him alarmed her, as it led her to conclude that his emotions were "dreadfully perverted." Yet his poem, she insisted in a letter to her mother, "proves that he *can* feel nobly but he has discouraged his own goodness." It was said he was an infidel, and this the pious Annabella could not condone. Yet her heart went out to him when she heard him murmur that he had not a friend in the world. On the whole, she was intrigued, but put off by the other women who were making fools of themselves over him.[9] "I made no offering at the shrine of Childe Harold," she wrote tartly, and went back to her mnemonics.

Annabella's cousin by marriage, Caroline Lamb, proved to be much less cool. An author herself, she went out of her way to seek an introduction to Byron. She had written poetry and an unpublished piece whose plot turned on the seduction of a girl by an infidel nobleman—a plot with at least superficial affinities to the theme of Byron's poem. Though put off at first, Caroline warmed to Byron after he began calling on her, and very quickly became hopelessly infatuated. He found her enchanting, scintillating and a little fey; he too was enamored, though not so fatally.

For Byron, a provincial nobleman unaccustomed to London society, to ensnare the heart of one of that society's chief ornaments was thought to be a great coup. Caroline had been raised in the ambience of Devonshire House, one of the most influential of the aristocratic Whig establishments. Her mother, the Countess of Bessborough, we have already met as one of the Regent's trusted intimates; her father the earl was a leading political figure and Lord Lieutenant of Ireland. Caroline's late aunt, the Duchess of Devonshire, had been one of the loveliest and most sought-after women of her generation, and had made Devonshire House a glamorous

.

gathering place, the scene of elegant parties and earnest political talk.

Through her husband William Lamb Caroline had been
brought into yet another great Whig circle—that of Melbourne House. Mistress here was Viscountess Melbourne,
William Lamb's mother and Caroline's nemesis. Lady Melbourne was handsome, imposing, formidably intelligent and
shrewd in her judgments of people and politics. Her grasp
of what made the world run was unparalleled, and a wide
variety of her contemporaries turned to her for advice. Melbourne House was a favorite resort of the Regent, and he
was only the most distinguished of an impressive array of
guests.

Caroline's fashionable circle dazzled Byron, but her explo-
sively original personality dazzled him even more. "She possessed an infinite vivacity of mind," he wrote, and in truth
her quicksilver facility with words and love of wordplay was
like his own, though more heated.

"My most sanative elixir of Julep, my most precious cordial
confection," she wrote, addressing her cousin Lord Harting-
ton as if he were a medicine chest, "my most dilutable sal
polychrist and marsh mallows paste, truly comfortable spirit
of hartshorn tincture of rhubarb and purgative senna tea!"[10]
Her letters were a quirky, eccentric jumble of exclamations,
playful archaisms, deft verbal dodges and feints, the whole
working together to scan like poetry. Sometimes they were
in poetry, or rather light verse. Her conversation, it is safe
to suppose, was as brilliantly eccentric as her writing, intense
and full of curiosity and wit, with abrupt changes of mood
and subject that kept her listeners enthralled.

Though she was three years older than Byron, Caroline
seemed much younger, more a willful child than a grown
woman. Slight, nervous and ethereal, with a piquant, heart-
shaped face and close-cropped hair like a boy's, she darted
here and there with the agility of a fawn. Constrained by
the role of wife and mother—her one surviving child, Augustus, was feebleminded—she liked to escape into fantasy, dis-
guising herself as one of her own pages or as a cart-driver
and slipping out into the street on some adventure or other.

In 1812, when she met Byron, her marriage had grown stale and she was chafing under the stern correction of her domineering mother-in-law, Lady Melbourne. The two women were unalike in every respect save strength of will, and as Caroline and William Lamb lived at Melbourne House, conflict between them was unavoidable. The ill feeling reached new heights, however, when Caroline and her famous lover began to cause scandal.

Everything Byron did in April and May of 1812 was watched, discussed and analyzed by his captivated public, and so when he began paying frequent calls on Caroline Lamb at Melbourne House, and sending her letters and gifts, and when her distinctively dressed pages were seen coming in and out of his lodgings several times a day, tongues began to wag. Soon they were being invited to parties together, just as if they were a married couple. (Possibly this was seen as expedient since, if Byron attended a soirée to which Caroline was not invited, she would walk conspicuously up and down in front of the house, waiting for him, until he came out to go home.)

The affair deepened, there were quarrels, noisy scenes and late-night reconciliations. Byron said later that he had never been completely faithful to Caroline, even during what he termed their "delirium of two months," but she insisted that no woman had ever been loved more than he loved her. Certainly he found her "the cleverest most agreeable, absurd, amiable, perplexing, dangerous fascinating little being that lives now," her dizzying charm so overwhelming that she made more beautiful women seem plain.[11]

For him the affair was part of the larger experience of sudden fame. Caroline idolized him, to be sure, but so did dozens of other women, many of whom pledged their love in anonymous letters or offered to meet him in secret rendezvous. "I adore you, how can I convince you that love is my only motive in writing?" "I live but in your image." "Nothing could give me more joy on earth than a lock of your hair."[12] He kept all these tokens of adoration, and showed them to friends, boasting that there were enough of the effusive love letters to fill several large volumes. Celebrity was dizzying,

.

if gratifying; celebrity compounded by violent infatuation was vertiginous indeed. For a few months it sent him reeling, but by summer he was finding his balance again, especially as Caroline had begun to lose hers completely.

As Byron's passion cooled, Caroline's grew ever more heated and explosive. Infatuation was one thing, her desperate, frenzied hectoring of him another. Caroline's nerves were on edge at the best of times; at her worst she gave way to manic fits, assaulting her pages, tearing her clothes and going wild. Byron called her "little Mania," and likened her heart to a volcano that "poured lava through her veins." Sensing that he was cooling toward her, and realizing that there were a hundred women eager to take her place, waiting only for Byron to turn his thrilling "under-look" on them, she became even more reckless in running after him. She went to his friends, sometimes waking them up in the middle of the night and begging them to put in a good word for her. She made a spectacle of herself by waylaying his coach and leaning in at the window shamelessly. He asked her to leave him in peace, but she pestered him anyway, coming in disguise to his rooms, sending him letters by the hour, threatening him and making scenes.

She could still charm Byron, but her antics were becoming tiresome and his friends warned him that through her he was beginning to look ridiculous. His celebrity would become tarnished if he wasn't careful. Besides, Caroline was all wrong for him, thin and irritable where he preferred women buxom and good-humored. "A delicate woman, however prettily it may sound, harrows my feelings," he wrote. Delicacy went inevitably with vapors, hysterics, nerves, megrims and intermitting fever. It was not for him. He wrote to Caroline, telling her how foolish their attachment was. "A month's absence would make us rational, you do not think so, I know it, we have both had 1000 previous fancies of the same kind, and shall get the better of this and be ashamed of it."[13]

A month's absence then might have been exactly the thing to wind down Caroline's obsession and put a stop to all the damaging gossip. "People talk as if there were no other pair of absurdities in London," Byron complained. It was hard

.

to bear, especially now that the pinnacle of social distinction was within his grasp. The Regent had asked that Byron be introduced to him, and he had received an invitation to a levée at Carlton House. Though the levée was ultimately postponed, Byron prepared for it with elaborate care, dressing in a full-dress court suit and applying a liberal amount of hair powder.[14] If he were to be admitted to the Regent's circle of friends he would have to be circumspect in his personal life—far more circumspect than he had been up to now.

Predictably, however, Caroline refused the entreaties of her distraught mother Lady Bessborough and her furious mother-in-law Lady Melbourne that she leave London and Byron for a while. She kept up her threats and storms, sleeping badly and looking careworn. She had been known to harm herself while in such states and her relatives were tensed for an explosion. It soon came: at the climax of a terrible scene with her parents she ran out of the house and into the street, disappearing before the servants could catch up with her. Her mother and father searched everywhere—including Byron's lodgings—but couldn't find her. She was finally found hours later in Kensington, where she had bribed a hackney coachman to take her, but her childish flight had upset all her relatives and caused further talk. Clearly someone had to take her in hand.

By this time another side of Byron's own capricious nature had begun to assert itself. He had made the acquaintance of Caroline's fair, blue-eyed cousin Annabella Milbanke, and had been drawn to her studious intelligence and preternatural gravity. Annabella was as much unlike Caroline as possible, composed and serene where her madcap cousin was nervous and excitable. Caroline had brought out the worst in him, Byron decided; Annabella would work to bring out his best. If Childe Harold could be redeemed, it would be at the hands of a young woman like Miss Milbanke.

Annabella was something of a prodigy. She wrote poetry, had a talent for mathematics, and was a proficient Latinist. At seventeen she had made a critical study of Bacon's *De Augmentis Scientiarum*, weighing the philosopher's observa-

tions and arguments and writing a commentary on them.
Byron was perhaps a new and interesting object of study
to her, ripe for experimentation and overdue for spiritual
ministrations. She became interested in improving him, and
he seemed eager to be improved.

He seemed eager—and in fact he began to court her in
earnest. Yet Byron, who could be strongly misogynistic, had
a certain contempt for Annabella's learned seriousness. "She
is too good for a fallen spirit to know or wish to know,
and I should like her more if she were less perfect," he remarked shortly after meeting her. He admired her intellect
and the breadth of her learning, but like most men of his
era he tended to think of learned women as bluestockings,
faintly ridiculous and more than a little tiresome. When he
called Annabella "my Princess of Parallelograms"—a reference to her enjoyment of mathematics—the epithet was a
mocking one. Two lines from *Don Juan*, which Byron wrote
long afterward, capture his attitude:

> But—Oh! ye lords of ladies intellectual,
> Inform us truly, have they not henpeck'd you all?[15]

The ambivalence he felt toward Annabella's endowments
was offset by other factors. She was an heiress with a large
fortune, and he was deeply in debt and in need of a wealthy
wife. Then there was her aunt, Lady Melbourne. She befriended Byron and gave him the benefit of her hard-headed
good sense. A sympathetic attachment developed between
them. Lady Melbourne was sixty years old and a grand-
mother, but Byron was a little in love with her; one of the
reasons he wanted to marry Annabella Milbanke, he confessed, was that she was Lady Melbourne's niece and he liked
the idea of becoming related to her.

Lady Melbourne helped Byron to put all his affairs of
the heart in perspective. Love affairs, she insisted, ought not
to interfere with more serious things, such as getting on
with one's career and advancing one's social status. Above
all, love affairs ought to be conducted discreetly and, when
they had run their course, broken off with a minimum of
recrimination.

.

Still handsome in a strapping, strong-featured way, Lady Melbourne was herself a veteran of numerous liaisons. (Her husband, whom she had married at sixteen, was little more than a cipher in her life, save that his fortune paid the bills.) Among her former lovers were the Regent, who was said to be the father of her son George, and the wealthy, eccentric Lord Egremont, father of her son William. Rumor had it that another of her lovers, Lord Coleraine, had "sold" her to Lord Egremont for thirteen thousand pounds, a portion of which she had taken as her own fee. Such an amorous history was nothing unusual for an influential Whig lady, but it did show exceptional shrewdness. Lady Melbourne had chosen her lovers, as she did her friends, her dress, and the décor of her mansion, with her social ambitions in mind. She counseled Byron to do the same.

"Anyone who braves the world sooner or later feels the consequences of it," she liked to say. However irregular one's private life might be, it was important to appear guiltless. Her rebellious daughter-in-law Caroline had not only ignored this social rule, she flaunted her extravagant passion for Byron, and for this Lady Melbourne could not forgive her. Her strong animus against Caroline worked to curdle Byron's remaining feeling for her, as did Caroline's unrelenting importunities.

In September Caroline finally agreed to leave London. With her mother and her husband she went to Ireland, to her father's estate, where she alternately brooded and erupted into nerve storms. But her departure did not put an end to her nuisance. The post from Ireland brought Byron letter after letter from her, letters full of accusations, avowals and entreaties. He showed them to Lady Melbourne—a breach of loyalty that would have made Caroline furious had she known of it. Together, man of the world to woman of the world, they dissected the problem. Finally Byron declared Caroline to be "the most contradictory, absurd, selfish, and contemptibly wicked of human productions."[16] He wrote her a curt, cruel letter of good-bye.

By this time Byron was detached enough to reflect dispassionately on his own emotions. With one exception, he had

.

never known himself to carry on even the most tumultuous love affair for more than three months, he told his confidante, Lady Melbourne. In the autumn of 1809, he recalled, he had been "seized with an *everlasting* passion," a good deal stronger than his late passion for Caroline. He had been on the point of eloping with his lover, Constance Spencer Smith, when circumstances had forced them apart. But that great passion had withered as rapidly as any of the others.

"She is now I am told writing her Memoirs at Vienna," he added cynically, "in which I shall cut a very indifferent figure; and nothing survives of this most ambrosial amour, which made me on one occasion risk my life, and on another almost drove me mad, but a few Duke of Yorkish letters [a reference to the promotion scandal involving Mary Ann Clarke] and certain baubles which I dare swear by this time have decorated the hands of half Hungary, and all Bohemia."[17]

Such an attitude toward love on Byron's part was underscored in the fall of 1812 by several light liaisons he entered into—all the while endeavoring to persuade Annabella to agree to marry him—with an actress and a dark-eyed Italian woman who reminded him of other Mediterranean amours. Marriage seemed more and more an urgent necessity; the heavily encumbered Byron estate at Newstead had been put up for auction, but as the bids had been too low to cover the debts it remained unsold, and the debts unpaid. Byron's valet William Fletcher suggested a solution. Fletcher had taken up with the maidservant of a Dutch widow "of great riches and rotundity." How ideal it would be for all concerned, he told his master, if Byron and the Dutch widow were to get married. She would have a husband, Byron would have her money, and Fletcher and the maidservant would have each other.[18]

In October Annabella, after weighing the matter almost as carefully as she had weighed Bacon's treatise, declined Byron's offer of marriage. Caroline, back in England the following December, staged a solemn little pagan ritual in which she burned Byron's effigy along with his book, his ring and chain, and copies of his letters to her. The ceremony

.

was, like Caroline herself, odd and childlike, with village maidens dancing around an open-air fire, chanting rhymes Caroline wrote for them. It was a minor revenge, but it could not exorcise his charm over her. Byron had meanwhile found new satisfaction with Lady Oxford, as learned as Annabella but infinitely more accessible, at once motherly and alluring. He installed himself at her country house and gave his fame and his temperament a rest. He thought of writing more of *Childe Harold's Pilgrimage,* for the opposing forces which had helped to inspire the poem still warred within him. He described himself as "daily repenting and never amending," though to think seriously of amendment in the company of the loose, complaisant Lady Oxford would have required a much sturdier conscience than Byron possessed.

In the interim fashionable London was celebrating a new literary production. *Christian Morals,* the newest work of the famed religious reformer Hannah More, had been published to much acclaim and the first printing had been sold out before publication. Several more printings had been ordered, and still the demand for copies could not be met. To be sure, *Christian Morals* did not elicit quite the same sentiments in its audience as Byron's poem had, but then Byron's career was just beginning, while the celebrated Hannah More had been widely read for decades and would continue to be, one critic predicted, for "as long as sensibility and good taste shall exist among us."

7

*W*hat Hannah More thought of Byron and *Childe Harold's Pilgrimage* can only be conjectured, but it seems likely she saw both the poet and his poem as very much products of their spiritually divided age.

"It appears to me that the two classes of character are more decided than they were," she declared. "The wicked seem more wicked, and the good, better." Byron's wickedness was flagrant and all-pervasive—and so was the joyless restlessness it drove him to. Much as she deplored his immorality she recognized in him an example to others of the poverty of the godless life.

The profane, the enemies of goodness, seemed to her to have their place in God's plan, if only because they "served to confirm the truths they mean to oppose." Thoroughgoing vice enhanced virtue by contrast, and Byron, by making a trademark of his boredom and sullen disaffection, made vice

.

more repellent than attractive. And if the fashionable world was titillated and seduced by Byron, it revered Hannah More and the comfortable decency she stood for. She represented regeneration, the pale young poet, stagnation and regression. Or so it seemed to the large and growing segment of the public that was serious-minded.

"Holy Hannah" was nearly sixty-eight when *Christian Morals* was published. She was the best-known, most read and most widely respected of the Evangelicals, moral reformers whose program of religious renewal and social betterment reached its height during the Regency. With William Wilberforce, Hannah More led the Evangelicals, exerting her influence through her voluminous writings and winning an extraordinarily wide audience for her views.

For a quarter-century, since before the outbreak of the Revolution in France, More had been addressing the "good sort of people" in England, "those who count," as she put it. She meant the upper classes, and especially the aristocracy whose behavior was all the more influential for being conspicuous to their inferiors. She addressed them in a straightforward, commonsensical way, without self-righteousness. What she told them was very simple: she told them that they were not really Christians.

It was a sobering message, and a great many people took it to heart. (A great many others didn't. "Things are coming to a pretty pass," Lord Melbourne said, "when religion is allowed to invade private life.") It was the heart, in fact, that mattered, More taught. Religion began and ended in the heart's devotion, and it was just this devotion that most churchgoers who called themselves Christians lacked.

"The fear of God begins with the heart, and purifies and rectifies it," she wrote, quoting Matthew Hale, "and from the heart thus rectified, grows a conformity in the Life, the Words, and the Actions." From the heart outward: it was a credo of the Evangelicals, and it coincided with a broad cultural shift toward feeling and sentiment in the later eighteenth century. More's "religion of the heart" appealed to the same yearning for emotional nourishment as did the popular novels that flooded the marketplace, tales of love and loss, Gothic horror, virtue triumphant. (That religious conversion and novel reading might spring from the same impulse would have dismayed More, who thought popular fiction "debased the taste, slackened the intellectual nerve, let down the understanding, set the fancy loose, and sent it gadding among low and mean objects."[1])

But More's works outsold even the most successful novels, despite their somewhat daunting titles, such as *Thoughts on the Importance of the Manners of the Great to General Society* and *An Estimate of the Religion of the Fashionable World*. Her books were sold out within days, sometimes within hours, of their appearance; edition after edition came out, and still the hunger for her message was not assuaged. She went on writing throughout the 1790s, into the early years of the new century, until by 1813, when *Christian Morals* was published, More was a cultural fixture, her eminence beyond dispute.

Hannah More had a genius for popularization, and she set out to make Christian morality popular. She was a supremely eloquent writer—before turning to religious subjects she had written well-received plays, and had great facility with words—yet hers was an eloquence that never called attention to itself. Her directness and sincerity were disarming, her down-to-earth tone engaging. She was not a scold, and certainly not a fanatic. Her style was calm and classical, her language that of a well-bred gentlewoman speaking to her equals.

Her "true religion" had nothing wild or extreme about it. It did not demand that one "renounce the generous and important duties of an active life for the visionary, cold, and fruitless virtues of an hermitage, or a cloister." But it was completely, uncompromisingly at odds with worldliness. Worldliness, more than outright vice, was to More the enemy of Christianity. "Religion was never yet thoroughly relished by a heart full of the world," she admonished, and she was well aware that the public she addressed was a product of a thoroughly—and in some respects gloriously—worldly culture.

Cultivated, sophisticated, reasonable and urbane, the English aristocracy prided itself on an easy toleration and good manners. Moderation was its watchword, with all things viewed in human scale. Its world was self-contained in its comfortable secularism, with no spiritual agonies or ultimate questions to disturb its equilibrium. Its church, the established church, did nothing to upset this equilibrium. Clergymen were frequently as worldly as their parishioners, and commanded little respect. One of their number, Sydney Smith, commented that in England men of the cloth were "no more regarded than cheesemongers," and other kinds of evidence bear him out.

In singling out worldliness as the primary enemy of the true Christian More touched a nerve, for her own generation was the last to embrace cultivated secularism without qualification. Upper-class English who came to maturity in the closing years of the century, and even more those who matured during the Regency were, many of them, oppressed by the emptiness of the old easygoing ways of their parents and grandparents. Toleration seemed to them indecision, moderation an excuse for mental laziness. To many of the young their elders seemed morally benighted, adrift on a tide of irresolution. They sensed, as Byron did, a canker at the root of things; grand as their elders might appear, many of the young believed them to be in fact trapped in a hall of mirrors, pursuing nothing more substantial than their own infinitely receding reflections. Worldly grandeur, and the pleasure it bought, were illusory. They sought escape, out of the hall of mirrors and into the region of limitless horizons offered by Christian truth.

Of course, it was not only the young who felt this way. People of all ages were converted to Evangelicalism in increasing numbers, until by the time the Regency opened they constituted a very strong social force, growing stronger all the time. Serious-mindedness was moving into the mainstream of public life, and Hannah More had helped greatly to put it there.

An important dimension of the Evangelical movement was improving the lives of the poor. More, with one of her four sisters, set out to bring her "religion of the heart" into poor

·

rural parishes and to teach the children of agricultural laborers to read the Bible.

In her letters she described her efforts to found a school
at Cheddar in Somerset, how she and her sister took rooms
in a little public house and began to investigate conditions
in the parish. There were in all more than two hundred
people in the parish, all but a dozen of them very poor. The
dozen exceptions were prosperous farmers—"rich savages,"
More called them—who dominated affairs in the village and
without whose approbation her efforts were sure to be
useless.

"I was told we should meet with great opposition if I
did not try to propitiate the chief despot of the village, who
is very rich, and very brutal," she wrote in a letter to
Wilberforce.[2] Accordingly she approached him, only to find
him totally opposed to the idea of offering religious education
to the poor. Teaching them to read would only make them
lazy and useless, he insisted. When More argued that religion
would be likely to make the laborers work harder, for they
would learn to be honest and industrious, he was not convinced. Nor was he convinced of her own disinterestedness.
He "knew the world too well" to be taken in by such arguments.

More found the man "hard, brutal and ignorant," and the
other well-off farmers were no better. She visited them all,
flattering their vanity, fondling their ugly children, ca-
ressing their slobbering dogs, doing whatever it took to win
their trust. It was hard going, for they were "as ignorant
as the beasts that perish, intoxicated every day before dinner,
and plunged in such vices as make me begin to think London
a virtuous place." Finally one of the wives, coarse and immoral though she was, agreed to rent More a house, with a
dilapidated barn adjoining it. With her sister's help she re-
roofed the barn and made it into a schoolroom. Then came
the challenge of coaxing the children inside.

More and her sister went through the parish from door
to door, counting the women and children, and trying to
persuade mothers to send their sons and daughters to school.

.

At first the mothers refused, wanting to be paid before they would agree to part with their children; some feared that the children would be kidnapped and sold into slavery. But in the end the children came, and the improvised school opened, with the teaching shared between More, her sister, and two paid schoolmistresses. During the week a class of thirty girls was taught reading, sewing and knitting; on Sundays all the children learned to read (but not to write, as this was thought to promote "fanaticism," or political radicalism), from printed tracts framed and hung around the walls of the schoolroom. Bible passages such as the Sermon on the Mount and certain Psalms were committed to memory, and the younger children learned hymns.

In the beginning only the children came, but before long their parents were joining them, attending the school on Sunday nights to hear a sermon, then on two nights a week or even three. More organized the women into a mutual aid club which, if it acted as a sort of moral vigilante society to report on swearing, scolding and church attendance, also provided funds to rescue members when they were ill or in acute financial distress. As time went by the children became adults, and were launched into adult life by a little ceremony. Girls who completed the course of instruction were given, when they married, five shillings, a pair of white stockings and a new Bible.

This was charity work, and as such it was not unlike what Lady Bessborough did when she started a school for "the commonest poor beggar girls who are running ragged and dirty about the streets," training them to become cooks and housemaids and laundrymaids.[3] But while Lady Bessborough hoped for nothing more than to rescue her girls from being forced into thievery and prostitution, Hannah More and her helpers actually attempted to fill the void left by the absence of parish ministry in Cheddar and the other rural communities she evangelized. She herself distributed hundreds of Bibles, Common Prayer Books and Testaments, while her teachers "did just what a clergyman does in other parishes," visiting the sick and giving them medicine, praying with

.

those in distress, occasionally giving out small sums of money where the need was great.

Cheddar was badly neglected by the clergy. There was a vicar, appointed by the dean of the neighboring town of Wells, but he was an absentee, collecting the fifty pounds a year the living provided and never coming near his parish. The curate lived at Wells, and came to Cheddar only once a week to preach a sermon, usually to a half-dozen people at most. The only other local cleric, the vicar of Axbridge, was a tough, hard-living old man of sixty, drunk nearly every night, who More said was "very frequently prevented from preaching by two black eyes, honestly earned by fighting." Needless to say, few people in Cheddar had had any religious instruction of any kind. Their acquaintance with the sacraments was perfunctory; children came into the world without baptism, and frequently died without a funeral. "We saw but one Bible in all the parish," More told Wilberforce, "and that was used to prop a flower-pot!"

The hymns and Bible verses the children memorized, and the Bible study groups the younger people attended in the evenings, were rudimentary as Christian teaching, and hardly controversial. Yet they drew fire from all sides. Anonymous enemies broke the windows of the converted barn. Tipsy farmers besieged another of More's schools, at Wedmore, where several hundred people had gathered to hear a sermon, "loudly vociferating that they would have no such methodistical doings."[4] To be thought "methodistical" was potentially damaging to the Evangelicals' cause of social betterment, for Methodism was a lower-class phenomenon and the Evangelicals were determined to win and keep upperclass support.

Methodism, whose initial fervor was past when Hannah More began her campaign of religious education, was a reform movement led by the Anglican clergyman John Wesley. The Methodists placed great emphasis on conversion, and the passionate oratory of their preachers, who often spoke out of doors to huge crowds, made a strong appeal to the emotions. Methodist sermons brought the fires of hell very

.

close, and the terrified believers, near panic in their fear, threw themselves on Christ's mercy. Most of them were poor and uneducated; imbued by those who converted them with a strong sense of the demonic, they were carried out of themselves to such an extent that they "shrieked and roared aloud," now weeping, now falling suddenly to the ground, now bellowing unintelligibly like mad people. Some gasped and all but choked, their faces turning red, then black before they could be revived.

To outsiders, especially outsiders among the propertied classes, Methodism was indistinguishable from holy demagoguery. Crowds of the poor were driven to uncontrollable hysteria, and no one knew where that hysteria might lead. Methodists were stoned, assaulted, set upon by dogs. There were fewer than a hundred thousand of them in England at the turn of the century, but they were nonetheless feared for that. And "Holy Hannah" looked very much like one of them, despite the rational tone of her prose and her attempts to align herself and her cause with the upper classes.

More and her teachers were accordingly called Methodists, and accused of distributing Methodist books and pamphlets. The Wedmore farmers went "to the fortune-teller, to know if we are Methodists, and if our school is methodistical," she described in a letter. "The oracle returned an ambiguous answer, and desired to know what reason they had for suspecting it. The farmer replied, it was because we sang Watts' hymns." Methodists did sing the hymns of Isaac Watts, but so did others. When the fortune-teller remarked that this seemed inconclusive evidence, and asked whether the farmers had any better reason for their suspicions, they became indignant.

"Yes," they answered, "for if the hymns were not methodistical, the tunes were."[5]

There was no limit to the threats and accusations made against More. The clergy were among her worst enemies, calling her a Jacobin, a traitor to England, a supporter of the French who taught her converts to pray for Bonaparte. Her writings "ought to be burned by the hands of the common hangman," one pamphleteer wrote. It was said that she had hired two men to assassinate a priest, another story had it that she had conspired to assassinate the king. It was even alleged that she had helped to instigate the war with France. The outlandish allegations she could dismiss, but years of harassment in the courts by legal agents of the clergy wore her down. The "grief and astonishment" of it all, she confessed to a colleague, nearly cost her her life.[6]

By the time she wrote this Evangelicalism had won a major victory in Parliament. In 1807, William Wilberforce, with his block of like-minded M.P.s known as "the Saints," succeeded in pushing through an act to abolish the trade in slaves. (Slavery itself was not to become illegal for another eighteen years.) The abolition of the slave trade had been a major aim of the Evangelical movement since its inception. Wilberforce had first moved resolutions to end it fifteen years earlier, but the opposition of the West Indian interest and of the Prime Minister, William Pitt, prevented passage of the act. In the long run, though, the campaign succeeded, chiefly because of the singular impact of Wilberforce's personality.

He was undeniably a saintly man. His face was radiant with gentle innocence, his kindness was boundless and completely disarming. As sweet as a child, he was physically painfully frail and crippled, eliciting compassion and no doubt indirectly aiding his cause. His sight was so poor he seemed half blind, and with his unsteady gait and twisted limbs he was a grotesque figure. "Nothing can surpass the meanness of his appearance," Simond wrote when he saw Wilberforce in the House of Commons. Yet his overflowing warmth and liveliness, his quick sense of humor and urbane and diverting conversation drew attention away from the defects of his person. One admirer called him "a winged being in airy flight," and sugary as the phrase was it matched the idealized portraits of the reformer painted toward the end of his life.

Simond described Wilberforce at work in Parliament: "a little man, thin as a shadow, drawing one side of his body after him, as if paralytic, hurrying across the floor with a tottering brisk step, and awkward bow." The speech Simond

.

heard him give bore out the widely held view that Wilberforce was the most movingly eloquent speaker in the country,
delivering his message "with peculiar energy of feeling." Any
cause he championed became tinged with his rhetoric, his
ethereal presence. Throughout the 1790s and early 1800s he
had poured his energies into the task of winning public support for ending the slave trade, organizing meetings, making
speech after speech, going wherever he could gather an audience. Finally in 1807, with Pitt dead and the Evangelical
viewpoint gaining support, the abolition act passed.

Between Wilberforce's persuasive oratory and Hannah
More's persuasive writings the progress of Evangelicalism
was remarkable. Societies sprang up to promote innumerable
causes. There was the Society for Bettering the Condition
and Increasing the Comforts of the Poor, generally called
the "Bettering Society," the Bible Society, the Climbing Boy
Society, the Church Missionary Society and the London Society for the Promotion of Christianity Against the Jews. Other
societies aided French refugees, Austrian soldiers, foreigners
in distress and Irish serving girls. Living conditions in London cried out to be improved, and the Evangelicals addressed
themselves with vigor to efforts to close brothels and dance-
halls, to bring the law down on those who used blasphemous
language and promoted irreligion, to protect homeless children and redeem the outcasts who scavenged for their livings
in the streets.

The scope of these reforming energies was vast and somewhat diffuse. In some instances the Evangelicals were moved
by heartfelt benevolence, in others by holy wrath. Wilberforce envisioned grandiose and sweeping change, on a nation-
wide and even a worldwide scale. His Society for the
Suppression of Vice (formerly known as the Proclamation
Society Against Vice and Immorality) was intended to alter
England's living habits radically, while projects to send mis-
sionaries into Africa and India and the Far East had as their
aim nothing short of the Christianizing of the globe.

Yet the Evangelicals had a blind spot when it came to
purifying the upper classes whose support they needed. Hannah More might exhort the privileged to free themselves

from worldliness, but there were no societies to promote fidelity, thrift and sobriety among the aristocracy. The royal family, whose members, apart from the king and queen, were so inventively and untiringly immoral, were spared censure. Wilberforce was, after all, one of the privileged few himself, his radical opponents claimed. He was a wealthy man, and marrying a wealthy wife had brought him even more prosperity. He was a humanitarian when it came to black African slaves, but not when it came to poor English laborers, whose efforts to form unions he criticized as immoral. The Evangelicals were profoundly conservative, devoted to maintaining the social hierarchy intact and horrified by the prospect of people rebelling against their assigned roles within it. What did one's station in life matter, they asked, when all were equal in God's sight? There were no gradations, no degrees when it came to salvation, and salvation was what counted.

Wilberforce brought all his eloquence to bear in support of this view. Christianity, he argued, made the lower orders less discontent with their lot, and the Bible taught them to be diligent, humble and patient, "reminding them that their more lowly path has been allotted to them by the hand of God." God ordained poverty, therefore the poor should "bear its inconveniences" with Christian fortitude. Life is short, the reformer insisted, and its comforts and pleasures fleeting; the peace of mind religion brings is worth more than all the expensive pleasures the rich enjoy.[7]

For a man, however saintly, who had never known the pain of poverty to moralize about it in this way alienated many who might otherwise have been his natural allies in the cause of social betterment. The radicals referred to "the verminous Wilberforce," and renounced him—if not all he stood for.

A broad segment of society, however, venerated him, and it was this group that was coming more and more to dominate the social tone. For as the middle classes advanced, piety and serious-mindedness advanced with them. The worldliness and moral eccentricity which had found fullest expression among the fashionable were being ousted by godliness and propriety. Evangelicalism was driving libertinism into retreat. Moral purpose was ousting fashionable purposeless-ness. If Byron had defined the national malady, the serious-minded had defined its cure.

Everywhere they were on the march, distributing Bibles and pamphlets, agitating against immorality and vice, work-ing to close down theaters and other places of amusement that threatened to distract people from loftier meditations, founding improvement societies and plucking lost souls out of the gutters. Their energy matched their earnestness; zeal seemed to drive even the most fragile of them onward past the point of exhaustion.

"Sin wears a front of brass among us," trumpeted the *Christian Guardian*, "walking with shameless impudence through our public streets in open day." The effrontery of the worldly was a challenge to the godly, spurring them on to militant confrontations. The Bishop of London, Beilby Porteus, rang down the curtain in the middle of a ballet performance one Saturday midnight, so that the profane entertainment would not continue into the early hours of the sabbath. The specta-tors erupted in anger, but Bishop Porteus prevailed. Wilber-force attempted, unsuccessfully as it turned out, to stop the sales of newspapers on Sundays, and would have prevented the militia from drilling on the sabbath as well if he could.

Such creedbound sabbatarianism lent itself to ridicule, as did the reformers' absolute and thoroughgoing opposition to card playing, dancing, singing and country walks on Sun-days. Seen in an Evangelical light, almost any secular activity was impure, tainted as it necessarily was by love of the world. The most uncompromising of the Evangelicals led the rest into Puritanism, or something resembling it, with the result that the movement was made to seem myopic and petty.

In 1804 Thomas Bowdler published *The Family Shakespeare*, an edition of the plays from which everything was excised "which cannot with propriety be read in a family." Reading aloud was a common practice, and Bowdler was concerned to protect women and children from being subjected to Shakespeare's bawdiness and blasphemy. (The men could read the unaltered version to themselves, in private.) Entire passages were omitted from the plays, as were such scandalous characters as Doll Tearsheet. In Bowdler's version the plays contained no sex, no expletives and no bodily functions. There were no bodies either: the word "body" Bowdler replaced with "person," just as he replaced "God" with "Heaven" or "Nature" and added sanitized words or phrases to fill out the lines he edited. *The Family Shakespeare* presented a bloodless, gutless bard, his works truncated or suppressed. Bowdler found *Othello* impossible to bowdlerize; to alter it sufficiently to satisfy propriety was to sacrifice the play's very heart. Consequently he advised that it not be read aloud at all, and kept out of the hands of the more tender family members.

Bowdler was a physician by profession, well educated and, like Hannah More in her youth, a familiar figure in London literary society in the 1780s. Friendship with Wilberforce and membership in the Society for the Suppression of Vice occasioned his Shakespearean labors, which proved to be highly successful. *The Family Shakespeare* sold exceptionally well, with a new edition appearing every few years until by the 1820s it was on its way to becoming a perennial. Nor was it his work alone that was successful. His method, too, set a pattern for presenting classics to the reading public in a way guaranteed to safeguard its virtues and beliefs.

Bowdler himself edited Gibbon's *History of the Decline and Fall of the Roman Empire,* leaving out the historian's irreverent account of early Christianity. A Cambridge clergyman "purified" *Robinson Crusoe* for family reading. Educational reformers excised the fairy tales from children's books, as they were not only un-Christian but of dubious morality. Cinderella was thought to be particularly "exceptionable"—the term conveyed extreme Evangelical scorn—as it "painted some of the worst passions that can ever enter the human heart and of which little children should, if possible, be totally ignorant."[8] Cinderella encouraged vanity, a love of self-adornment, envy, jealousy, and hatred of stepmothers and half-sisters—all repugnant to the teachings of Christ. Worse than fairy tales were the pagan classics, and scholars were hard put to edit these in a way that honored both their learning and their faith.

.

Once the hunt for guilty texts was under way there was no moderating it, and a narrow literalism set in. With Bowdler and his imitators Evangelicalism took on the character of small-minded bickering over minutiae. It was one of the least attractive aspects of the movement. "The letter killeth," and the spirit—that spirit Hannah More had sought to reach and to move within people—began to be imperiled. More always emphasized that what mattered was not words, but what lay beyond them, the purer communication of the heart. "Prayer," she wrote in *Practical Christianity*, is

> the application of want to Him who only can relieve it; the voice of sin to Him who alone can pardon it. It is the urgency of poverty, the prostration of humility, the fervency of penitence, the confidence of trust. It is not eloquence, but earnestness, not the definition of helplessness, but the feeling of it; not figures of speech, but compunction of soul. It is the "Lord save us, we perish" of drowning Peter; the cry of faith to the ear of mercy.[9]

Yet the Evangelical fervor ran along many channels, and the thoughtful pursuit of meaningful religion continued to be among them. And it was this pursuit that continued to find a growing response among the population at large, whose sense of emptiness and drift and desire for fulfillment and direction grew year by year. That this societal anguish should express itself in the lexicon of religion was inevitable, given the time and place in which it arose. Peter's cry "Lord save us, we perish" came naturally to the lips of people bred, however casually, in Christian teachings and threatened by war, economic chaos and perpetual uncertainty.

It was also a populace haunted by guilt. "I am convinced that the French are permitted by the almighty to succeed as a scourge for our sins," one aristocratic dowager told her son at the outset of war between England and France.[10] For centuries the English had interpreted their calamities as brought on by divine displeasure, just as they attributed their triumphs to divine intervention. God had afflicted his people with plague and war and with the violent weather that made the crops fail and left the people to starve; God had rescued

.

his people from disease and from their enemies, strengthening their armies and causing the sun to shine on their abundant harvests. The cycle of sin and repentance, punishment and redemption seemed inescapably clear to many. It was the ground stuff of human history, providence at work in earthly affairs.

"We have offended. Oh my countrymen;/ We have offended very grievously," Coleridge wrote as he watched the sea, expecting the French invasion fleet. "Therefore evil days/ Are coming on us, O my countrymen!" The evil days were at hand, and the Evangelicals presented a timely and salutary—indeed a providential—counterforce. In a time of severe trial and underlying distress they held up the banner of faith, and many rallied to it.

"I do not like Evangelicals," Jane Austen commented. She particularly disliked Hannah More's one work of fiction, the highly successful *Coelebs in Search of a Wife*. To be sure, the novel told a story, yet it pointed any number of somewhat intrusive morals at the same time, and berated readers for allowing their imaginations to be beguiled into "unparalleled vice and infidelity" by poetry and romance. Yet the appeal of Evangelicalism was not lost on the younger novelist. "I am by no means convinced," she noted, "that we ought not all to be Evangelical and am at least persuaded that they who are so from reason and feeling must be happiest and safest."

.

8

*T*he first dispatches describing Wellington's stunning rout of the French at Vitoria reached England early in July of 1813, and within hours special editions of the newspapers were announcing "the most complete defeat of the enemy yet experienced in the peninsula."

Fifty thousand British, Portuguese and Spanish troops had engaged 60,000 of the French, entrenched behind 138 guns in the plain of Vitoria in northern Spain, and had beaten them so badly that they abandoned all but one of the guns and fled toward the Pyrenees. In their haste the French had lost everything, not only artillery but ammunition, baggage, provisions, even money. The two French commanders, Joseph Bonaparte, who had been enthroned King of Spain five years earlier, and Marshal Jourdan, had been so precipitate in making their escape that the former had left behind all

·

his personal possessions and the latter his marshal's baton—
a prize that sweetened the English triumph.

Vitoria meant the end of Bonaparte rule in Spain—and
the resurgence, on the part of Russia, Prussia and Austria,
of determination to defeat the French. Earlier in the year
that determination had wavered, for Bonaparte had shown
amazing resilience following the overwhelming defeat of his
army in Russia the previous fall. He had raised yet another
army, and had beaten the Russians and Prussians at Lützen
and Bautzen only a month before Wellington's victory. An
armistice had been signed—which excluded Britain—and for
a time it looked as though there might be a permanent peace,
arranged on terms favorable to France and greatly to England's disadvantage. With the continent at peace Bonaparte
could turn his full attention to driving the English out of
Spain and Portugal and then to invading Britain itself, as
he had long been threatening to do. And the seriousness of
this threat would be compounded by the fact that England
was at war with the United States, and could not use her
full forces to repel a French assault.

But Wellington's victory reversed all this. Britain's continental allies were heartened, they began to envision success
once again. Only a few garrisoned towns now stood between
Wellington and the French border. If he could sweep up
from the south, while the other powers pressed the French
from the east, the momentum of the war might shift decisively.

In London there was a scramble for the *Courier* and the
Gazette, which carried accounts of the battle and printed the
names of dead and wounded officers (only the numbers, not
the names of enlisted men wounded and killed were printed).
The casualties were heavy, but those of the French, the papers
said, were far heavier, redeeming the national sacrifice. In
any case, the magnitude of the victory outweighed all. "Everybody, as you may well suppose, is wild with joy," George
Jackson wrote on July 3. "People are in the very highest
spirits. . . . The public look for much, their hopes are placed
upon the very loftiest pinnacle."[1]

•

The excitement lasted for days, with gala public celebrations and, every night, displays of lights illumining the squares and public buildings. Balconies were hung with lamps, theaters and shops were festooned with garlands of colored lanterns and blazing flambeaux.[2] "Wellington" and "Victory" were spelled out in lights in every street and square, and the crowds that gathered in the warm July evenings cheered their hero and his triumph again and again.

A firm of professional illuminators designed the display at the Marquis's own house. A very large painting decorated the exterior, with a bust of Wellington—now a Field Marshal—at its center, being crowned with a wreath by a figure representing Victory, while another figure representing Fame "spread his achievements." The painting was framed in lamps in the shape of a temple, with a star crowning all. The Spanish Consul's establishment in the Strand was equally striking, with every window in each of its three stories bordered with brilliant lamps, more lamps draped across the roof, and a crown, a star, and the words "VICTORY, JUNE 21, 1813" painted in huge letters.

The pillars of Carlton House were outlined in white lamps, with "Wellington and Victory" spelled out over the center arch, but the effect of this display was lost amid the glare and crack of the multicolored fireworks set off every night in the garden, to the accompaniment of four booming brass cannon placed atop the colonnade and fired at intervals throughout the evenings.

Carlton House was the scene of a grand ball and supper and, a few days afterward, another lavish party which began in midafternoon and lasted until four the following morning. The four hundred guests arrived to find the Regent, his mother and sisters seated under a tent in the garden, flanked by one of the French battle flags captured at Vitoria and Marshal Jourdan's baton. (The baton, brought to England by the captain who carried news of the victory, had been hurriedly sent on to Windsor by the Regent's page, who delivered it to the queen and princesses.) The afternoon was very hot, and the guests refreshed themselves with ices as they promenaded through the gardens, listening to the lively

.

music of three bands and admiring the virtuosity of an Italian entertainer, Mr. Rivolta, who played seven instruments at once.

Most members of the royal family were present, including Princess Charlotte, the Regent's daughter and heir. Charlotte was seventeen years old, plump to excess, with "great intelligent eyes of pale blue" and a decidedly unladylike personality. She was strong-willed, blunt and coarse in her speech, and physically undisciplined to the point of immodesty. That was the view, at least, of her governess, the Dowager Duchess of Leeds, who was appalled at the careless, tomboyish way the princess wore her clothes, her lack of grace when she walked and stood, and her dangerous forwardness with men.

Charlotte had a cruel streak. Once when she was driving her phaeton through the streets of Windsor, one of the ponies shied, and the groom went immediately to calm it. "Her Royal Highness, who was indignant that the collected crowd should suppose her to be unequal to manage it, gave the poor groom a smart cut across his face, and dashed furiously on."[3]

The princess liked to drive out in public, nodding and kissing her hand to the people who invariably turned out to cheer her and to urge her, somewhat to her chagrin, "never to desert her mother." She was popular, the newspapers recorded where she went and what she wore. Her presence at Spring Gardens, an amusement park, in the week of Wellington's victory was reported in some detail. While she was there the remarkable musical instrument called the panharmonicon—"two hundred instruments played by mechanical power"—was demonstrated, and the princess patriotically announced that of all the pieces the panharmonicon played, she liked "Wellington's March" best. "Her Royal Highness never appeared more elegant," another paper noted in its account of the Regent's ball held a few days before the afternoon fête. Her embroidered dress of pink satin and lace with silver borders had been set off by diamonds circling her round arms and at her neck and ears; her headdress of diamonds, pearls and ostrich feathers had been commanding.

In truth, Princess Charlotte was often overdressed and

her showy gowns called attention to her bulging proportions. She had inherited her mother's gaudy bad taste along with a good deal of her insouciant spontaneity. Sedate ladies thought her a hoyden, but to others she was merely awkward; a kind observer alluded to her "very cheerful and natural manners" and praised her for her lack of hauteur.[4]

The princess's appearance at her father's gala came as a surprise, for under his orders she had been living a somewhat constricted life—constricted, at least, as far as public gatherings were concerned—since the start of his Regency. It was widely believed that Charlotte took her mother's side in the increasingly acerbic quarrel between her parents, and that she got on badly with her father. An incident in March of 1813 seemed to confirm this.

The Regent suspected that his daughter's flirtation with a handsome young Hussar, Captain Hesse, had gone much too far, and that she was communicating with Hesse through a go-between, her friend Margaret Mercer Elphinstone. He demanded to see Charlotte's letters to her friend, and when Charlotte, who was every bit as stubborn as he was, refused, he ordered her desk broken open. The letters were read, his suspicions were confirmed, and the princess was furious. She had never had much respect for her father, she said, but now that he had acted in such ungentlemanly fashion she had even less.[5]

This happened in March, but by early July father and daughter appeared to have put the quarrel behind them, for there was Charlotte at the gala, looking plumper than ever and asking the bands to play "Mrs. McLeod of Eyre," "The Tank," and "Lord Dalhousie"—Scottish dances that were much in fashion that season. Also present at the gala was Prince William of Orange, a slight and sickly-looking young man with a weakness for drink whom the Regent favored as a potential son-in-law. Charlotte thought him so ugly she could barely force herself to look at him, but no doubt they exchanged polite conversation and may even have danced one of the Scottish dances together.

After supper the cannon boomed and the fireworks exploded, and the huge crowds outside Carlton House broke into shouts as the guests began to leave in their carriages. The shouting and huzzaing went on until shortly before daybreak, long after the illuminations were extinguished and the warm night turned chilly. The war, the intensity of the rejoicing seemed to hold Londoners in its grip, as it did Britons throughout the country.

There was a growing sense that the long war was at last approaching its climax, and that, contrary to the prevailing belief for most of its duration, the French might well lose. Bonaparte no longer seemed invincible. The "Tyrannical Destroyer," as some called him, had been unable to conquer Russia, and had left his route of retreat clogged with mounds of unburied French corpses dozens of feet high; the streets of Vilna, it was said, had been made impassable by the broken carriages and dead horses and pitiable human debris of the remnant Grande Armée.

Now the French had been beaten again, by the first English commander since Nelson to inspire confidence in an English victory. A generation of children who had been frightened by the specter of "Boney" now played at being Wellington defeating Boney, and took heart. All the children in England in 1813 were children of war. They had never known any other condition, and to many of their parents peace was only a remote memory. But habituated as they were to the conflict they sensed a definite change now in its pace and urgency. Vitoria was only one, though admittedly a highly significant one, in a rapid series of diplomatic and military events presaging a decisive French defeat. Soon after it came word that the continental allies had reopened hostilities, and that Wellington had gained further victories. In October Bonaparte was defeated at Leipzig, in the following month Holland threw off the yoke of French occupation and the Prince of Orange returned to Amsterdam from his exile in England to begin his reign. By December peace negotiations were under way.

The excitement of those months was long remembered by those who lived through them as "among the hottest of the war period." Thomas Cooper, who spent his boyhood at Gainsborough in Lincolnshire, recalled how his little town

.

"was kept in perpetual ferment by the news of battles, and the street would be lined with people to see old Matthew Goy, the postman, ride in with his hat covered with ribbons, and blowing his horn mightily, as he bore the news of some fresh victory—Ciudad Rodrigo, or Badajoz, or Salamanca, or Vitoria, or St. Sebastian, or Toulouse."[6] Word of battles lost and won, of casualties suffered, of relatives maimed or killed kept small towns and large in a constant state of war fever. More and more troops were in evidence, marching smartly down the roads in gaudy new uniforms, bound for Spain. Many among them were pathetically young, war children grown into soldiers, with dreams of valor that would soon be tarnished by the grime and severe hardships of the peninsular war.

The war fever bred criticism. There were those who stayed indoors while London was celebrating Wellington's victories, condemning the colored lights and fireworks on the grounds that they encouraged further conflict instead of promoting peace. Disaffected veterans told stories of wanton slaughter and brutal floggings in Wellington's army, of the bestial behavior of the troops following battles, of rapine and corruption and dishonor. An antiwar poem was found written on the back of a pound note:

> Is it not a wicked thing
> To suffer men to serve the king?
> Count up the widows that were made
> The day that Nelson prostrate laid,
> Amid the cannon's dreadful roar
> And decks that swim with human gore!
> Tell me, ye Bishops, if you can,
> How Christians may destroy a man?
> Since Christ their patron has decreed
> That none shall make a brother bleed?
> A Brother bleed!—nay e'en our foes
> Should share our love, but not our blows;
> Oh! why is all the horrid war?
> And what kill they each other for?[7]

Yet everyone, critics and supporters alike, was caught up in what Lady Bessborough called the "military mania" of the times. It was inescapable, a circumambient awareness of struggle and suffering, of triumph and loss, against a backdrop of military pageantry and symbolism. The war consciousness permeated civilian life and civilian pursuits. Byron referred to publishing two works at once as "firing on the public with a double barrel," and said he preferred discharging one barrel at a time. Walter Scott, writing of literary critics, called himself "a veteran who has stood the fire of at least forty reviews." Women's fashions reflected the current preoccupation. Military epaulets decorated coats and the short jackets called spencers, morning walking dresses were cut in imitation of the "Cossack mantle," and for evening, women were advised to wear "Prussian helmet caps" of canary yellow frosted with silver, ornamented with a diadem and tassels and a curling ostrich feather. Even the language of courtship took on martial overtones. Writing of an eligible heiress and her suitor, George Jackson remarked that "Miss Long has at last surrendered, and Marshal Pole is forthwith to be put in possession of the citadel and all its stores."[8]

No one was more caught up in the military mania than the Regent, with his battle trophies and huge collection of weapons, his passion for uniforms and for the paraphernalia of soldiering. He liked to dress up as the medieval warrior king Henry V, who led England to victory over the French four hundred years earlier at the Battle of Agincourt. At other times he put on the court dress of a Chinese mandarin of war, or brandished one of the costly swords he had ordered, embossed in gold, or a golden saber. He was so elated by the victories in the summer and fall of 1813 that his trembling hand could barely hold his pen to send word of them to his mother at Windsor.

"GREAT EVENTS, GREAT EVENTS, GREAT EVENTS," he scribbled at the top of one note to her giving her news from the continent. "My first impulse was and is, before I can allow myself to collect my ideas, to communicate to you best and dearest of mothers these joyful tidings."[9] Good news sent his spirits soaring, but put his always unsteady nerves on edge. Confusion and agitation followed,

.

whereupon he took to his bed and called for his doctors. "I shall fly and embrace you the first moment I am able," he assured the queen, but more often than not he was disabled by drink or laudanum, or by the sheer exhaustion of heaving his great bulk from bed to sofa and back again.

He got little exercise—he seldom rode on horseback and never walked—yet he imagined himself on the battlefield with Wellington's troops, and boasted that he deserved "some little merit" for engineering the alliance against the French. Queen Charlotte humored her favorite son's fantasies, and congratulated him on the steadiness of his government which had turned the tide against "the tyrannical oppression of the upstart Corsican self made emperor." She was proud of her son, and lent her presence to his entertainments even though she was criticized by the newspapers for joining in his "promiscuous assemblies" with their notorious "midnight bowers and miscellaneous companionships." She took his side, it was as simple as that. He had been through a great deal, his political enemies were hounding him and the work of ruling taxed him heavily. He deserved better. "I hope," she told him in her slightly odd English, "that after so many storms double the number of sun shining days will follow."[10]

But the storms that surrounded the Regent, far from abating, were growing more tempestuous, and his ability to battle them was eroding.

His outlandish wife, Princess Caroline, was continuing what she called her "warfare with the royal family," emboldened more and more by the political opposition. The Whigs, chief among them Henry Brougham and Samuel Whitbread, were using Caroline and the scandal surrounding her to attack the Regent and the Tory government of Lord Liverpool, who had succeeded Spencer Perceval as Prime Minister in June of 1812.

Ever since 1806, when an investigation into Caroline's behavior brought to light an array of allegations, stories and gossip about her, her husband refused to let Caroline see their daughter oftener than once a week. Neither mother nor daughter seems to have been much distressed by this, but Caroline pretended to be, and when in 1812 the Regent reduced Princess Charlotte's visits to no more than one every two weeks his wife wrote to him to complain. Or, rather, Brougham wrote her letter for her, and she signed it. Predictably, the Regent refused to read Caroline's letter, in keeping with his long-standing policy of never reading any communication she sent him, and returned it unopened. This gave Brougham his opportunity. He arranged to have the letter published in the *Morning Chronicle*.

It was the opening salvo in a battle neither side could win, but in which the Regent had much the most to lose. At stake for Caroline was her reputation, which had never been good; at stake for her husband was his ability to keep the government and the country from political chaos. The newspapers became the arena of combat, with the prince ordering the publication of the scurrilous tales told about his wife during the "Delicate Investigation." The details made risqué reading: according to her housemaids and pages, and others, the princess had entertained many lovers at her rented house at Blackheath; these lovers had been seen in her bed, she had been observed kissing them, she had boasted of "having a bedfellow whenever she liked." One of her footmen told the investigators that Caroline was "very fond of fucking," and any number of witnesses deposed that she had been pregnant.

Taken together, the allegations were damning. But there was no proof, only hearsay, and the investigators had concluded as much in 1807. The Whigs rushed to the princess's defense, turning the entire sordid combat into a persecution, on the part of a debauched and profligate husband, of a friendless and ill-used lady in distress. Never mind Caroline's own shortcomings, whatever they might be; she was the Princess of Wales, and might, should the old king die, become queen at any time. The prince sought to rid himself of her, her supporters argued, solely in order that he might pursue his licentious pleasures unshackled.

To a society thirsty for causes, and eager to lend charitable assistance, the cause of the Princess of Wales was irresistible. Had Wilberforce organized a Society to Prevent the Impugning of a Certain Lady's Reputation he would have

.

found subscribers by the thousands. As it was, Caroline's plight led to loud outpourings of popular support. The issue of how often Princess Charlotte could visit her mother was submitted to the Privy Council and others in the government. When, as expected, they supported the Regent's position the Whigs protested in the House of Commons, leading to more publicity and further scandal. Everywhere she went Caroline was applauded. People shouted encouragement to her, and shouted down her odious husband. Jane Austen spoke for many when she wrote that she hated the Regent for treating his wife so badly. She would support Caroline, she vowed, "as long as I can because she is a Woman."

Even those who found Caroline a highly imperfect exemplar of womanhood felt some sympathy for her as a victim of her position. "The poor Princess of Wales," Walter Scott remarked, "surely her fate has been a hard one and no less so to have fallen into the hands of her present advisers whose only object in making these scandalous anecdotes public is to disgrace the royal family in the eyes of the public." It all reminded him of a hand of cards, he said. "The present ministers while out of office held the Princess in their hand—a court card to be sure but of no great value—they have the luck to take up the prince (cast by the blunder of their opponents) and they discard the princess as a matter of course: while the Outs equally as a matter of course take her up and place her in their hand as being a kind of *pis aller.*"[11]

Pis aller or not, Caroline was receiving an increasing amount of attention. With her bright blue eyes beneath heavy dark eyebrows, her cheeks rouged a startling red and her fair hair hanging in masses of curls on each side of her throat "like a lion's mane," she was a clownish figure. Her gowns were more like costumes for the stage than regal attire. "Her Royal Highness was of a showy turn," wrote the Countess of Brownlow, who saw Caroline frequently at Kensington Palace and elsewhere. "Her gowns were generally ornamented with gold or silver spangles, and her satin boots were also embroidered with them. Sometimes she wore a scarlet mantle, with a gold trimming round it, hanging from her shoulders, and as she swam, so attired, down an English dance, with no regard to the figure, the effect was rather strange."[12]

Grossly fat, her overabundant flesh free of corseting, her expression bold, the Princess of Wales strode out into society, sometimes going incognito to public masquerades, sometimes taking lodgings in the city unbeknownst to her husband, riding in her open carriage and nodding enthusiastically to the people who cheered her. She had always had her own circle of friends, drawn from every social rank, making her parties, Countess Brownlow thought, "marvelously heterogeneous in their composition." Several of the Regent's brothers attended her dinners, her sister-in-law, the Duchess of York, called on her, and a variety of aristocratic ladies, among them Byron's mistress Lady Oxford, were her familiar companions. All else aside, Caroline was a refreshing, if alarmingly eccentric, personality, a complete contrast to her punctilious husband.

But much as she enjoyed "teasing and worrying" him, and gratified as she was by Brougham's and Whitbread's support, Caroline was finding life in England tedious and restricting. Nothing the Whigs could do could really compensate for the fact that Caroline was excluded from her husband's court. Her daughter seemed to be drawing closer to her father, despite the intermittent friction between them, and Caroline was finding that there was a limit to the pleasure she could derive from tormenting her in-laws. Her usual diversions were no longer satisfying, she was restless and talked of leaving the country. Warned by her advisers that to go abroad might give her husband the opportunity he needed to deprive her of her title, she stayed on in England, frustrated and embattled. When not entertaining men in her room or swimming across the dance floor, Caroline shut herself away and fretted. In private she sang or played her harp, or amused herself sitting in front of the fire, making wax models of her husband and sticking pins in them until they melted away in the heat.

An exceptionally cold winter set in in January of 1814, freezing the Thames and making travel all but impossible

.

along the snowbound roads. The stages were halted, no mail came or went except by special messenger. In London the horses slipped and slid their way along the frozen streets and all the windows of shops and houses were opaque with ice. Icy nights succeeded cold, frosty days until people said it was the coldest season in memory, the harshest in twenty years.

Prince George, who had been abusing his fragile constitution by drinking with his brother the Duke of York until both collapsed under the table, felt the effect of the severe weather and complained about it. He had set off for the country in the last days of the old year, only to be forced back to the capital when a dense fog blocked his way. The cold gave him a sore throat, which lowered his spirits and caused him to weaken himself further with brandy and laudanum. "You cannot conceive how mortally I do hate this weather," he told his mother, adding that he was suffering "symptoms of lowness." His quarrels with Parliament and the debilitating embroilment with the Whigs over his repellent wife had taken their toll, and the more he tried to escape his troubles by dulling his senses the more he weakened himself to face fresh onslaughts from his enemies.

For some months he had been trying a new medical treatment. Every morning a physician administered to him a potion "of a very nauseous kind" to strengthen his general health. He took it manfully, then spent the rest of the day and night undermining its effects by overeating and overdrinking. His girth grew prodigiously. A sculptor who made a bust of the prince was disconcerted to find the likeness spoiled by the rapid change in the sitter's appearance. "Your Royal Highness had increased in fullness of face the thickness of two fingers since I modeled your face," the man told him, but the prince only smiled and took more snuff.[13] The twitching in his hands, his tendency to collapse in tears in even the most minor household crisis were clear indications of ill health, and only those privy to court secrets knew how ill he really was.

In February, with the extreme cold continuing without letup and the Regent's spirits at their lowest ebb, he arranged

.

a special entertainment for himself which kept him at the pitch of exaggerated stimulation all night. Instead of becoming intoxicated and subsiding quietly under the table as usual, he became more and more red-faced and agitated, quivering in a fever of excitement until finally he had an apoplectic fit.

His guests and servants rushed to him, doctors were summoned, he was carried to bed and there relieved of twenty-seven ounces of blood. "It was thought he would never again rise from that bed," wrote one of the few people who knew of the incident.[14] The Regency tottered. Prince George lay in a stupor, pale from loss of blood and terrified of dying.

The bleeding alone might have been fatal to another man, but the Regent was accustomed to it, having been bled, so one of his doctors said, "more than a hundred times" with twenty ounces taken each time.[15] For weeks afterward he was very weak, and did not stir out of his apartments. But gradually his strength began to return. "His constitution seems proof against everything," one observer wrote, amazed that the prince had not succumbed.

No word of the emergency reached the newspapers, where Londoners read instead about record snowfalls and low temperatures, and about the continuing success of Wellington and the allies. In the week of February 21 a rumor swept the capital that the war was over. Bonaparte had been killed, the story went. His forces were in complete disarray. The armies of Austria and Prussia were about to enter Paris.[16] The rumor was dispelled, but it was not far wrong. Six weeks later Paris capitulated to the allied armies and Bonaparte, with his greatly reduced army more than a hundred miles away, was helpless to prevent it.

.

On the seventeenth of June, 1814, the Regent issued a proclamation announcing a public thanksgiving for the allied victory.

"Whereas it has pleased Almighty God, in His great Goodness, to put an end to the long, extended, and bloody warfare in which we were engaged against France and her allies," the proclamation read, "we, therefore, . . . appoint and command, that a General Thanksgiving to Almighty God for these His mercies be observed throughout those parts of the United Kingdom called England and Ireland, on Thursday the Seventh Day of July next."

A special prayer of thanksgiving was to be recited in all places of worship, and all loyal subjects were to be present, "upon pain of suffering such punishment as may be justly inflicted upon all such as shall condemn or neglect the same."

On the appointed day St. Paul's was crowded with ele-

.

gantly dressed worshipers watching for the dignitaries who were to make their way in procession into the cathedral.[1] At a quarter to ten the Speaker of the House of Commons and many of the Members arrived, and at almost the same moment Field Marshal von Blücher appeared, a great favorite of the Londoners, and took his place of honor. Blücher, hero of the battle of Leipzig, was only one of a host of foreign visitors in London that summer, among them Tsar Alexander of Russia and King Frederick William of Prussia. But the populace had taken the white-haired Prussian general to its heart, and in the weeks since his arrival he had been hounded by well-wishers wherever he went.

The Regent kept the congregation waiting for an hour and a half, during which time they studied the cathedral's magnificent interior and admired the abundant display of gold plate on the communion table, and of course scrutinized one another. Finally the Lord Chancellor, Lord Eldon, entered followed by four of the Regent's brothers and his cousin the Duke of Gloucester. All wore their trailing ducal robes. The Regent came in next, with Wellington on his right bearing the Sword of State. It was a noble procession, though people remarked disapprovingly on the fact that no ladies were included. The queen, her daughters, the Duchess of York, the Princess of Wales and Princess Charlotte all should have been present, but the Regent decreed otherwise. To include any of the royal ladies would have put him under an obligation to include his wife, and that he was most emphatically unwilling to do.

For three hours the thanksgiving service went on, with prayers and anthems and a sermon delivered by the Bishop of Chichester. Finally it was over, the dignitaries filed out and the Regent got into his yellow carriage and sped away, eager to escape before he was mobbed by his hostile subjects.

For four weeks, ever since the arrival of the continental princes and their glittering entourages, London had been in a frenzy of excitement. "The peace, and the sovereigns and the princes, and Wellington, and Blücher, and Platov, all coming at once, upset the sober mind of John Bull. Night and day, everybody was rushing everywhere."[2] Even earlier,

.

in April, they had rushed to see the new sovereign of France, scion of the restored Bourbon monarchy, Louis XVIII, pass through London on his way to the Channel ports.

"Louis the Gouty," as Byron dubbed him, who had been living quietly in Buckinghamshire for seven years, rode into London escorted by his friend and protector the Prince Regent. That the French Senate had voted to make Louis king was immensely gratifying to the English, who in the main had vehemently opposed any peace proposal that allowed Bonaparte to remain Emperor of France. ("You can scarcely have any idea how insane people are in this country on the subject of any peace with Bonaparte," the Prime Minister, Lord Liverpool, commented in February.) They showed their approval of Louis's elevation in dignity by wearing white cockades—white being the Bourbon color—and yelling loudly as his carriage went past, accompanied by a military guard and outriders in gold lace.

Louis cut a sorry figure, immensely fat and so crippled by gout that he had to be helped out of his coach. But he had presence, and bowed "very gracefully for a person of his size," and when he addressed the onlookers his tone was regal and his words well chosen.

"It is to the counsels of Your Royal Highness," he said with a gesture to the Regent, "to this glorious country, and to the steadfastness of its inhabitants, that I attribute, after the will of Providence, the reestablishment of my House upon the throne of its ancestors."[3] The king's words moved his hearers to cries of *"Vive le roi!"* and many were in tears. His presentation to the Regent of the Order of the Saint-Esprit—an honor never before offered to any Protestant ruler—brought him further praise, and when he left for the coast he carried with him the hearty good wishes of thousands of Londoners.[4]

Their appetite for celebrities seemed inexhaustible. When early in June Tsar Alexander, King Frederick William and Field Marshal von Blücher arrived in the capital, along with the Austrian Chancellor Prince Metternich, the Prussian Chancellor Prince Hardenburg, and a number of lesser princes and princelings, the citizens reacted by abandoning

.

shops, businesses and families and rushing to besiege the foreigners and follow them through the streets. "Every day is passed in seeing these great people," wrote Lady Shelley, whose prominent social position brought her into frequent contact with the distinguished visitors. "The whole population of London is in the streets!"[5] A holiday mood swept the city. Rather than pursue their own humdrum lives, people adopted the schedules of the tsar and his lively sister, the Grand Duchess of Oldenburg, following them from the Pulteney Hotel in Piccadilly where they lodged to Hyde Park or Kensington Gardens, where they took their morning walk, then on to other points of interest and in the evening to dinners and parties and the opera or theater. Crowds gathered to watch King Frederick William and his sons drive here and there, admiring their natural manners and enviable military bearing. Blücher was mobbed, his silver hair and "beautiful countenance" making him a kind of military saint in the eyes of the English. People fought with one another for the privilege of pulling the shafts of his carriage; when he rode through Hyde Park on his war-horse, "the broadest, stoutest old fellow that ever was seen," men and women alike chased after him on their own mounts, risking their lives to get close to their hero.

Part of the visitors' charm was that they were not English, and their foreign ways had an exotic fascination. The Russians were particularly exotic. The grand duchess, with her flat Eastern face, high cheekbones and broad nose, and the tsar, with his unfathomable religious views and his lofty hopes for European peace, caused endless curiosity in the early days of their stay in the capital. Another Russian, Matvei Platov, leader or hetman of the Don Cossacks, attracted even more attention. Like his troops, whose barbarism and ferocity made them dreaded by friends and enemies alike on the continent, Hetman Platov was a fierce, almost demonic figure riding among the genteel horsemen and carriages in the park, attended by two menacing Cossacks armed with long spears. Platov spoke no language but his own, making conversation with his admirers impossible. Unable to gratify their curiosity by talking to him, the English traded rumors

·

117

about him: that though he looked forty, he was really sixty-four; that the magnificent white horse he rode was a charmed beast, sixteen years old, that had carried him safely through all his campaigns; that he had in all twenty thousand horses, and could call out an army of vassals eighty thousand strong.[6]

Day after day the popular amusement of celebrity-watching continued, along with illuminations and fireworks, and an elaborate fair in Hyde Park. For the dignitaries themselves, however, there was serious business to attend to, and much of their time not spent in the public eye was devoted to the brokering of Europe's future.

Much progress had already been made. King Louis reigned in Paris, and Bonaparte had been banished to the island of Elba off the Italian coast with a generous pension and a sizable guard. Peace had been made with France, but the fate of the rest of Bonaparte's former empire was in dispute. There were arguments over Saxony, over the Low Countries, and over the date of the peace conference to be held at Vienna. The diplomats and rulers did agree eventually that Belgium and Holland should become the kingdom of the Netherlands, ruled by the House of Orange, and they reached other understandings about the dispositions of their respective armies. But the meetings were contentious, with the Russians conducting themselves in an overbearing fashion and the Austrians stirring up trouble wherever they could. Metternich mocked the vaunting, self-important tsar when he talked with the Regent, and made fun of the Regent when in the presence of the tsar; by widening the growing rift between the English and Russian sovereigns, he reasoned, he could improve Austria's leverage at the bargaining table.

That Tsar Alexander and Prince George should have taken a dislike to one another was perhaps inevitable, given their temperaments and their politics. Tall, fair and imperial in his tight green uniform and gold epaulets, the tsar was vain of his handsome face and considered himself superior to all other sovereigns. He talked easily and pridefully of his own spiritual enlightenment, of how the burning of Moscow in 1812 lit his soul, and of how "if men were vital Christians,

.

there could be no wars." His condescension was almost as galling to the Regent as his slimness, though these were as nothing compared to the insulting way he cultivated the Whig leaders, as if trying his best to infuriate his royal host.

The tsar's liberalism was sincere, if somewhat shallow, and from his point of view the Regent was a posturing figurehead whose disreputable private life made him unworthy to serve as his father's deputy. Alexander cannot have been pleased to see the Regent dressed up in the uniform of a Russian general ("and looking wonderfully well"), or to hear him claim, in effect, that it was England that had made the peace. His Toryism, his love of exaggerated court formality, his obvious alienation from his subjects all made the Regent contemptible in the tsar's eyes, and so they were irreconcilably at odds.

Complicating their enmity was the nettlesome presence of the grand duchess, who saw through the Regent's oily charm and pronounced him to be dissipated, disgusting and obscene. His licentious conversation, his "brazen way of looking where eyes should not go," and his drunken habits were repulsive, she thought, and she disapproved of the way he kept his daughter and his estranged wife under excessive restraint. The grand duchess had a great influence over her brother, and her opinions helped to mold his. Moreover, she went out of her way to make herself objectionable, by announcing her intention of visiting Princess Caroline (she was dissuaded) and by disrupting social events with endless complaints about the music or demands for special treatment. In her defense let it be said that the grand duchess was in mourning for her late husband, killed in battle, and was suffering from epilepsy brought on by the trauma of her wartime experiences. But ill or not, she set out to make herself disagreeable to the Regent, and succeeded.

The grand duchess was blamed, in fact, for a turn of events which altered the Regent's plans for the succession and dealt him yet another domestic blow.

His daughter, Princess Charlotte, had agreed some months earlier to marry the man he chose for her, Prince William

.

of Orange, but had begun to waver in her decision. Her wavering, the Regent believed, was due to the meddling influence of the tsar's sister, who had a Russian nobleman in mind for Charlotte and who, in concert with her brother and his ministers, wanted to prevent a dynastic link between England and the Netherlands. Charlotte objected strongly to living in Holland, as she would have to do for at least part of the year when she married Prince William, and her objections became more pronounced after the Russian duchess befriended her and she encountered some of the young princes in the tsar's entourage.

Charlotte's acquaintance with men was limited. She had had one passionate infatuation—with the gallant young Hussar officer, Captain Hesse—but because her father kept her relatively secluded her encounters with eligible young suitors were few and far between. But in June of 1814 she met Princes Augustus and Frederick of Prussia, her cousin Prince Paul of Württemberg and, most important, Prince Leopold of Saxe-Coburg-Saalfeld. These made the slight and sickly Prince of Orange look positively loathsome to Charlotte, who regretted having allowed her father to talk her into becoming engaged to him. She rebelled, informing poor Prince William that their engagement was "totally and for ever at an end." Never mind the diplomatic consequences, or the embarrassment to her father, or the fact that the queen had already begun to order her granddaughter's trousseau: Princess Charlotte had to have her way.

The Regent blamed his daughter's defection on the wicked influence of the grand duchess, and though he contained his fury behind an ever-smiling, well-bred exterior he wished fervently that the Russian guests would leave. Instead of doing him honor they had exposed him to ridicule, and they continued to insult his hospitality and ignore his consummate abilities as a host.

The people too, after weeks of excitement and disruption, began to weary of their exotic, glamorous visitors. Some of the lesser potentates dispersed into the countryside, where they were assured of fresh acclamations. In Bath the Grand

·

Duke of Weimar was "almost pulled to pieces by the crowd," and others encountered similar displays of adulation. But the initial excitement had worn off, and if ball guests could still take delight in watching Blücher "skip down the middle of the room" with his partner, and Platov "stamp his feet like a horse" in time to the music, such pleasures were growing thin.

Seen up close, the celebrities soon lost their glamour. Lady Shelley described how at a ball "the Royalties appeared, late, and stayed less than an hour." The tsar and the King of Prussia disappointed her. The tsar was "shy, and very deaf." "He has a bad figure," she added, "tightened in at the waist, and has a chest like a woman. His epaulets are large, and placed very forward; and his arms hang in front very awkwardly."

In truth the English had ceased to care very much about their guests. "Long before the departure of the sovereigns public curiosity had been completely satisfied," Lady Shelley thought, "and their stay became, at last, a positive nuisance. When the date for their return home was fixed, the joy felt by the higher ranks of society was universal."[7]

Amid all the commotion over the sovereigns, one sovereign was completely forgotten. George III sat in his cramped, dark apartments at Windsor, knowing nothing of the comings and goings of his monarchical colleagues in London, or of the momentous events which had brought them there. He no longer remembered the war, or Bonaparte, or the state of the continent; he only dimly remembered himself, and then spoke of himself in the third person, as "the king."

King George had become progressively calmer and more indrawn since the most recent onset of his illness. The "dreadful excitement" that had once held him in its grip, driving him to frenetic activity and incessant talking and eventually to pitiable wailing, rarely troubled him now. Instead he was overcome by listlessness at times, sitting and staring sightlessly ahead or lying motionless on his narrow, unadorned bed, his purple dressing gown enshrouding his thin body. His long white hair hung unkempt over his shoulders, and a scraggly beard filled out his hollow cheeks. The servants who looked after the old king grew accustomed to his long periods of inactivity, as they did to the peculiar habits he developed when active.

He played the flute and harpsichord "in an irregular manner," received visitors (though he had no idea who they were) and discoursed on politics or on the events of his early life. His memory for some things was flawless, though his imagination often led his memory astray. In his imagination he was married to Lady Pembroke, and was being kept from her deliberately. "Is it not a strange thing that they still refuse to let me go to Lady Pembroke," he asked his son Adolphus, "although everybody knows I am married to her?" Dr. Halford, "that scoundrel," was present at the marriage, the king insisted, "and has now the effrontery to deny it to my face."

Often the king's mind was "occupied with ideas of former times and persons." Lost in a dream of the past, he would talk earnestly with the Earl of Bute, his mentor in young manhood, or with other Prime Ministers long dead.[8] From some remembered history lesson he conjured the shades of Henry VIII and his infamous minister Cardinal Wolsey, and interrogated them "respecting their political and other proceedings," and "putting questions to them for reasons of their conduct."[9] Those who listened to him were impressed by the range of his knowledge, and by the kingly authority he displayed. But then all at once his kingliness would dissolve, his features would contort with grief or dread as new phantasms haunted him. Visions of his beloved daughter Amelia, dead on her bier, or of the imagined deaths of his sons tormented him. Or he became convinced that England was drowning, the seas submerging the land, and he began vainly trying to gather together the state papers before they were destroyed, to take with him to Denmark.

In such a state his emotions blended into one another. Apprehension rapidly gave way to laughter. He laughed easily, but then the laughter turned just as easily into tears. Extremes of feeling racked him, and he lost control of himself completely. Then, bewildered and pathetic, he became uneasy, and began to play nervously with the contents of his wardrobe, tidying his handkerchiefs, knotting and unknotting them, buttoning his waistcoat and unbuttoning it again. Or he lapsed into deep depression.

One evening his attendants noticed that he had been sitting for hours with his head lowered, unmoving. When his usual bedtime came, they tried to rouse him, speaking to him and then touching him.

"Let me alone," the king snapped. "I am looking into hell."[10]

There was general agreement among the doctors that King George would not recover, yet he continued to receive constant medical supervision. Each of three physicians attended him two days a week, in addition to his long-standing doctors, John and Robert Willis (whose presence filled him with terror), who took turns keeping watch over him. The Windsor apothecary also visited the royal apartments twice a week, and there were in addition servants of the various doctors who waited on the king.

The cost of all these consultations ran to the very large sum of 35,000 pounds a year, and as it all came from the king's estate—the Treasury paid nothing—the household budgets of the queen and princesses were being undermined. But the doctors continued to make their calls, and to send large bills, and the Regent, who administered his father's property, had no choice but to pay them.

With the old king frail but stable, his mind fragile but his body fairly sound, it began to look as though the Regency might outlast the Regent. One of the king's doctors announced that his patient was "in a state happy for himself, amusing himself," his bodily health good. "He would probably live longer being in this state," the doctor added.[11] Meanwhile the Prince Regent's prospects for longevity were rapidly darkening, or so his own physicians told him. He might never live to be king.

From time to time there were rumors that the king was much worse—or much recovered—or that he was dead. The

·

first few times these stories appeared in the newspapers people took them seriously, but then they became skeptical. The
rumors about the king's death were started by shopkeepers,
it was said, who could count on selling every bit of black
cloth they had on hand once the story began to spread. As
for the rumors of his recovery, they were undoubtedly started
by wishful thinkers weary of the Regent, longing to have
the plain, straitlaced old king back to govern them once again.

10

*T*he country that had fought, supplied and to a large extent financed the victory over the French was something of an enigma to outsiders. Two small, agrarian islands, inhabited by between fifteen and twenty million volatile if broadly patriotic people, had managed to sustain and eventually to win a prolonged war against a far more powerful enemy.

The secret force that had led to this monumental achievement, the wellspring of Britain's strength, was not easily discovered. That her insularity provided a natural defense, that her laws were equitable (if harsh) and her unwritten constitution uniquely poised between the authority of the crown and the countervailing weight of the landowning minority, that her people had so far resisted political extremism and that her world-ranging trade brought her great wealth were benefits too obvious to be denied. Yet Bonaparte's inva-

.

sion fleet had challenged Britain's charmed isolation, and her laws and the integrity of her government were coming under increasing attack. Radical politicians and the destructive followers of General Ludd had brought popular dissatisfaction to a head, amid widespread cries that the war had strangled trade and starved the poor.

Where then did Britain's strength lie? The Evangelicals saw the English success against Bonaparte as part of the advance, along a broad front, of good over evil. The French were godless, the British increasingly godly. "A new era has begun betwixt Christ and Belial," wrote one Evangelical, addressing the London Missionary Convention. "The adherents of both are arming on either side." The servants of God were "declaring offensive war against the kingdom of the devil."[1] Worldly power, the *Morning Chronicle* proclaimed, flowed ultimately from the moral qualities of a nation, and whereas the English possessed sterling moral qualities, the French were woefully deficient in them. "France may be mischievous," the editors affirmed stoutly, "but she will never be great."

Others pointed to Britain's economy, and in particular to the output of her factories, as the determinants of her victory. "To Arkwright and Watt, England is far more indebted for her triumph than to Nelson or Wellington," a contemporary historian wrote. "Without the means supplied by her flourishing manufacture and trade, the country could not have borne up under a conflict so prolonged and exhausting."[2] The inventors of the water frame and the steam engine had made it possible for England to send her continental allies the matériel they needed to fight the French—flints, powder, hundreds of cannon, millions of muskets. Beyond this, prosperous factory owners had paid hundreds of thousands of pounds in income taxes to support the war; customs and excise taxes on manufactured goods had been another major source of revenue.

England's burgeoning industries, though they employed as yet only one-fifth or less of her national work force, were expanding at a rate too dizzying to comprehend. Decade by

.

decade, since the 1780s, her exports of iron and cotton and coal had shot upward, far surpassing those of France—her nearest rival—and putting the other European nations in her debt. Bonaparte's Continental System and the British Orders in Council had gravely disrupted the trade vital to this industrial expansion, but in 1812 both sets of laws had been revoked, allowing for rapid and widespread business prosperity. Rising profits in turn helped to subsidize an enlarged war treasury, from which Britain's continental allies had been financed.

But if trade and manufacturing had strengthened the nation, they had also sapped its strength, while straining its fragile cohesiveness to a dangerous point. The confusing rapidity with which imports and exports grew, and the wrenching shock waves that ran through the marketplace and the work force when they suddenly contracted, then just as suddenly resumed their growth, made for anxiety. Owners and workers alike were nervous in prosperous seasons and desperate when profits failed; they felt vulnerable, unable to outguess, much less control, the blind economic forces they served. There was prosperity, but it was always short-lived. Inevitably periods of depression and severe unemployment followed any season of abundant work and high wages, and even when work was plentiful and wages rising the cost of food and other necessities rose still faster.

Every economic group faced its own peculiar dilemma. Rural laborers and urban workers were beset by the extreme fluctuations in the availability of work, by ever-increasing prices and, in addition, by the costly duties charged on goods and by periodic food scarcity when harvests were bad. Businessmen and merchants knew boom times but lived in fear of bankruptcy, many succumbing to it; those who prospered lost a high proportion of their profits to income tax which went to support the war. Landowners benefited from high rents but suffered when crops failed in 1809, 1811 and 1814; an overabundant harvest in 1813 glutted the market and caused prices to fall drastically. The income tax fell heavily on owners of agricultural land, who found it particularly

·

burdensome at a time when they were under pressure to bring new acreage under cultivation to meet wartime demands for food.

Overall, England's economic transformation was a source of great enrichment, won at great social cost, and though there was truth in the assertion that Arkwright and Watt made heavy contributions to the victory over the French still the core of the nation's fortitude lay elsewhere.

To suggest that England derived her strength from her haphazard, unsystematic, essentially medieval form of government would have been to ignore its obvious deficiencies. The country was administered through a network of archaic institutions, overwhelmingly local in their jurisdictions, dominated by the gentry and aristocrats whose interests they served.

In the countryside, five thousand unpaid Justices of the Peace carried the full burden of governmental responsibility, as they had since the fourteenth century. Appointed by the crown, like the other local officials—the Lords Lieutenant and the sheriffs—whose offices had been in existence since the Middle Ages, the Justices of the Peace were in practice answerable to no higher authority. They enforced the law, brought lawbreakers to justice, levied taxes, kept the highways in a poor but passable state of repair, kept the destitute from starving, regulated wages and performed a wide variety of other basic tasks. Amateurism, corruption and bias were pervasive, and perhaps inevitable in a system in which the chief function of law was to protect property and the chief function of government to prevent change of any kind.

Town governments were a jumble of feudal liberties, manorial custom and antiquated offices. Beadles, High Stewards and Bellringers were ill equipped to cope with early nineteenth-century economic stresses, not to mention the exigencies of sanitation and peacekeeping. In practice, merchants dominated municipal governments, and ran them in their own interests.

Parliament too was an antique institution, where landowners exerted a heavily disproportionate influence. Five out of six Members of the House of Commons were chosen by the peers or gentry, and while the Commons was in theory an elected body, representative of the more substantial portion of society, in actuality most of the seats were controlled by a tiny fraction of the population.

The Tory government of Lord Liverpool, who became Prime Minister in 1812, was hampered both by the lack of cohesion among its own ministerial group of Members and by the whimsical interference of the Regent, who treated the Prime Minister as if he were "a sort of maître d'hotel," to be noticed or disregarded at will. Liverpool's own personal integrity, and his ability to hold warring factions together, proved in the long run to be the salvation of his government but this was not yet apparent in 1814. The Tories seemed to stumble on, unable to provide strong leadership yet surviving each crisis they encountered, more unified than the increasingly divided Whigs yet incapable of rising to indisputable preeminence.

Neither her habits of governance, nor the forward thrust of her commercial energies, nor whatever moral or constitutional virtues she possessed could fully account for Britain's extraordinary triumph. Tsar Alexander believed that she owed her underlying strength to the British people themselves. The high state to which the country had advanced, he told an English acquaintance during his stay in London, owed something to her constitution and her laws, but more to a quality inherent in her population. The English possessed a certain temper of mind, a soberness of thought, a reflectiveness other people lacked.[3]

Though not notably sober or reflective, the British soldiers had displayed a stolid, dogged, almost obstinate perseverance on the battlefield that seemed to bear out the emperor's judgment. To stand firm, to face enemy fire bravely, without ducking or flinching, to hold formation no matter how fierce the oncoming attack: such was honorable soldiering, and the British held to the code of honor. Not every man was honorable, to be sure, and there were shameful episodes of cowardice, brutality, betrayal of fellow soldiers, unchivalrous treatment of defenseless prisoners and civilians—a long list of crimes and tragedies. But these transgres-

·

129

sions were the exception. The qualities that impressed observers most were the steadiness, hardiness and sheer endurance of Wellington's men, and these same qualities leavened the entire population.

Unlike their continental neighbors, the English showed a coolness and endurance in the face of adversity that made them governable—though at any moment that governability might evaporate, as it had most recently with the outbreak of Luddite violence. Patriotism, loyalty to the crown and deference to authority in general helped to preserve order, and that order tended to ensure the continuity of a way of life centuries old.

But if England's strength lay in the hardihood and equanimity of her people, it was all the more disturbing when that equanimity was shattered. The last of the Luddites had been tried and sentenced early in 1813, and there had been no recurrence of their militancy, yet many of the grievances that had precipitated Luddism remained. People remembered other mass risings—the naval mutiny at the Nore in 1797, the Gordon Riots of the 1780s, which had terrorized London—and trembled for their security every time an influential popular orator spoke or a crowd gathered. Periods of quiet were viewed with distrust by the propertied classes, who feared that beneath the surface calm, hatreds and destructive urges were building up among what they called "the lower and riotous class of people."

The fact that the country lacked an effective police force made these fears more acute. Neither in rural areas nor in towns was there anything resembling a paid professional constabulary, and as a result, crime flourished. To be sure, there were severe penal laws, calling for hanging, not only in cases of murder or robbery but for what we would now consider very minor crimes against property. Yet in practice the majority of criminals brought to trial in capital cases were pardoned rather than executed, and many, probably most, of those guilty of lawbreaking were never apprehended.

Murderous assaults, rapes, arson and thefts were commonplace. Highwaymen waylaid travelers along the roads, gangs

.

of smugglers operated in coastal towns and villages. Burglars were in every street, or so it seemed.

Lady Bessborough's London house was ransacked by burglars while the family was away in the country. "I arrived in London in a great fuss about an hour ago," she wrote to Lord Granville, "on hearing our house was broke open last night, and every thing that could be got at taken." The thieves had been interrupted in their work, and had left many valuables behind in their haste to get away, but the brazenness of the theft left Lady Bessborough shaken. "The boldness and ingenuity with which it was managed quite terrifies me," she wrote. The burglars had sawed out the panels of the shutter, then managed to open the windows from the inside, undetected by the neighborhood watchmen and undeterred by gates and barred windows. "Bars and bolts, walls and watchmen, are perfectly useless," she told Granville in despair.[4] No defense was possible against such a determined attack.

It was less the presence of widespread crime than the climate of lawlessness that made people feel insecure, especially in the towns. Public order, always precarious, was being undermined, it seemed; the "lower and riotous class" was getting out of hand.

In Edinburgh a gang of fifty apprentices, the youngest of them only twelve years old, came together in a "formal association" sworn to assault and rob anyone they encountered. They kept their association a secret from their masters for months, holding clandestine meetings, keeping records and amassing arms. Carrying bludgeons loaded with lead, they swarmed into the narrow streets at night, and when a likely victim came in view they shouted "Mar him!" and bludgeoned the man to the ground.[5] The boys were eventually caught and their gang disbanded, but not before they had killed several people and severely injured many others.

The manufacturing towns, chaotic and crowded, where anonymous laborers were thrown together in squalor, invited lawbreaking. On the outskirts of Birmingham "Mud City" sprang into existence, a squatters' village inhabited by crimi-

.

nals who preyed on the burgeoning town. Nearly every town had its protests and marches, its bread riots, its noisy, turbulent celebrations when, drunk on gin and beer, the volatile populace gathered to cheer the king, curse the French and the Regent, and vent their frustrations in violence.

The danger of crowd fury was worst in London, whose dark streets lent themselves to murderous affrays and casual viciousness and whose huge outlaw population—allowed to flourish uncontrolled in slums no watchman ever attempted to enter—was always primed to explode. The London crowd formed spontaneously and quickly, its mood shifting uncertainly from joyous excitement to nervous suspicion to defiant hostility. The slightest incident could set it off—an accident in the street, a tavern brawl, the appearance of a dignitary or a piece of news. Cries of distress or panic, hoots of derision, cheers and applause, or growls of resentment rippled through the knot of massed bodies. People jostled one another, clapped one another on the back in their exuberance, trampled one another in their rush to flee danger or catch sight of some curiosity.

Often, when the crowd had been out in the streets for hours, its exuberance edged over into something sharper and more menacing, a surge of power, an impulse to harm. On the night that Londoners celebrated Wellington's victory at Salamanca, they roved from street to street, shooting off guns and setting off firecrackers, shouting to the well-dressed gentlemen and ladies who passed in their carriages. The shouting turned to abuse. Carriages were assaulted, women screamed, and ruffians set fire to lengths of cord dipped in turpentine and hurled them through the carriage windows. Horses reared and plunged, and some of the carriages overturned.

In Piccadilly, where earlier in the evening the illuminations had been bright and elaborate, shouts went up for them to be relit. The householders hurriedly lit candles in hopes of satisfying the mob, but in vain; the people in the street began breaking windows and kept up their tumult until their throats were hoarse. By now there was serious danger. Arms and legs were broken, heads bleeding, women with

·

their skirts on fire tore at the burning cloth and scorched their hands.

The rioters, armed with stones and clubs and brickbats as well as with firearms, terrorized whole neighborhoods. Sounds of gunfire, of shattering glass and neighing horses filled the streets until three in the morning, and respectable people who tried to escape the violence found themselves caught up in it. A woman taking refuge in a churchyard was so badly frightened by the report of a blunderbuss going off near her that her heart gave out.

In the Strand the mob stopped a hackney coach carrying two men and two women. They forced open the vehicle and threw handfuls of fireworks inside. Instantly the straw that covered the floor went up in flames, and in their struggle to get out of the coach the passengers, their clothes on fire, were burned and blinded.

The crowd surged on past them then, toward the City, where the cattle market was coming to life in the last hour before dawn. No watchmen tried to stop it, no magistrate or militia troops appeared. But as suddenly as it had flared up, the mood of ugliness began to dissipate. Exhaustion overtook the rioters, they had spent themselves. They dispersed, disappearing in twos and threes into alleys and courtyards, blending back into the silent, dark retreats from which they had come.

.

11

"*A*ll the world's in Paris," went the words of a popular song in the autumn of 1814. Upper-class English men and women went abroad by the hundreds that season. Brighton was "crowded by persons on their way to and from France," and everyone who could afford it booked passage, packed and joined the emigration.

Except for a brief period in 1802, following the Peace of Amiens, the English had not been to France in twenty years. Young men who in normal circumstances would have spent several years on the continent taking the Grand Tour, polishing their manners and improving their skill in languages, had acquired what polish they possessed in the army instead. A few, like Byron, traveled to Greece and the Levant, avoiding the theaters of war, but nothing could replace a prolonged stay in France and Italy and there was concern that the next

.

generation of Englishmen would be "barbarous" for lack of proper travel.[1]

The English descended on the French capital in large parties, taking lodgings together and going out in groups to see the city, to dine and to attend the receptions and assemblies of English hostesses. Fashionable people tended to re-create in Paris the closed world they occupied in London. They went where their compatriots went: to the British embassy, where lavish dinners and balls were held, to the Café des Anglais on the Boulevard des Italiens, where they could dine on good English beefsteak and potatoes, and to the soirées held by Lady Oxford in her hotel on the rue de Clichy, where they met French people, to be sure, but French people carefully selected for their civility and wit and for their pro-British politics.

Few of the visitors broke away from this social pattern. One who did was John Croker, Secretary of the Admiralty and a man of letters, who had made a scholarly study of events in France over the past two decades and who planned to write a history of those events. Croker had a large library of journals and broadsides published in Paris after 1789, and once he got to the French capital he lost no time in visiting every site made memorable by the revolution.[2]

A good many of the English grumbled and complained. Paris was no place for respectable people, they said. The streets were narrow and dirty, and unpaved. Stinking gutters running with filth divided the roadways, and one could not cross them without sinking ankle-deep in mud. After sundown the only light was provided by strings of lamps suspended from cords, and these were few and far between. It was not safe to go out at night without an armed escort. Everyone knew what horrors the Paris mob had committed; as for the upper classes, they were either impossibly snobbish and superior or depraved, drunk on pleasure and utterly lacking in any sense of decency or delicacy. Why, the very walls of the hotels were covered with pornographic pictures.[3]

Yet even the most self-righteous of the English had to admit that eating *suprême de volaille* or *côtelette à la Soubise*

.

at Beauvilliers in the rue de Richelieu was unlike any gastronomic experience available in England. The elegant Parisian restaurants, where candlelight gleamed on marble tables and thick carpets and where splendidly dressed people came to savor the art of fine dining before retiring upstairs to the private rooms, were a far cry from the few clubby hotel restaurants in London. At the Rocher de Cancalle, where one of Bonaparte's former cooks presided, the wines were superb and the cuisine so exquisite that travelers were said to come to Paris expressly to enjoy it. Tortoni's was famed for its ices, the Trois Frères Provençeaux for its Provençal specialties, the Café des Milles Colonnes for its hostess, a demimondaine who presided over the establishment seated in a royal throne and swathed in velvet.

If the English were offended by the older parts of the city they could not help but be impressed by the stately, classical edifices Bonaparte had erected, and by the old Bourbon palace of the Tuileries with its spacious grounds and formal gardens. The palace of the Louvre, filled with the plundered artworks that were among the chief spoils of French conquest, was an aesthetic wonderland. The soaring victory monuments, the wide tree-lined boulevards, Bonaparte's former residence at St.-Cloud where his private apartments were on view, filled with his furnishings and mementos of his imperial ascendancy, all called forth at least a reluctant—and somehow nervous—respect.

For the former emperor haunted his city still, even though he was in exile on Elba hundreds of miles away. His monuments stood guard over his continuing glory, even in defeat. His empty bed and desk at St.-Cloud, his emblems carved in stone, the Bonapartist slogans scrawled on walls throughout the city all proclaimed his ongoing influence, as did the scowls of the French and their vituperation of the English.

Far from seeming a beaten, dejected people the Parisians were defiant and full of fire. There were French officers everywhere, and they took it upon themselves to challenge their English counterparts (along with any Russians or Austrians or Prussians) to duels as often as possible. The officers in the Garde du Corps were reputed to be the most belligerent duelists. They strode into Tortoni's or Silves's, a well-known Bonapartist café, eager to pick quarrels. Swords were drawn, and challenges issued. The French preferred to duel with swords or sabers, but their foreign opponents, fearful of the renowned French swordsmanship, chose pistols. Each morning, shortly after dawn, shots rang out in the Bois de Boulogne; afterward, the survivors treated their comrades to champagne at Tortoni's and boasted of the men they had killed.

The English officers became accustomed to such pugnacity but the civilians found the bloodshed distasteful. Duels were sometimes fought in the streets, and the corpses of young men left to lie where they fell. Skirmishes in cafés or restaurants left dozens dead. Paris was a gilded battlefield, a "bloody and ferocious" place that gave the lie to the dearly bought European peace.

The French seemed to fling themselves headlong into pleasure as they did into dueling and brawling. A fierce hedonism gripped them; they were mad to hazard all on a single cast of the dice or a single night of dissipation.

The Palais-Royal was their mecca, a vast building whose corridors and gardens were thronged with "the particular class of ladies who lay out their attractions for the public at large." The women were to be seen at all hours, even early in the morning, dressed in revealing evening clothes and wearing sparkling paste diamonds and ropes of false pearls. "Casting their eyes significantly on every side," the prostitutes walked up and down in search of companions. They were at once brazen and alluring, as bold, in their strutting confidence, as the duelists of the Garde du Corps. The officers flirted with them, bought them jewelery in the shops of the Palais, then took them upstairs to rented bedrooms.

At night the Palais-Royal was the only well-lighted place in the city, and it drew multitudes of Parisians (and foreigners) who patronized the shops, flocked to the cafés to gossip—

•

loudly maligning the British—then went on to dine and, usually, to gamble afterward. "It was a theater in which all the great actors of fashion of all nations met to play their parts," a contemporary wrote of the Palais-Royal. "On this spot were congregated daily an immense multitude, for no other purpose than to watch the busy comedy of real life."[4]

The most crazed, and the saddest, of the pleasure-seekers were the confirmed gamblers, the unhealthy-looking, wild-eyed "hawks," whose one passion was roulette or *rouge-et-noir*. These men had lost their fortunes and forfeited their place in society. Their property was mortgaged, they were in debt to moneylenders, they could not sleep for anxiety. Still they came, night after night, to the gambling parlors, mesmerized by their own destructive compulsion.

The Salon des Étrangers catered to these desperate fanatics, and many visiting Englishmen were drawn into its poisoned ambience. An opulently furnished set of rooms, the Salon offered fine food and wine and an emollient host, the Marquis de Livry, who on Sundays when his establishment was closed opened his villa to his clientele. What went on at the tables of the Salon des Étrangers was extraordinary. Reckless risk-taking led to extravagant losses. Men appeared one evening, tossed fortunes on the table, lost them, and then disappeared, never to be heard from again. Occasionally, of course, a patron would enjoy a run of luck. One night the secretary of the English embassy, a habitual gambler, surprised himself by winning sixty thousand francs, breaking the bank. Another patron, the Hungarian Count Hunyady, won two million francs over a period of time and used it to turn himself into an envied celebrity.[5] The Parisians aped him, eager to imitate his dress, his carriage, his perfect house. Women wore cloaks "*à la Huniade*," and the chef of the Rocher de Cancalle created new dishes and named them after the fabulous count. In the end, however, Hunyady yielded to his addiction and gambled away his entire fortune, having to borrow money to take himself back to Hungary.

Many an Englishman who survived the deadly duels in the Bois de Boulogne succumbed to the Salon des Étrangers.

·

Eager young men worth fifty or sixty thousand pounds a year borrowed against their inheritances and then sacrificed everything they borrowed. Suicide seemed the only honorable way out. Most used pistols, but one flamboyant loser put a canister of "fulminating powder" under the table where he was sitting and lit a match to it. There was a tremendous explosion, but miraculously no one, not even the overwrought gambler, was hurt.[6] De Livry, his tact fully equal to the situation, sent for the English ambassador who had his compatriot shipped quietly back to England as a madman.

The British were drawn to the grandeur and flash and even the violence of Paris, yet they could never quite fit into its rhythms. They seemed flatfooted and wooden compared with the showy, volatile Parisians. Some Britons blended in, but many stuck out painfully as they walked the boulevards, stodgy and more than a little indignant at the Parisians' hard frivolity. The French language was treacherous. One Alderman Wood, who had at one time been Lord Mayor of London, inscribed on his visiting cards "Alderman Wood, feu Lord Maire de Londres," thinking that the words meant "former Lord Mayor." The French were greatly amused, and joked to one another about the "dead Lord Mayor" and his calling cards. When the British became loud and belligerent, "behaving themselves à la John Bull, in a noisy and swaggering manner," they seemed to the French far more ridiculous than frightening. They went about picking quarrels in a curiously stuffy and formal way. Two officers went into Silves's, primed to fight, but instead of insulting the French or striking them the British took out their visiting cards, placed them over the chimneypiece and calmly announced that they would fight any man in the room. The gesture was gentlemanly, but without bravura; the offer was ignored.

When it came to fashion the Parisians ridiculed the English mercilessly. The English men, with their brass-buttoned, long-tailed blue coats, short, tight pantaloons and waistcoats, cravats and frilled shirts made a quaint contrast to the black-coated French men. But the English women were far worse. They still wore the simple, classical narrow white shirts and colored spencers that had become fashionable in the 1790s. Their bonnets were small and modest, often untrimmed, and the effect was, in the flattering words of an English newspaper, "domestic, simple, chaste, sedate." The French women had discarded such styles long before in favor of high-waisted, wide-sleeved gowns that belled out extravagantly and were tiered with endless ruffles and ribbons. Crowning all were enormous bonnets that projected far outward from the face and rose high over the back of the head, festooned with flowers, feathers and more ribbons.

Initially the English women recoiled from the foreign toilette, especially the huge bonnet. French women, a critical observer wrote, "are chiefly distinguished by a sort of bonnet three stories high and by far the most horrible superstructure that was ever piled upon the human head."[7] But within a few months the old, domestically simple style had disappeared and the English were wearing wide skirts and full sleeves—and even the towering headgear originating in Paris.

In any clash of styles the French were bound to win out, for the English, despite an enmity nurtured through a generation of war, deferred to them. French couture was the hallmark of fashion, just as French culture was the hallmark of refinement. All well-brought-up English children of the upper classes learned to speak French as a matter of course, though there were those who argued that this was undesirable. The universality of French, wrote the author of a pamphlet called *Latium Redivivum*, was a contributing cause of France's ascendancy in Europe. It would be far better to return to Latin as the language of schools and universities, the common tongue of diplomats and international travelers.[8] But the educational tradition persisted, and as the French war drew to a close the demand for teachers of French rose. "To French Ladies," began an advertisement in *The Times* in September of 1814. "Wanted, in a respectable Ladies' School, in Bath, a French Lady, who can teach her own language grammatically; none need apply who are not Parisians."

.

The strong cultural ties that united the French and English upper classes were a counterforce to their patriotism. Aristocrats understood aristocrats; in some ways they had more in common with one another than with the lower classes of their own country. An English colonel who dined with Lady Bessborough told her how English and French officers conversed and eventually fraternized across the battle lines in Spain.

It had begun, he explained, one night when a young English officer guarding an outpost grew bored. There was nothing for him to do but watch the French officers guarding their outpost a short distance away. The Englishman began bowing to his French counterparts, who bowed back. More civilities were exchanged, in pantomime, and then the English officer, after removing his sword and laying it on the ground, shouted to the French asking whether he might come across the lines to them in safety.

They gave their word not to harm him, so he took the risk. The result was an acquaintance that quickly spread among the officers on both sides. The French complimented the English on their soldiering, the English said that their opponents were "excellent soldiers and intelligent, well informed men," the colonel told Lady Bessborough. The two sets of officers exchanged views of the war, the French expressing admiration for Wellington and confessing to hate what they called Bonaparte's "tyranny." Yet they believed their commander to be invincible, and this belief made them recklessly brave, ready to "march into a cannon mouth simply at his bidding."[9]

The dueling that went on between the French and English officers in Paris was in a sense fratricidal; the men were fighting for the honor of their countries, but under rules that bound them together as gentlemen, regardless of country. They were brothers in rank, as in taste and outlook.

And there was another, much odder, bond between them. Many of the upper-class English admired Bonaparte almost as much as the French did.

That strange figure, unquestionably the dominating personality of his time, enigmatic, magnificent in his ambition

.

and nearly as magnificent in the scale of his achievements: Bonaparte commanded awe. He was morally contemptible, the English told themselves, yet the terms of opprobrium they reserved for him—The Flagitious Tyrant, The Impious Wretch, The Outlaw, The Brigand, The Monster, The Bloody Miscreant—seemed feeble beside his demonic energy and brooding genius. He was Mephistophelean, his dark conquests held a strong temptation. He was Childe Harold on a Europe-wide scale, an errant prodigal standing outside moral bounds, the incarnation of a fissured age. Aloof and visionary, Bonaparte was a prisoner of his destiny, and while he was not a self-destructive voluptuary like Byron's character he shared Childe Harold's powerful, complex personality and overwhelming sense of fate.

Bonaparte elicited sympathy and infatuation—and the chill of the numinous. His basilisk stare, his power over his soldiers, his apparent invincibility set him apart from ordinary men, as did his simply stated goal of global domination. "I wished for the empire of the world," he told an admirer after his defeat, "and, to ensure it, unlimited power was necessary to me."

Bonaparte was the Angel of Death, moving across the face of Europe spreading carrion. Throughout the war Londoners were obsessed with the prospect of his own death. Speculation on his survival went on constantly, with people taking out gambling policies at varying rates of interest, depending on how much danger he was in at the time.

Such a being, combining as he did great generalship, a great capacity for leadership and an even greater capacity for mayhem, was bound to provoke at least an ambivalent response. The English had vilified and vituperated him, hated and feared him throughout the war. Yet they had always been fascinated by his uniqueness, his genius and magnetism. His portraits had filled the London printshops ever since the days of his Italian campaigns in the 1790s, portraits immortalizing his handsome, sallow-complected face, his catlike features and enormous, intense eyes. "Attachment to Bonaparte's person" was common among the English even when they despised Bonaparte the Tyrannical Destroyer, as the

.

painter Joseph Farington christened him. "I hate Bonaparte," Lady Bessborough commented when she heard the rumor that his baby son, the King of Rome, was dead, "but I should be sorry for him if this is true; it is not the kind of punishment I wish him."[10] After his defeat she conceded that "if it were possible to forgive his rapacity he might be thought very agreeable." Her friend Lady Holland referred to him as "the poor dear man," and sent him gifts to brighten his exile.

While the English were in Paris the sovereigns of Europe and their diplomats continued to wrestle with the task of peacemaking. They had been lenient and generous to France. Under the terms of the First Peace of Paris, signed on May 30, 1814, France had been granted considerable territory beyond her traditional boundaries—an area including nearly half a million people—and had not been required to pay reparations or any indemnity. The generosity was self-interested: the European powers wanted to promote stability in France, to shore up the government of Louis XVIII and prevent Bonapartist agitation.

In September the formal peace conference convened at Vienna, and over the ensuing months the complex and divisive search for a satisfactory territorial compromise went on. Conflict arose over Poland and Saxony, and in December it appeared that war might break out among the former allies. What had begun as a negotiation among the four leading states—Russia, Prussia, Austria and Great Britain—was broadened into a five-way conference when Louis XVIII's cynical, sardonic minister Talleyrand maneuvered himself into a position of influence.

By midwinter of the new year 1815 the delegates at Vienna were addressing, among other issues, that of Bonaparte's exile on Elba. King Louis preferred to have him moved farther away, to the Azores, and the chief English negotiator Castlereagh agreed. The Bourbon throne was tottering, the army wanted its great general back, and the king was growing increasingly ill at ease.

Then, before the proposal to remove Bonaparte to a more distant place of exile could be acted upon, he himself acted.

·

He had been chafing within the confines of the tiny island of Elba for months, afraid that an assassin might slip past the guards and stab him or that pirates might land in the harbor and kidnap him. Apart from the Elbans, his servants and soldiers, Bonaparte had only his mother and one of his sisters for company. They spent long, empty evenings together playing cards.

When winter came the confinement seemed more oppressive. Elba was a very dull place, and when Bonaparte read the messages his informants sent him from the mainland, telling him of the quarreling among the diplomats in Vienna and the turmoil in France, it seemed even duller. Then there were the disturbing reports that he might be moved to some more remote island, where life would be even more insupportable. Bored, restless, irritated at the French government for withholding the annuity he had been promised, and above all, spurred to action by the news from France, he decided to risk his fortune again.

With his meager force of eleven hundred Guards and militia he embarked from Portoferraio on the night of February 26, 1815. The little flotilla of five ships sailed along the Italian coast, hoping to escape detection while battling the capricious winter seas. After three days and nights the men came ashore near Cannes, and began a rapid march that led over the mountains through Grasse and Digne to Grenoble. The icy roads were treacherous, and the cold of the mountains daunting, but the men marched resolutely with their commander. When they reached the outskirts of Grenoble they encountered a battalion of royalist troops, sent to arrest the escapee from Elba.

"Soldiers of the Fifth!" Bonaparte shouted, ordering his own men to put down their weapons, "I am your emperor; do you recognize me?"

He opened his coat, making himself vulnerable, throwing himself on the mercy of men who had once obeyed and adored him. "If there is among you a soldier who would like to kill his emperor," he shouted, "here I am!"

Discipline melted away, the men put down their arms

.

and cried, *"Vive l'empereur!"* as they rushed forward to welcome him.

When word reached Paris that Bonaparte had landed there was a frisson of excitement, but no great alarm. The National Guard was called out, the military commanders sent to their posts at Metz and Cambrai and Lyons. But when Parisians heard that their former emperor had reached Grenoble—always a staunchly republican city—and had been mobbed there by thousands of well-wishers, including the mayor and the military officers, panic began to spread. Bonaparte was proving to be invincible once again.

"Frenchmen," he had proclaimed on landing, "I have heard, in my exile, your lamentations and your prayers. . . . I have crossed the sea, and am coming to reclaim my rights." With the immediacy of biblical prophecy he was predicting his triumph. "Victory will march at full speed; the eagle, with the national colors, will fly from steeple to steeple, even to the towers of Notre-Dame."

Lyons capitulated, the royalist troops deserted. The soldiers of the garrison joined Bonaparte's forces, which had grown from eleven hundred to twelve thousand, with more joining him every day.

By this time the English had left Paris, scrambling to buy what horses there were at exorbitant prices, bribing their way past soldiers and roadblocks, racing for the coast. All was confusion and commotion, neither the king, the deputies nor the military could keep order. The Palais-Royal, the Salon des Étrangers were nearly empty. In the Faubourg St.-Germain the former émigrés trembled at the thought of the emperor's revenge.

Fierce March storms lashed the roads that led northward to Boulogne and Dieppe and Ostend. The wind and rain punished the fleeing English, drenching them and threatening to keep them stranded in the mud forever. In the overcrowded ports they waited to make the Channel crossing, fearful of the wild water and praying for safety. Finally they made it home, sick and anxious, to learn that the Tyrannical Destroyer was in Paris and that Louis XVIII had fled to

.

Lille. Wilberforce, who had not joined the exodus to France the previous fall and who thoroughly disapproved of the hedonistic, frivolous French, gave it as his opinion that Bonaparte's escape was a divine judgment for the sins of his fellow countrymen, and in particular, for their wicked sojourn amid the corruptions of Paris.

12

*I*n the first week of March, 1815, before word of Bonaparte's escape had reached England, a reporter for a provincial newspaper was struck by the mood of unrest in London. "Every man who has walked the streets of London for the last fortnight," he wrote, "has seen the inscriptions on the walls, attempting to inflame the public mind and excite riot and disturbance." Street orators drew crowds to hear their violent harangues, people gathered to sing anti-government songs, and to cheer the memory of Oliver Cromwell and other popular heroes "who so gloriously dissolved the Parliament."

Parliament was the villain—or so it seemed to the tens of thousands who signed petitions urging the government to vote down the bill introduced on February 17 calling for restrictions on the importation of foreign grain.

The issue was far-reaching, for it threatened to affect not

.

only the price of bread, and therefore the survival of the laboring classes, but the economic future of the landowners and, indirectly, of the manufacturers as well. The bill, if passed, would subsidize domestic agriculture by excluding imported grain priced below a specified figure (80s. per quarter), thus ensuring that English "corn"—wheat, oats and barley—would continue to bring a high price in the marketplace. Rents on land had risen tremendously during the war, and would not fall now that the war was over. Farmers could not afford to grow wheat if the price was allowed to drop significantly—as it had begun to do the previous spring. The subsidy was vital, and the urgency of the situation was obvious to a Parliament overwhelmingly dominated by the landed interest.

Yet if some form of subsidy was vital, affordable bread was even more of an imperative. The average Englishman and Englishwoman ate a pound of bread a day. It was the chief staple of their diet (potatoes had not yet replaced it), even in the slums of the capital where chalk-white loaves, bleached with alum, filled the rumbling bellies of the very poor. Affordable bread was a necessity to employers as well, for though the ratio between the two fluctuated wildly, prices had an impact on wages; at a time when bankruptcies were commonplace, manufacturers had to do all they could to keep wages low.

The Corn Bill was a crisis measure, necessitated by the threat of severe agricultural depression. But to the hundreds of thousands who signed petitions against it the measure appeared to be a purely selfish one, initiated by rich and greedy landowners bent on enriching themselves still further at the expense of ordinary citizens and manufacturers. The number of petitions reaching the House of Commons increased day by day, sent from nearly every region of the kingdom. Fifty-four thousand signed their names to a catalog of grievances in Manchester, five thousand in the small town of Frome, tens of thousands in the capital itself. The petitions were read aloud in Parliament, where the Tory ministers, worried over falling prices for manufactured goods and overstocked inventories, and disheartened by the lack of progress in the peace talks at Vienna, marshaled their arguments in defense of the bill and braced themselves to ride out the storm of public controversy.

The bill entered the committee stage in the Commons on March 6, and that night the storm broke. Immense crowds gathered to block the entrances to the building where the Commons was sitting, shouting at the Members as they attempted to go in and out.[1] The city constables could not control the crowd, and troops were called in to keep the lobby and its approaches clear. Inside the chamber, the debate went on, but the Members could hardly hear each other for the crowd was shouting and booing incessantly, their "insolent and threatening language" drowning out much of what was said. Elsewhere in the city mass meetings were held, and people took to the streets by the hundreds.

The angry crowd surged through the West End, making for the house of the Chief Justice, Lord Ellenborough, where they smashed all the windows, and then going on to the Lord Chancellor's residence in Bedford Square. "Where is Lord Eldon?" a voice demanded, and when there was no reply the rioters tore out the iron railings that stood in front of the doors and used them to force their way into the house. The arrival of a group of Horse Guards sent the rioters running, but they regrouped at the home of the Member who had introduced the Corn Bill and broke in. Here the work of destruction went on unimpeded for the better part of an hour. After breaking every pane of glass in the house the crowd began on the furnishings, destroying the larger pieces and tossing the smaller ones into the street to be trampled underfoot. Valuable paintings were ripped apart, china shattered, books and papers destroyed.

By this time some seven or eight hundred people were engaged in the looting, by one estimate, and they went on to damage another half-dozen houses that night. The Horse Guards succeeded in dispersing the crowds by eleven o'clock or so, at least in Westminster, but they massed again on the following night, and again the night after that, their numbers growing and their mood more ugly. In an attempt to appease the rioters the Court of Aldermen ordered the price

.

of bread in the city lowered immediately, but the crowd took no notice; they continued to roam the streets of the West End, dodging soldiers, taking aim with stones and brickbats at unbroken windows, "hullooing and huzzaing as they went along."

Parliament went on with its deliberations, and on March 10, the Third Reading of the Corn Bill was carried in the Commons by 245 votes to 72. By this time the city was full of soldiers. The 10th Dragoons, the Regent's regiment from Brighton, guarded the King's Mews, the 16th Dragoons were quartered at the Queen's Riding-house and there were militia posted at Knightsbridge and in the Tower. Artillery was conspicuously displayed and soldiers guarding the looted houses were ordered to fire on anyone who attempted to approach them. Several people were killed, others wounded from saber cuts, and the jails were full of surly dissidents who cursed the troops and the government.

At this juncture Lord Liverpool and his Tory ministers learned that a new crisis was at hand.

"Bonaparte's landed!" the newsboys shouted. "And with eleven hundred men!" People fought one another to get copies of the newspapers at twice their usual price. *The Times* announced the "lamentable intelligence of a civil war having been rekindled in France, by that wretch Bonaparte, whose life was so impolitically spared by the Allied Sovereigns." The Corn Bill was, for the moment, displaced in the popular consciousness by the prospect of a renewal of the war with France. And in that moment Tories and Whigs were agreed on what course to take, what leader to turn to. The Foreign Secretary, Lord Castlereagh, sent word immediately to the Duke of Wellington.

Arthur Wellesley, Duke of Wellington, occupied a unique place in public life and public esteem in the spring of 1815. A national hero, he inspired boundless admiration. He was "like a Divinity," wrote an officer who had served under him. He was a wonder-worker, an exorcist who had rid the world of the demon Bonaparte. His campaigns in the Peninsular War had, after a rocky beginning, made his name great. In 1811, with French success at its height, Wellington was

The Prince Regent c. 1814–1815 by Thomas Lawrence

Caroline of Brunswick in 1804 by Thomas Lawrence

The Prince Regent. Studio of Thomas Lawrence

Princess Charlotte in 1815 by T. Heaphy

Mail coaches setting off for the West of England from the "Swan with Two Necks" by Pollard

The assassination of Spencer Perceval in the lobby of the House of Commons, 1812, anonymous engraving

Carlton House, the Gothic Conservatory

Carlton House, the Rose Satin Drawing Room

George Gordon, Lord Byron, by Thomas Phillips

Lady Caroline Lamb dressed as a page, 1813, by
Thomas Phillips

Hannah More in 1827 by A. Edouart

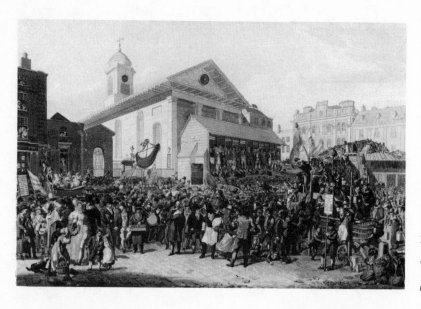

*The election of Members in Covent Garden, 1818, by
R. Havell and Son after G. Sharf*

Brighton Pavilion, the Music Room

Brighton Pavilion, the Banqueting Room

An execution outside Newgate Prison

Regent Street, the Quadrant, 1827

denounced as a reckless and ambitious—though undeniably courageous—commander. When in the following years his series of victories began to unfold, first Ciudad Rodrigo, then Badajoz, then Salamanca and later Vitoria, reverence succeeded reproof and Lord Wellington became the Marquis of Wellington and, in 1814, Duke of Wellington.

Those who had followed his career throughout its course were not surprised by his superlative distinction. Even as a young aide-de-camp, on the staff of the Lord Lieutenant of Ireland, he had shown exceptional promise, and when he obtained his own command his talent for thoroughness and keen judgment began to be evident. With the aid of his eldest brother Richard, Lord Mornington, Wellington sailed for India in 1796, a lieutenant colonel. Over the next eight years he learned the craft of command, deploying his troops against the much larger forces of the ferocious Mahrattas and coming away the victor. The chief obstacle to military success in the subcontinent—besides the unbearable heat—was disorganization. The young lieutenant colonel had a genius for bringing order to the chaos of a poorly provisioned, poorly supplied army, and with it a special gift for appreciating to an exact degree the strength of his fighting force.

"One must understand the mechanism and power of the individual soldier," he once told his friend John Croker, "then that of a company, a battalion, a brigade and so on, before one can venture to group divisions and move an army. I believe I owe most of my success to the attention I always paid to the inferior part of tactics as a regimental officer. There were few men in the Army who knew these details better than I did; it is the foundation of all military knowledge."[2]

Wellington's attention to what he called "the inferior part of tactics" served him well in the subcontinent, where distances were great and movement of the army, with its hundred thousand bullocks and hordes of native attendants and camp followers, was crucial to success. Other commanders had difficulty moving the huge animal and human swarm along at five miles an hour; Wellington managed to make it move nearly three times as fast, and on occasion even faster

.

than that. Furthermore, he managed to reach his destination without the usual appalling losses of life from climate and harsh terrain, so that once the troops arrived they were ready to fight effectively.

And there was another side to his leadership. He was extraordinarily collected, no matter how turbulent the situation in which he found himself. In the thick of battle, assaulted by the thunderous din of cannonades and hampered by blinding smoke and dust and widespread confusion, he remained level-headed, able to appraise his position and make judicious decisions. Battle transformed him, an aide wrote. He became "like an eagle," inspired and inspiring, wondrously courageous and seemingly invulnerable. At Assaye he and his men faced the massed batteries of the Indian enemy, a hundred guns mowing down the men in rapid and terrible slaughter, but Wellington, though he had two mounts killed under him, led his remnant force on to victory. "Wellesley Bahadur," his native troops dubbed him. Wellesley the Invincible.

The qualities that distinguished him in India brought him success against the French: care for the details of provisioning and supply, understanding to an uncanny degree the precise strength of his own men, brilliance in deploying them against a more numerous enemy—plus icy calm and magnificent courage. The English, eager for victories after so many years of defeats and eager too for a leader whom they could admire, glorified Wellington and made him their hero. Each of his victories compounded his fame, and when at last the war ended and Bonaparte was dethroned the duke came home to a hero's welcome. When his ship landed at Dover in June of 1814, a crowd of well-wishers was waiting to greet him and to cheer his carriage as it passed. He was cheered, in fact, all the way to London, and the crowd would have loosened the shafts and drawn the carriage themselves had he let them.

So immense was his popularity—and so immense the unpopularity of Lord Liverpool and the Tories—that many people thought Wellington would become Prime Minister. But where politics were concerned he was in an awkward position. His flamboyant brother Richard, Marquis Wellesley, a member of the Regent's inner circle and formerly Foreign Secretary in Spencer Perceval's cabinet, was on the outs with the present Tory leadership. Richard Wellesley had in 1812 been a leading candidate to replace Perceval but had fallen from power, unable to command the allegiance of the prominent men of either party. The duke could hardly join a government that had treated his brother so shabbily, and besides, his own expressed views on politics were not a little negative. "I never felt any inclination to dive deeply in party politics," he told his elder brother William. "I may be wrong but the conviction in my mind is that all the misfortunes of the present reign . . . are to be attributed in a great degree to the Spirit of Party in England."[3] Beyond this, a military man, Wellington felt, had to be above politics; though he was a firm Tory the duke believed he ought to be free to serve the Whigs should they come to power.

Whatever his status was to be in civilian life, Wellington was idolized. He was the "conqueror of the conqueror of the world," with statues rising in his honor all over the country. In 1815 he was still a youngish forty-five, hale and energetic, his blue eyes clear and his close-cropped brown hair untouched by gray. He looked every inch a classical hero, with his Roman profile and lean, muscular body, his abstemious habits and air of sober self-reliance. His loud laugh shattered the classical image, though, and he was prone to pleasant self-mockery. ("It's a fine thing to be a great man, is it not?" he remarked to a companion as they made their way through a dense knot of admirers.)

The duke's brusqueness was in time to become proverbial, but the succinctness and precision of his speech—which in a flowery age seemed like understatement—should not blind us to his very considerable social accomplishments. In youth he had been good-looking, charming, very much a ladies' man, and he retained these characteristics into middle age. His capacity for collected judgment made him an able mediator. Moreover, he had the polish of a continental education. He had been sent to France in the 1780s, before the revolution, to study riding, fencing, military science and good manners at an elite academy at Angers. His years there were

·

very happy, he later recalled, and beyond acquiring a mastery of French he acquired an appreciation for the chivalrous code of the ancien régime, with its scrupulosity and courtly gentlemanliness. Young Wellington had been a young man of the world; Wellington in middle age, broadened by his experience in India and tempered by the sorrows and frustrations of twenty years of campaigning, was England's man of the hour.

Given all this, the duke's indifference to honors and to his own appearance was all the more striking. He was unpretentious, direct, disarmingly simple. His utter lack of self-importance was conspicuous in an era of personal magnificence and ostentation. He had none of the Regent's unctuous grace, and in fact was put off by his prince's emollient affability. But he had something far more valuable. More than any other prominent Englishman of his time, Wellington incarnated the hardihood and equanimity peculiar to his countrymen. He not only incarnated these attributes, he inspired them in others. He brought out the toughness in his soldiers, and they loved him for it, calling him "Old Nosey" and swearing to fight to the death for him if he asked it of them. His plain appearance—he liked to wear an old blue frock coat, and disdained elegantly tailored uniforms—and occasional gruffness were more effectual than any other commander's pomp and harsh punishments.

And it was not only the soldiers who responded to Wellington's sturdy equanimity. The public at large discerned in him a uniquely steadying calm. He was a cool, reasonable man in an impassioned age. Unlike Byron, who filled them with fascinated horror by hovering on the brink of self-destruction, or Hannah More, who aroused their fear and contrition by her visions of virtue triumphing over rampant wickedness, or the Regent, who exasperated and distressed them by his shallow debauchery and periodic hysteria, the duke reassured and steadied them. He was undaunted by the Olympian tragedies and dramas of the times. He simply faced them with Olympian equanimity.

So when word of Bonaparte's escape reached England in

March of 1815, Castlereagh sent at once for the duke. He was not only England's greatest general, he was her greatest asset in a crisis. He was Wellington Bahadur, Wellington the Invincible.

Castlereagh's message reached the duke in Vienna. He had been on the continent since the previous fall, when he had accepted the post of ambassador to the court of Louis XVIII. It was a dangerous if glamorous posting, for Wellington was understandably hated by the French army and there were plots against his life. He proved to be an able ambassador, and an able diplomat, but when he narrowly escaped assassination while attending a military review it was clear he would have to be recalled. In January of 1815 he left Paris for Vienna, where he replaced Castlereagh as principal British representative at the peace conference.

The delegates to the conference, startled by the news from Elba, had immediately closed ranks and determined to unite in opposition to Bonaparte. Wellington agreed to command an allied army, under a mandate that empowered him to confront "the disturber of world repose" who by his challenge to Louis XVIII's throne had "placed himself outside the pale of civil and social relations." The duke left at once for Brussels to take up his command.

By the middle of March the London streets were quiet, the nightly ravaging of mansions in the West End had stopped. The dragoons and the militia, brought in in increasing numbers to dampen the rioting, kept order—though their presence created resentment. "The spirit of the mob is as bad as ever," the Regent wrote in a letter to his mother. Yet the soldiers were effective, he assured her, and had in one case fired on the crowd, "and killed two, a man and a woman, et *tant mieux* (God forgive me for saying so)."[4]

The Corn Bill, having passed the Commons, passed the Lords on March 20, rousing the street orators to new denunciations of Parliament, the ministers and above all, the Regent.

The Regent was believed to be among the Corn Bill's strongest supporters, and the angry crowds would gladly have attacked Carlton House had it not been heavily guarded

.

by troops. As it was, opponents of the bill succeeded in making a symbolic gesture; a loaf of bread, dripping with blood, was placed atop the outer wall, where its accusing message could be plainly read.

Carlton House was on everyone's mind, for the prince's Whig critics were currently publicizing the extravagant expense of its upkeep. The grandiose palace, with its exquisitely ornate décor, its costly furnishings and priceless art treasures, was never finished to its occupant's satisfaction. He was forever renovating it, ordering the sumptuous rooms redecorated, suggesting improvements, expanding his collections of statuary and china and Old Masters. Antique dealers, picture dealers, gilders and dyers, carvers and cabinetmakers filed in and out of Carlton House, each with an appointment to consult with His Majesty on his collections, or to obtain his approval on a point of design. The Regent was a perfectionist when it came to ornament, and it mattered very much to him that the curtains in the Rose-Satin Drawing Room should be a particular shade of rose, and made of a particular weight and quality of satin, and that the patterns in the varnished wooden walls of the new Gothic Dining Room should complement those used in the Conservatory. The number of such details was infinite, and overseeing them took almost as much of Prince George's time as his meetings with tailors and haberdashers and wigmakers. He took particular pains with the newest additions to the mansion—a dining room so large and so elaborate it had five separate apartments, a Gothic Library more splendid than the original gilded and columned library, a new Golden Drawing Room and several other ornate rooms. The furnishings were supplemented, rearranged, or replaced; many of the superseded pieces were sent to the Marine Pavilion in Brighton to complement renovations going on there.

The Pavilion, the Regent's treasured private retreat, was undergoing even more alteration than Carlton House. John Nash, who on James Wyatt's death in 1813 had become the prince's chief architect, began to enlarge the Pavilion and was in time utterly to transform its exterior. In 1815, Nash was at work refashioning the interior, designing new cast-iron staircases with bamboo balusters, modifying the color scheme of the South Drawing Room (four times) and redoing the North Drawing Room in bright Chinese yellow with innumerable dragons and lanterns. Nash had already rebuilt the royal lodge in Windsor Park to the Regent's taste; now he was undertaking the same sort of thoroughgoing alteration at Brighton, much to the distaste of the Regent's detractors. The Pavilion was an embarrassment to them, its luxury-loving occupant a sybarite who, in the words of one Whig M.P., "resembled more the pomp and magnificence of a Persian satrap seated in all the splendor of Oriental state than the sober dignity of a British prince seated in the bosom of his subjects." The Pavilion was a den of vice; that the satrap should need to renovate his den at public expense seemed wicked and shameful.

Relatively few of the prince's subjects had ever seen the interior of the Marine Pavilion, but a great many of them had seen it caricatured. George Cruikshank, with Thomas Rowlandson and James Gillray the most popular of the Regency caricaturists, drew "The Court of Brighton à la Chinese!!!" in 1816. In Cruikshank's depiction the Regent sits at the center of the scene, his huge round body clothed in the robes of a Chinese mandarin, a Chinese moustache cascading over his wide triple chins. Beside him lolls a rotund Lady Hertford, escaping voluptuously from her skimpy gown, while to the left of their canopied bed servants pour out gold from the privy purse.

"Get fresh patterns of Chinese deformities to finish the decorations of ye Pavilion!" the Regent demands of his ambassador, Lord Amherst. Other officials and judges stand in the background ready to do their master's bidding, their dignity destroyed by their silly-looking Chinese hats.

In the prince's own mind, of course, the Pavilion and Carlton House were only the beginning. He proposed to make all of London a monument to his reign—and a backdrop for his personal splendor. What Bonaparte had done for Paris, he would do for England's capital, he boasted to his friends.

.

To this end he had Nash draw up an ambitious scheme of "Metropolitan Improvements."

At the heart of Nash's grand design was an expanse of undeveloped ground—Marylebone Park, which had just become crown property. Here he proposed to build a summer palace for the Regent, who dreamed of having a palace spacious enough to house a museumlike sculpture gallery accommodating three hundred casts from the antique. The palace was to be surrounded by a verdant "garden city" for the Regent's privileged friends. Dozens of luxurious villas were to be built amid groves of trees and stretches of shrubbery and lawn. A dramatic shrine, a "National Valhalla," was to rise in the midst of the development, along with lakes and terraces and broad promenades. To connect the new royal palace with Carlton House Nash designed a new street—Regent Street—which in time became the city's principal north-south axis.

The "Metropolitan Improvements" as Nash proposed them were rejected by the Treasury; though Regent Street and Regent Park took form neither the palace nor the shrine nor the array of villas were ever built. But the Regent persisted in his lofty aspirations for the capital. England, after all, had no public buildings of any significance, no imposing state palace where important ceremonies could take place. Windsor was more a fortress than a royal residence, and sadly decayed, the Tudor palace of St. James's was quaint but hardly imposing, and the Queen's House—Buckingham House—had not been designed with formal occasions in mind. England's greatness—and his own—deserved better.

After all, the Regent had, with the aid of his generals, of course, put an end to the long war and had recently regained his continental kingdom of Hanover. His achievements cried out for recognition. He saw himself the way an admiring artist had imagined him a decade earlier, as a deified prince, handsome and serene, standing aloft on a pedestal of integrity. Below him lesser mortals were embroiled in strife, but he belonged to a higher realm above it all. His being radiated qualities the artist carefully identified: Conde-

·

scension, Liberality, Honor, Dignity, Fortitude, Benevolence, Tenacity, Charity and Justice. He was glorious, unsurpassable. "No prince was ever idolized by the people of this country as I am," he told one of his courtiers. And why not? At everything pertaining to princeliness he was, in his own estimation, superb.

One night at Brighton Pavilion a select group of the Regent's friends amused themselves thinking up names for one another. The brilliant but perpetually bankrupt Richard Sheridan was given the witty but cruel title "The Man Who Extends England's Credit." Then came the Regent's turn to be given a name.

"*The* Man," suggested another guest, Philip Francis.

"Go on," Sheridan encouraged.

"I've done," said the canny Francis.

He knew he had pleased his host. "I'm content," the Regent said, and bowed gracefully to everyone in the room.[5]

Dressed in his splendid Field Marshal's uniform, his curving ornamental saber strapped around his huge waist and his false curls in place, the Regent indulged his fantasies of military glory as he waited for news from Brussels. On his chest were gleaming medals presented to him from the other European sovereigns, and in his own mind he believed that he had won them in battle. He had only to close his eyes to recollect the glorious scenes he had witnessed at first hand—the plunging and rearing of the horses, the clash of swords, the cries of exultation and of agony from his valiant men. He shared these recollections with his friends, who were too loyal to tell him that his imaginings bore no resemblance to the truth, and too tactful to upset his nerves by reminding him that Bonaparte was gathering strength day by day in Paris.

Londoners were busy, as in every crisis, placing bets on Europe's future. They wagered on the day Bonaparte would march into Brussels, then into Vienna. He would soon have half a million troops at his disposal, people said, while Wellington would be lucky to raise a hundred thousand. Russian troops were on their way to him, but were coming slowly,

.

171

through Poland. Austrian troops were to join him too, but for the time being were needed in Italy. The Prussians were the nearest, but even they might not be able to reach the duke's miscellany of British and German forces in time to support him when Bonaparte attacked—as he was certain soon to do.

.

*T*he French attack, when it came, was bold and aggressive. Bonaparte knew that the longer he waited, the higher the probability that he would have to face a combined assault by the allied armies. With only about 200,000 men in all—albeit excellent men, trained veterans of many campaigns and completely loyal to him—Bonaparte could not risk having to defend France against four large invading armies. In mid-June he led his men into Belgium, defeating the Prussians under Blücher at Ligny and moving on toward Brussels where Wellington awaited him.

Wellington had by this time assembled an army of something less than ninety thousand men, less than a third of them British. Of the remainder, many were Belgians, whose loyalty could not be assured, and many others were Hanoverians, who were loyal but poorly trained. Of his stalwart penin-

.

sular veterans there were relatively few, and a high proportion of the duke's British troops were recruits. Still, once they were soundly deployed, he hoped for the best from his men, and put them in position spread out along high ground at a site near the main road to Brussels. The rising ground gave them one advantage; another was provided by two farms, Hougoumont and La Haye Sainte, whose buildings stood fortresslike in front of the British lines.

A violent rainstorm swept the area on June 17, and Wellington's soldiers told one another that it was a good omen.[1] All the duke's peninsular victories had been preceded by pouring rain, and this storm was uncommonly fierce, lasting through the night and turning the hard ground to deep, sticky mud. The hope of victory made the long, uncomfortably wet night more bearable, but it meant that the troops who faced each other the next morning were sodden and chilled, and had slept badly or not at all.

Some fourteen hundred yards separated the English on their ridge from the French who occupied the heights opposite them called La Belle Alliance. Both armies had about seventy thousand men, but the French soldiers were far superior in training and experience and the French artillery, gun for gun, far outnumbered that of the English. Bonaparte was contemptuous of his enemies, and of their general. He was fresh from victory over the Prussians, and he thought less of the English than he did of Blücher's men, despite the warnings of his own officers who considered Wellington's infantry "impregnable." As for Wellington himself, Bonaparte belittled him. "I tell you, Wellington is a bad general, the English are bad troops, and this affair is nothing more than eating breakfast," he insisted, though he did acknowledge the significance of the impending battle. "The battle that is coming will save France and will be celebrated in the annals of the world," was his portentous pronouncement—and the words were prophetic. No battle has ever been quite so celebrated.

Between the two long lines of troops were the two farms, and Bonaparte, hoping to draw men away from the strong English center, decided to launch his attack against one of

.

these, the château of Hougoumont. He sent his youngest brother Jerome to capture the château and its grounds, but though Jerome and his four veteran regiments fought their way forward into the courtyard, they were repulsed by the firepower of the defending English—and by the thick old walls of the building itself—and after further futile assaults the battle for Hougoumont ended in a costly loss for the French.

A thunderous cannonade, so deafening that the ground shook as in an earthquake and the very air seemed to vibrate with the noise, signaled the French infantry advance that began in early afternoon. Sixteen thousand men swept down from the heights of La Belle Alliance and across the valley toward the English, swirling around the second of the two farms, La Haye Sainte, and forcing its defenders to take refuge inside the farm buildings. But the English answered the assault, first with an infantry charge and then with a pounding cavalry charge that forced the French back and chased them across the valley the way they had come, pursuing them to their own lines and, in a furor of blind heroism, seizing two of their standards and a number of their guns. Their own momentum betrayed the English horsemen, for the French infantry cut them off from behind and few made it back to their own positions alive. A quarter of the English cavalry lay dead or dying, but the French too had lost thousands of men, and Bonaparte was having to admit that defeating the English was proving to be harder than he thought.

It was midafternoon now, and still the English center held. In the far distance Wellington could see the Prussians advancing—at a snail's pace, it seemed to him—to reinforce his troops, and Bonaparte, who had refused to believe that Blücher could manage to reach the battle site for several days, saw them too. Yet the thought of a British victory was preposterous: all the weight of superior fighting men, superior guns, vastly superior generalship was surely on the French side. Bonaparte ordered Marshal Ney to take La Haye Sainte, and then to breach the English defenses.

The tragedy of Ney's cavalry charge—light cavalry riding suicidally against a solid wall of musket fire—would long be remembered, but at about six o'clock the French infantry managed to do what the cavalry could not and take the farm. By this time, however, skilled combat had given way to haphazard chaos and brutal attrition. The battlefield was obscured by the thick black smoke belched out by the cannon, and fog descended periodically to obscure it still further. Men, horses and guns on both sides were covered in mud, making recognition difficult, and late in the day many men were accidentally killed by their comrades-in-arms. Riderless horses, wild with fear, dashed here and there, impeding the orderly deployment of troops and colliding with the onrushing cavalry. Dazed men, deafened by repeated cannonades and numbed by seven hours and more of exhilaration and terror, wandered aimlessly among the piles of corpses, or joined the hundreds of walking wounded filing slowly and silently away from the melée toward safety.

Amid the disorder the killing went doggedly on. Miraculously, Wellington's men did not give way, though at one point the French came within a few hundred yards of them and even though their ranks were thinned again and again by heavy bombardment. In the end Bonaparte had not enough troops both to defend himself against the Prussians and to force the English to yield their ground. When at last he led his "Immortals" against the English, his indomitable Moyenne Garde, they were turned back—something that had never happened before—and when they fled, the English pursued them.

From then on, with the Prussians attacking on one side and the English on the other, it was only a matter of time before Bonaparte, fearing encirclement, got into his carriage and hastily left the battlefield. Behind him came the Prussians, driving the retreating French before them like harried animals, giving no quarter. The pursuit went on all night, while the moon rose over the scene of carnage, making easy work of the slaughter. Wellington returned to his headquarters, and after a meal and a few hours' sleep, wrote a dispatch to the War Minister, Lord Bathurst. He had lost thirty-five thousand men, but allowed himself only a little time to weep for them. "The army never, upon any occasion, conducted

.

itself better," he told the War Minister. "There is no officer nor description of troops that did not behave well." The battle of Waterloo had been won.

The battle was over, but the Waterloo legend was just beginning. The men who survived it sensed that they had taken part in a supernal struggle, a brief, intense distillation of human experience into a few hours of elation, glory and tragedy. All battles heighten the passions, but Waterloo, because of its decisiveness and drama, and because of the heavy loss of life on both sides—and, no doubt, because of the unprecedented prolixity of the survivors—has always seemed monumental among battles, classic in its execution and exemplary in its collective heroism.

Time and again, in their memoirs, men recalled acts of remarkable courage: officers who led their men on even after they had received fatal wounds, calling on their last reserves of strength and concealing their pain; sergeants who gave their lives to protect the regimental colors, seizing the staff when the man who held it went down and holding it aloft until they too were cut down; infantrymen who fought with superhuman savagery, hewing down the enemy and, when needed, holding back their advance by sheer muscle and determination. There were stories of men joking over their wounds, of cavalry officers riding recklessly into furious fire in order to capture an enemy gun—and dying in the attempt, of Scots pipers stepping outside the safety of their regimental squares to play defiantly while in range of the French cannon. Personal honor was paramount, whether it meant standing tall and still while French grapeshot rained down on all sides or showing mercy to a gallant enemy.

The charge of the Scots Greys and the Life Guards, the Inniskillings and the King's Dragoons, their huge horses churning the mud as they galloped madly across the cornfields and into the thick of the French lines, had the stuff of immortality about it. The trumpeters called the charge, the sound quickening the nerves and making the men steel themselves, their hearts racing, to unleash their battle fury. The riders rushed forward, shouting, "For England!" "Scotland Forever!" as the sound of cannonfire drowned out the

.

trumpets and drums and the screams of wounded men and horses all around them. They galloped on, exhilarated by the danger, filled with an exalted sense of murderous purpose, until with a final dash they were closing with the Cuirassiers and clashing, sword on sword, fighting for their lives.

The French fell back, overwhelmed by the onslaught of raging men on giant horses. But then, instead of re-forming and riding back to safety as their officers urged them to, the English horsemen rode on forward, crazed by their success and tempted beyond endurance by the sight of the fleeing French. "Every officer within hearing exerted themselves to the utmost to reform the men," one officer wrote afterward, "but the helplessness of the enemy offered too great a temptation to the dragoons, and our efforts were abortive." The trumpets called the retreat again and again, but in vain. The inevitable happened; the French reserves were called in, and the English, from being the hunters, suddenly became the hunted. The French horses were fresh, while those of the English, though they continued to slash and bite at the enemy in a frenzy, were winded. Too late the English realized their peril and tried to turn and regroup. But the French Lancers were already upon them, riding them down with the long pointed lances against which the shorter English swords were useless. The strongest horses carried their masters back to safety, but by then most were too slow and weak to get away. Mercilessly the Lancers mowed them down, unhorsing, maiming, and finally dispatching the English as they tried desperately to run or crawl away. Not a man was spared. Of the three hundred Greys who rode out in glory, only a few dozen rode back.

The nimbus of high valor soon came to surround every man who had fought at Waterloo. Each man became a "Waterloo man," with a medal to prove it and two years' extra service time credited toward his pension. All the regiments that had taken part in the battle were allowed to carry on their badges, colors and other appointments the word "Waterloo," and received other marks of distinction. The Prince Regent announced that "as a mark of his high approbation of the distinguished bravery and good conduct of the First and Second Life Guards at the battle of Waterloo," he was "pleased to declare himself Colonel in Chief of both the regiments of Life Guards." There were Waterloo panoramas, spectacles, songs and poems in abundance.

> Oh, shame to thee, land of the Gaul!
> Oh, shame to thy children and thee!
> Unwise in thy glory and base in thy fall,
> How wretched thy portion shall be!
> Derision shall strike thee forlorn,
> A mock'ry that never shall die;
> The curses of Hate and the hisses of Scorn
> Shall burthen the winds of thy sky;
> And proud o'er thy ruin for ever be hurl'd
> The laughter of Triumph, the jeers of the World!

So wrote "Brutus" in the *Morning Chronicle,* and his sentiments were widely shared.

As for the triumphant commander responsible for the victory, no amount of praise could do him justice. "Everybody is wild with admiration of our wonderful hero," wrote Charlotte Grenville, Lady Williams Wynn, some ten days after the battle. "All the private letters are filled with enthusiastic encomiums on him, even in the first moments of individual suffering." The duke's battlefield heroism and his providential escapes from harm were on everyone's lips. One man had been killed while turning the head of Wellington's horse Copenhagen, but both Copenhagen and his rider were unscathed. Another officer had been resting his arm on Wellington's knee when a ball struck it, amputating the arm but deflecting the ball so that the duke was saved.[2] Clearly he had been spared so that through his inspiration and exhortation, his soldiers could carry the day.

He had been at the heart of the battle, riding here and there, taking note, it seemed, of every soldier and every gun. When reinforcements were needed, he somehow found them, despite his shortage of troops; his presence, always composed and reasonable, reassured the men and kept them at their fateful labors. Wherever he was needed, he appeared, rallying the fleeing Brunswickers, leading his cavalry into position,

·

pointing out where the guns should be placed and, on one occasion, showing a fine sense of chivalry by deterring an eager gunner from taking a shot at Bonaparte, who was just then in range. Long after the battle men recalled hearing his voice—"There my lads," to the infantry, "Now, gentlemen," to the cavalry—and feeling a renewed surge of enterprise, even though they were near the end of their endurance.

Honors rained down on the duke after the battle. The King of the Netherlands, William I, made him Prince of Waterloo. Tsar Alexander pronounced him "the Conqueror of Waterloo," and gave him a sword encrusted with diamonds. There was talk of building him a palace which, like Blenheim erected for Marlborough, should bear the name of his victory.

With Waterloo the "military mania" of the Regency built to an exultant, glorious climax. The grand battle to end battles had been fought and won. No further glory was attainable, no further sacrifice conceivable. "Grant, O merciful God," churchmen prayed from their pulpits in thanksgiving, "that the result of this mighty battle, terrible in conflict, but glorious beyond example in success, may put an end to the miseries of Europe, and staunch the blood of nations." Europe had reached a new turning. An age of war was closed.

The tide of victory was at the full, but almost at once it began to ebb. On the night that word of Waterloo reached London, people poured out into the streets, relieved at the triumphant outcome of the battle but apprehensive about its cost. So many families had received private word of sons, fathers, husbands killed that the scale of the slaughter was beginning to be apparent, even though no detailed figures of the losses had yet been released. None of Wellington's officers had escaped unhurt, it was said. Many were dead. Unofficially, men in the government were trying to prepare people for the worst, while at the same time arguing that the Waterloo dead ought to be viewed not as the casualties of a single battle but as part of a grand tally of fatalities arising from a generation of warfare. The argument was unconvincing. By the end of June, half the people in the West End were wearing mourning, or so it seemed, while the other

·

half were desperately attempting to get word of relatives who had been in the battle. Many were embarking for the continent where wounded kin lay in makeshift hospitals. Suddenly, in the aftermath of one destructive battle, the war-hungry populace was awakening to the stark truth of war. The phantasms of horror they had lived with for so long were dissolving. A horrible reality was taking their place.

Crows feasted on the Waterloo dead for days after the battle ended. The ditches were full of bodies, bloated with putrefaction; the sweet stench of death was everywhere, over-powering and nauseating. The dead had to be neglected while the few available orderlies and surgeons attended to the living, but thousands of wounded men died before they could be reached and treated. Fever, internal bleeding, gangrene took their toll of wounded; so did the looters, who lost no time in stripping the men of their valuables as they lay helpless, and then in finishing them off so they could tell no tales.

One of the wounded who survived the looting was Lady Bessborough's son Frederick Ponsonby. He had taken part in the cavalry charge at midday, and, wounded in both arms, was knocked off his horse near the French lines.[3] A Lancer saw him struggling to get to his feet and plunged his lance into Ponsonby's back, but though the lance pierced his lungs, making him cough up blood and nearly choke on it, the wound was not fatal. Later a French field officer gave him a drink of brandy from his flask, and put a cloak over him and a knapsack under his head before returning to his own responsibilities.

Ponsonby lay where he was while the battle went on around and over him. According to the account he wrote later, a French sharpshooter plundered him, then when the French retreated a pursuing squadron of Prussian horsemen rode over him, leaving him "a good deal hurt." Wounded in five places, with bones smashed and covered with severe bruises, he waited for help. Now some Prussians looted him, then left him for dead. At last an English soldier appeared who agreed to stay with Ponsonby until he could be treated. "I suffered but little pain from my wounds," he wrote, "but

·

I had a most dreadful thirst, and there were no means of getting a drop of water. I thought the night would never end."

In the morning a dragoon from Ponsonby's brigade came by, and tried to get the wounded officer onto his horse, but he was too badly hurt. The dragoon rode to headquarters, and finally after more hours of suffering a wagon was sent to pick him up. Ponsonby had by this time been lying where he was for eighteen hours, and was near death from shock and blood loss. He was taken to the inn at Waterloo, which was already crowded with wounded, and there, despite the severity of his wounds, he began slowly to recover.

Brussels, a dozen miles from the battle site, became a vast open-air hospital, with men lying out along the streets because there was no room in the inns or private houses. Disease began to spread through the city, and as the English civilians poured in, hoping to rescue their injured family members, the congestion made the likelihood of an epidemic greater. Meanwhile at Waterloo, peasants, their noses and mouths covered with cloths to prevent them from gagging, raked the corpses into mass graves and burned the thousands of dead horses that littered the field.

About six weeks after the battle Walter Scott visited Waterloo. He was a keen student of battles, and had followed the course of Wellington's victories with avid admiration, at one point hoping to visit the army in the peninsula in order to experience the course of combat at first hand. He never got his chance to witness the peninsular campaign, but in August of 1815 he arrived in Belgium.

"On Wednesday last, I rode over the memorable field of Waterloo, now forever consecrated to immortality," he wrote to his patron, the Duke of Buccleuch. "All the more ghastly tokens of the carnage are now removed the bodies of both men and horses being either burned or buried. But the ground is still torn with the shot and shells, and covered with cartridges, old hats, and shoes, and various relics of the fray which the peasants have not thought worth removing."[4]

He walked over the bloodstained field, attempting to reconstruct the course of the battle and pausing here and there to pick up souvenirs—a French officer's memorandum book, filled with records of receipts and expenses and notations of punishments meted out to his soldiers, a cross of the Legion of Honor, a songbook. A Flemish peasant who claimed to have been by Bonaparte's side throughout the battle attached himself to Scott and told him a stream of anecdotes. The peasant was no doubt making good money recounting his experiences to visiting English travelers, for by late summer Waterloo had become a ghoulish tourist attraction. Grieving parents came to see for themselves where their sons had died, sweethearts in black veils arrived to pay tribute to their fallen lovers. The more reverent of the visitors left flowers, the irreverent carved their names on the walls of Hougoumont. Some took back macabre reminders of the battle—severed limbs or fingers preserved in alcohol.

The looters had become businessmen. "At Waterloo and all the hamlets in the vicinage," Scott wrote, "there is a mart established for cuirasses; for the eagles worn by the imperial guard on their caps; for casques, swords, carabines, and similar articles." The writer himself bought two cuirasses to take back to Scotland with him as decorations.

But the greatest relic of the battle, Bonaparte himself, was not in Belgium but in Torbay harbor, aboard the British ship *Bellerophon*. After Waterloo, Bonaparte had abdicated, hoping to be granted the right to live in exile in England, the only country where he believed he would be safe. He had surrendered to the captain of the *Bellerophon*, and had been allowed to go aboard the ship with forty or fifty attendants and a great deal of imperial baggage.

While the English deliberated his fate, he made himself at home aboard the ship, taking over the captain's quarters, dining in splendor, ingratiating himself with the seamen— who pronounced him "a devilish good fellow"—and familiarizing himself with every detail of the *Bellerophon*.

The English rowed out to see him by the thousands, their boats bobbing up and down in the Channel waters while they waited for him to take his regular daily promenade. He appeared, in uniform, spyglass in hand, and paced the

.

deck for the benefit of the crowd every afternoon at five o'clock. At first the English jeered him noisily, shaking their fists and gesturing angrily. But as the days passed the crowds became less hostile, and larger. Detailed accounts of his person and behavior began to appear in the papers. The latent admiration many of the English felt for him came to the fore. Soon the people who greeted him were wearing red carnations in token of their sympathy, and writing letters to the *Morning Chronicle* calling him the "greatest of living men" and hoping that his "great and firm mind" would be able to withstand whatever future the government decreed for him.

For two weeks the people continued to be fascinated with the celebrity aboard the *Bellerophon,* and were quite crestfallen when on August 7 he was put aboard another ship, the *Northumberland,* and sailed away bound for exile on St. Helena.

14

*T*he Crimson Drawing Room of Carlton House was fitted up with a velvet-covered altar near one of the fireplaces for Princess Charlotte's wedding to Prince Leopold of Saxe-Coburg-Saalfeld on the evening of May 2, 1816. Chapel ornaments, including two handsome candlesticks six feet high, were brought from the military chapel at Whitehall for the ceremony, and some fifty privileged guests, having been treated to a fine supper beforehand, were now assembled to await the bride.

Her husband-to-be, Prince Leopold, took his place in front of the altar. He was a good-looking young man, his well-proportioned figure set off by his military uniform. An ornamental sword hung at his side, fastened in place by a wide belt sparkling with diamonds. His expression was, some thought, rather severe—others said it was merely melancholy—but the grave look on his face only heightened his

.

princely dignity as he stood waiting for the princess. Leopold was the third son of the Prince of Saxe-Coburg-Saalfeld, and as such hardly a figure of consequence, yet he had proven his worth as a cavalry general in the Russian army and promised to be the sort of manly, dependable consort who could be relied on to sire a long line of British monarchs.

For the past several days the prince had been staying at Clarence House, the London residence of Prince William, Duke of Clarence, and the usual crowds of spectators had come to gape at him there, shouting for him to acknowledge them until he stepped out onto the balcony to gratify their curiosity. They approved of him, liking the way he greeted them with sober courtesy, the way he rode about in an unadorned green carriage—so unlike the Regent's ornate yellow one—and the plainness of his dress. His simplicity of style came more from penury than principle, but Londoners did not know this, and as the days passed the cheering crowds grew. On the night of the wedding, as the prince came out to enter his carriage to go to Carlton House, a great many women came to see him off. They waved their handkerchiefs in the air enthusiastically, those nearest to him "approaching him closely, patting him on the back, and invoking upon him all sorts of the best blessings."[1]

The Archbishop of Canterbury, flanked by the Archbishop of York and three other bishops, took his place in front of the altar. To his right was the frail old queen, seated in a chair of state as it taxed her strength to stand for any length of time. The wedding pleased her, temporarily melting her rather cantankerous disposition and calling forth words of advice for the father of the bride. Prince Leopold, she wrote to the Regent, "must be the head of the family, and she [Charlotte] must submit to him as his wife."[2] However incongruous this submission might seem in a future sovereign, it was necessary to ensure a happy marriage, and especially in this case where the bride had never been accustomed to submitting to anyone. Beside Queen Charlotte were Princesses Augusta, Elizabeth, Mary and Sophia, and the Duchess of York. Across from the royal ladies were three of the royal dukes, Frederick, William and Edward, and beyond them,

.

positioned here and there, were the members of the cabinet, the officers of the Regent's household and several foreign ambassadors.

At a nod from the Lord Chamberlain Prince William left his place and went out. He returned escorting the bride. Charlotte, fat and ungraceful—her tread, an unflattering observer remarked, was like that of Henry VIII—approached the altar "with much steadiness," a look of happy triumph on her revealing face. Her wedding dress was all in silver, layer upon layer of costly fabric sewn with metallic thread, embroidered at the borders with patterns of shells and bouquets. The dress was cut full below the high bodice, emphasizing Charlotte's corpulence, and the endless frills and lace trimmings and garlands of diamonds served to draw attention away from her blue eyes and appealingly pretty round face and to fix it firmly on her doughy arms and heavy torso. A wreath of rosebuds and leaves, formed of brilliants, crowned her blond hair.

There was nothing demure about Charlotte as she joined Leopold and stood before the archbishop to recite her vows. Nor was her stammer in evidence when she repeated the words, "giving the responses with great clearness, so as to be heard distinctly by every person present." (Leopold was "not heard so distinctly.") She spoke with all the authority, if not the decorum, of a future queen, though her manners, as a rule, were "very much below her situation," and reminded people to a frightening extent of her absent mother.

Yet despite the tacit understanding that she would one day succeed her father, there was an air of tentativeness about Charlotte's position as next in line, after her father, for the throne. It was not just that a male heir would have been preferable to a female—though that was certainly true—or that the princess's underdeveloped sense of decorum could be expected to hamper her once she began to rule. There were strong rumors that the Regent would divorce Charlotte's mother before long, and fainter ones that, should the Regent die before he obtained his divorce, the Duke of York would attempt to remove Charlotte from the succession by having the Regent's marriage to Maria Fitzherbert declared

.

legal. Either way, Charlotte would lose her succession rights.

Certainly Charlotte had not been educated to become queen. To remedy this deficiency, at least in part, Hannah More had published in 1805 a book with the modest title *Hints Towards Forming the Character of a Young Princess.* In it she discussed the importance of forming the future sovereign's mind along sound lines. A knowledge of history was vital, she taught, along with the scriptural evidences of Christianity, the "graces of deportment" and "the art of moral calculation." Charlotte ought to learn how to discriminate, in her reading, between instructive and merely amusing books—with novels assigned lowest priority on her reading list. She ought to follow the example of her illustrious predecessor Queen Elizabeth, More advised, and to shun imitating such exceptional models of female rulership as Queen Christina of Sweden. "Had the royal pupil been a prince," More wrote in her preface, "these hints would never have been obtruded on the world, as it would then have been naturally assumed, that the established plan adopted in such cases would have been pursued." But since there was no established plan to educate Charlotte for her future role, More saw fit to provide one.

Charlotte's domestic conduct was at least as important as her adroitness in statecraft, and here More advised those who had charge of the princess to restrain her vivacity and wit, and encourage in her the virtues of patience, industry, and humility. She should be led to distrust her own judgment, to bear chastisement meekly. "It is of the last importance to their happiness in life," More wrote of young women, "that they should early acquire a submissive temper and a forbearing spirit. They must even endure to be thought wrong sometimes, when they cannot but feel they are right."[3]

The irrepressible princess bore little imprint of this advice, which was just as well for her self-assurance. *The Times* loyally acknowledged her prospects in expressing the hope that she would one day reign—"the third instance in our history of the wisdom and glory of the reign of a British queen." (Charlotte would in fact be the sixth Queen of England, but *The Times* did not like to recall any earlier queens than Elizabeth and Anne; Mary I had been a Catholic, and by reputation a sanguinary tyrant, Mary II had been a cipher, and the shadowy twelfth-century Queen Matilda had borne a disputed title and was now all but forgotten.) And the people who shouted "loudly and incessantly" to her on her wedding night clearly expected her to ascend the throne one day, and were delighted at the thought. They were much more delighted, however, at the idea of a royal wedding, to be quickly followed, they hoped, by a series of healthy royal births. For whatever her ultimate dignity was to be, Charlotte's principal role as a woman was perceived to be that of wife and mother, dutifully subordinate to her husband, contentedly confined to the private sphere.

The view of women was changing, and the popular attitude toward Charlotte reflected that change.

Though women were still occasionally accused of witchcraft, and persecuted, in Regency England and though the range of legal punishments for women still included whipping and burning at the stake, a gentler ethos had begun to prevail. Women, it was felt, required protection, both the physical protection of fathers, brothers and husbands and protection on the part of society from the defilements of worldliness. The older generation of aristocratic women notorious for their sophisticated amorality was dying out. Byron's confidante Lady Melbourne died in 1816, Lady Bessborough was aging. Women such as these, with their convenient but passionless marriages, their lovers and illegitimate children, their public roles as cultivated hostesses and political patronesses were gradually disappearing. In their place were women who, though they might not always adhere to it, subscribed to a far more confining moral code and had no public roles to speak of.

"Lady Holland once told me," Lady Bessborough wrote to Lord Granville, "all women of a certain age and in a situation to achieve it should take to politics—to leading and influencing."[4] That advice had been offered decades earlier.

.

189

By 1815, the number of prominent women exerting political influence was exceedingly small. Decorous patriotism was replacing partisan intrigue. A ladies' subscription was organized to pay for a monument to Wellington, "to be formed of the cannon taken by the duke in various engagements," the subscription to be sponsored by the Duchess of York. Raising funds to commission war memorials, to rescue soldiers' widows and children from destitution, or to aid the Waterloo wounded, were permissible activities for women. Yet even in undertaking charitable endeavors they ran into opposition. Wilberforce would not accept help from any women in his antislavery campaign, insisting that such work was "unsuited to the female character as delineated in Scripture."

Opposition to slavery was scripturally sound; what was unsuitable was the appearance, in women active in the arena of the world, of immodesty. St. Paul had defined the female character in the New Testament, and anyone who might have forgotten what he wrote there had only to read Hannah More's study of his doctrine published in 1815. Women, St. Paul taught, ought to "adorn themselves in modest apparel, with shamefacedness and sobriety; not with braided hair, or gold, or pearls, or costly array." They ought to keep silence, "for it is not permitted unto them to speak," lest they usurp men's authority. "Let the women learn in silence with all subjection," he cautioned. Let them learn from men, their divinely ordained superiors, whose primacy had been established beyond question at the time of creation. Adam was virtuous, Eve sinful; women suffered from an inherent weakness and sinfulness, and so ought to try to redeem their deficiency through living modest, quiet, passive lives "in faith and charity and holiness with sobriety."[5]

More herself, of course, breached St. Paul's precepts by usurping male authority and immodestly presuming to teach others. But at least she refused membership in the Royal Society of Literature, saying it would be inappropriate for a woman to belong, and her prefaces were full of shamefaced apologies for her presumption in writing.

.

Female morality went hand in hand with religious piety, and immoral women, the Evangelicals taught, deserved punishments that were akin to penance. Among those Wilberforce condemned as immoral were divorcées, many of whom sought freedom from their husbands in order to marry their lovers. (Divorce was a relatively rare phenomenon, and limited to the aristocracy, since a special act of Parliament was necessary to institute it.) His Proclamation Society made strenuous efforts to pass a bill in the House of Lords making a divorced woman guilty of a crime if she married her corespondent. The bill passed the Lords, but not the Commons. Still, divorced women bore a weightier stigma in the Regency than they had a generation earlier, and many Evangelicals thought that a divorcée ought to shut herself away from society and devote the remainder of her life to repentance.

If divorcées were expected to immure themselves like anchoresses, women conspicuous for their virtue were all but deified. That a morally weak woman should triumph over her infirmities was thought to be a near miraculous achievement, especially in an age when wickedness was on the rise. Byron recorded with amusement how his friend Wedderburn Webster talked on and on about his wife's good qualities, ending his harangue by asserting that "in all moral and mortal qualities," she was "very like Christ." (The poet had reason to doubt Webster's judgment of his wife, for she had made an un-Christlike proposition to him.[6])

Webster was deceived, but in seeing his wife in beatific terms he was not unique. Men spoke of the women they respected as superhuman, angelic beings, pure and untainted, uncorrupted by any stain of vice. And once they became accustomed to seeing them that way, it was only natural for men to want to keep them pure by screening them off from contamination. Hence the bowdlerization of the classics, the sanitizing of fairy tales, the increasing segregation of women from worldly pastimes. Card playing, which had been the usual evening entertainment, was abandoned and piano playing and singing took its place. Women began to make a point of leaving the room when the men made jokes, even innocent ones. They toned down their dress; the most serious-minded of them put aside their jewels and wore diamond or amethyst crosses. More and more the lives of women were becoming closed in by a narrowing circle of propriety. They were defined as either well-bred or ill-bred, pious or impious, pure or impure. There was no middle ground, at least in theory, and only by strenuous efforts at self-improvement could they attain the propriety, purity and piety that made them truly worthy.

One of those who succeeded at the arts of self-improvement was Annabella Milbanke, whom Byron courted intermittently and with whom he maintained a correspondence "of a most improving nature, mainly concerned with religion," even after she turned down his proposals. He had always felt that she was too good for him, yet he found himself longing for some of that goodness to rub off on him, especially after he discovered, to his great joy and greater guilt, that he was capable of becoming his half-sister Augusta's lover.

In the fall of 1814 he proposed to Annabella once again, and she accepted. It was agreed that the wedding would not take place for several months, by which time the bridegroom—and probably the bride—were having second thoughts. Byron loved and greatly admired Annabella, but found Augusta much more companionable. Annabella, he confided to Lady Melbourne, was "perfectly good," so good he wished he were better. She was "overrun with fine feelings—scruples about herself and her disposition," given to spells of anxious self-torment over her character and behavior. And what was worse, she was humorless and could not follow Byron's playful wit, far less respond in kind. And she had an irritating habit of watching his every expression and listening to his every word in order to detect changes in his quicksilver moods. She seemed to hound him. "The least word, or alteration of tone, has some inference drawn from it," he complained to Lady Melbourne.[7] At times he wondered whether there would be a wedding at all.

But they went ahead in the end and were married on January 2, 1815, and before very long Annabella was pregnant. At first Byron tried to accommodate to his new wife's severely introspective disposition, and to rise above the dampening effect she had on him, while she bore his eccentricities—he insisted on sleeping alone, he drank far too much, he stormed through their rented house carrying loaded pistols—in patient silence. Her suffering maddened him. Far from redeeming him, she drove him deeper into depression, and made him feel not only doomed and lost but guilty besides. Clearly the marriage was a misalliance, and Byron's continuing desire for his half-sister Augusta—which Annabella discerned—made it worse. A month after their child was born, Annabella left her husband in London and went home to her parents, full of stories about his cruelty and his unspeakable vices.

Inevitably, the stories turned into rumors, and when Annabella asked for a legal separation the rumors appeared to be confirmed. Byron, who had been muttering for years about leaving England, made preparations to go abroad. His fame had become infamy. While his staunch male friends stood by him, the social world that had lionized him now turned against him with a vengeance. "Byr'n—Byr'n—Byr'n" was still heard everywhere, only now the name was murmured with contempt instead of excited reverence. People continued to buy editions of his poems, especially his touching farewell to Annabella, but they shook their heads over his vileness. They were caught up in anticipating Princess Charlotte's wedding, only weeks away, and could not spare any pity for Byron, who had surpassed even his dissolute creation Childe Harold in wickedness. Ten days before the royal wedding Byron sailed for Ostend, glad to scrape the soil of England off his boots.

The same forces that led Byron and Annabella to make their disastrous marriage affected relations between men and women in the Regency decade, and resulted in tensions and estrangements. Like Byron, though to a moderate degree, men were wayward; like Annabella, women were correct. But to the extent that women represented goodness and recti-

.

tude, they represented restriction—and, as Byron found with Annabella, a kind of suffocating repression. The undue emphasis on morality drove a wedge between the sexes, so that they spent a great deal of time with their own kind and less in mixed company. The custom of men and women separating after dinner began at about this time, reinforcing the idea that women had to be protected from the coarseness and bawdry of all-male conversation. "Female society amongst the upper classes was most notoriously neglected," wrote Captain Gronow, reminiscing about his youth in the last years of George III. Men devoted their days to business or to their clubs, their evenings to politics or gambling or to keeping company with demimondaines who made no demands on their consciences.

To be sure, these were tendencies, not unvarying habits, and they affected people to varying degrees. The notion that women were destined to redeem men was only one in a complex tangle of ideas about how men and women ought to behave toward one another, but it was bound to be a prominent one at a time when Evangelicalism and reform were being broadly espoused. It also harmonized well with the character types and themes women read about over and over again in the novels they devoured.

Novel reading was the consuming pastime of young women, and they scarcely outgrew the habit as they got older. They read until their eyes were swollen, devoting entire days, evenings, and often entire nights to their books and then, once they had finished them, rereading them or going to the nearest subscription library for more. Sometimes they memorized them, cover to cover. Aristocrats, middle-class women, shopgirls, seamstresses and servants all read the same books—and those who couldn't read, listened as others read aloud to them. The stories were much the same, compounded of vulnerable young heroines, the attractive but dangerous men they encountered, mysterious houses and forbidding landscapes, charms, curses, prophecies, and endless vicissitudes. Tying all together was overriding passion, passion in every degree from unrequited to matrimonial.

Good and evil were sharply etched in these novels, and

the heroine's role was to bear up under the onslaughts of evil until, through her virtue and constancy, she won happiness in love. The message was clear and repetitive, and so was the plot formula. It was hardly surprising that assiduous readers were tempted to turn themselves into writers of novels, for the writing of them was scarcely less enjoyable than the reading and even more therapeutic to the emotions. "Everyone scribbles novels," Hannah More lamented. "Is a woman in low spirits? Let her console herself by writing a novel. Is she ill? bored? unhappily situated? Let her pour it all out into a novel." According to Walter Scott, writing ladies were the bane of the age, "the very cream of affectation." Byron's judgment was more misogynistic. "Of all bitches dead or alive," he said, "a scribbling woman is the most canine."[8]

Leaving England when he did Byron was spared the immediate impact of one scribbling woman's revenge on him. On May 9, 1816, Caroline Lamb published her novel *Glenarvon*, a *roman à clef* whose central character, a murderer and seducer haunted by melancholic brooding, was Byron himself. In the novel, whose overburdened plot winds through three volumes, Glenarvon is a mysterious, haunting figure with a dual identity and a number of mistresses. He behaves abominably, ordering the murder of a helpless infant, plotting and scheming, treating one of his mistresses so badly that she plunges on horseback off a cliff to her death. Yet he has his appealing side, and the heroine's impassioned love for him is plausible, if star-crossed. The heroine of *Glenarvon*, Calantha, is Caroline herself, sketched to the life with all "her violence, her caprices, her mad frolics." Calantha wants above all to elope with Glenarvon, who evades her; when Calantha's husband leaves her, intent on a lasting separation, she follows him and, overborne by the strain of too much emotion, dies in his arms. Glenarvon goes off to sea.

Along with Byron and Caroline, *Glenarvon* includes characters meant to represent, among others, William Lamb, Lady Oxford, Byron's wife Annabella and Caroline's hated mother-in-law Lady Melbourne. (The portrayal of Lady Melbourne is the most merciless in the book; near the end she

·

is stabbed to death, and the author describes her demise with unmistakable relish.) The novel was part mutinous assault on the Lambs, the Ponsonbys and the fashionable world, part *cri de coeur*. It was deeply felt, if hastily wrought, occasioned by a series of incidents which seemed to bring all the themes in Caroline's obstreperous life to a head. First came Byron's marriage, which upset her, then there was yet another of the scandalous episodes she was forever precipitating, when she assaulted one of her pages and left him bleeding, and finally her long-suffering husband decided that he could take no more, and made up his mind to obtain a separation from her. While the legalities proceeded Caroline, in low spirits and unhappily situated, wrote her novel in a month of secret late-night sessions.

There was something spidery about *Glenarvon*, a mood of hidden web-weaving and poisonous malice. Its plot is a fantasy of animosities and wish fulfillment, set against a melodramatic backdrop of Gothic horror and mystery. The web is cunningly spun, and the language occasionally poetic. Like many another young woman, Caroline was using the conventions of fiction to explain herself and her situation as best she could. "To write this novel was then my sole comfort," she said later; fiction seemed the suitable outlet for her fervent, largely misdirected intellect.

In the end William Lamb did not proceed with the separation, and was reconciled with his wife. But Caroline proceeded to publish *Glenarvon*, and it caused a minor furor. That she painted Byron as a dark libertine was to be expected, but her representation of Lady Melbourne as his sinister accomplice gave offense, as did her sketches of other prominent people as shallow and self-indulgent and generally worthless. The whole of cultivated society, it seemed, was under attack in *Glenarvon*. People bought the novel and read it, but whispered that it would only be a matter of time before Caroline's relatives put a stop to its further publication.

Meanwhile they turned with relief to contemplating the storybook happiness of Princess Charlotte and Prince Leopold. Charlotte's life had all the makings of a novel, and one with a happy ending. She was a rambunctious, somewhat errant heroine but on the whole a lovable one—or so her future subjects decided now that she showed signs of mellowing into her wifely role. She seemed to be overcoming the severe handicaps presented by her embarrassing mother and despised father, and had managed to avoid, in the manner of a heroine, marriage to the undesirable suitor her father had chosen for her. Instead she had married for love, and to her credit, had chosen a conspicuously sober, devoted, steady man—the sort of man any young girl would choose if she chose wisely.

Charlotte and Leopold began their married life under the happiest auspices. They had a country house, Claremont Park, in Surrey in addition to their London residence, and an income of sixty thousand pounds a year—beyond the sixty thousand they were allotted for furniture and jewels—on which to maintain their household. Yet wealthy though they were they led a staid, almost dull domestic life that was a complete contrast to the showy extravagance of the Regent and his brothers. The Prince and Princess of Coburg, as they were known, were often seen riding together in the park or on their way to and from church. They never gave wild parties or entertained disreputable people, they did not like to stay out late and were said to enjoy staying home in the evenings, reading aloud to one another. Leopold was markedly religious, studious and a little bookish; he preferred reading or drawing to field sports. Charlotte, though she still occasionally forgot her dignity and took to dancing around the room without a partner in an elephantine way, no matter who was present, was noticeably tamer under Leopold's calming influence. Her happiness made her quite radiant, and led to excited speculation that she might be pregnant, but months passed and no announcement was made.

Like the ill old king and his aging queen, Charlotte and Leopold were genuinely popular. Crowds cheered them when they entered the royal box at the theater or the opera, printmakers sold their portraits, the prince was sought after and the princess honored with concerts. A book on deportment was dedicated to her: *Remarks on Modern Female Manners,*

.

*as Distinguished by Indifference for Character, and Indecency of
Dress.* Tradesmen did a brisk business in anything related
to the royal couple: florists sold a variety of geranium called
"the Prince and Princess of Coburg," a Holborn milliner
advertised "The Coburg Hat, patronised by Her Royal Highness," and London dressmakers flourished when it became
known that, good Englishwoman that she was, Princess Charlotte disliked imported gowns and had all hers made in England. The monarchy was in esteem once again thanks to
the young royals. The Regent began to look more and more
like an aberration in the Hanoverian line, to be endured
until Charlotte and her admirable consort could come to the
throne.

When Charlotte's pregnancy was announced in February
of 1817, the populace was ecstatic. The baby would be George
III's first great-grandchild, third in line of succession. It
would secure the continuity of the family, it would provide
a new focus of public loyalty. Charlotte had had two miscar-
riages, but this pregnancy progressed well. She seemed if
anything too healthy, putting on a great deal of weight and
showing such lively high spirits that her obstetrician, the
eminent Sir Richard Croft, tried to calm her down by drawing quantities of blood from a vein in her hand and severely
limiting her diet. Not surprisingly, she responded badly to
the loss of nourishment, and became worried and depressed
about the approaching birth. She sensed vague dangers ahead,
and became morbid about her "joyless" future.

The last month was a very long one, with Dr. Croft ordering more bleeding and less food and the old queen, who
was keeping close watch on her granddaughter, muttering
about the odd shape and size of Charlotte's belly. The queen,
who was no mean expert on childbirth, having been through
it fifteen times herself, knew that something was wrong, but
Dr. Croft confidently predicted that the royal infant would
be born on about October 18 or 19, and if he foresaw any
difficulty he did not say so.

Charlotte languished, huge and melancholy, until the first
week of November, with Leopold constantly by her side.

•

She was so miserable that when her pains finally began on November 3 she must have felt more relieved than frightened. She struggled on through the night and into the following day, in terrible pain but without entering the final stage of labor. Dr. Croft, who refused to allow the prince or anyone else in the family to see Charlotte, reported that though her progress was slow, her pulse was regular and she looked well. By this time, however, it was evident that she was in grave difficulty. The baby was in a transverse position, and very large; a forceps delivery was called for. But though such deliveries were no rarity in 1817, the doctor, following common obstetrical practice, decided not to intervene. Instead he let the labor take its own excruciating course.

Charlotte soldiered on, bearing her agony "with a Brunswick heart," her will and pride too strong to let her cry out. The nurses who attended her were impressed by her fortitude, but saw that she was weakening, and as the hours passed their concern grew into alarm. Dr. Croft commanded all. He had two colleagues in attendance, but like Prince Leopold they were kept away from the patient. They waited, together with the cabinet ministers and the Regent, for the least bulletin. Charlotte sank lower and lower. She had eaten nothing, and had been in labor for two days and nights.

At last, fifty hours after it began, the ordeal ended. Charlotte's son, "a beautiful fine boy," was born dead. The birth had taken the last of her strength, and afterward she was too weak even to sense that she too was dying. Very likely the family disease, porphyria, set in and her debility made her fatally vulnerable to its symptoms. Dr. Croft and his colleagues gave her brandy and tried to keep her warm, desperate to save her, but her pulse began to fail and her chest and stomach hurt her terribly. She lost feeling, was confused, and had more and more difficulty breathing. Then came convulsions and death.

Public mourning for Charlotte was sincere and protracted. Queen Charlotte was distraught, the Regent deeply grieved over the loss, as he said, of "two generations at once." Dr. Croft and his colleagues were blamed for the princess's death,

.

but blame was futile. While Lord Liverpool and his ministers worried over the succession, Londoners bought memorial portraits of the princess and copies of a book purporting to be her memoirs. Those close to the court begged Charlotte's waiting women for a bit of ribbon from her wardrobe or a lock of her hair to wear in a brooch, but Prince Leopold, beside himself with grief, kept nearly all her hair for himself and refused all consolation.

15

The sidewalks along Skinner Street were railed off with sturdy wooden planks, and the nearby roads blocked off with posts and chains so that no traffic could come near the place of execution on the morning of March 12, 1817. John Cashman was to be hanged there, in front of Mr. Beckwith's gunshop, where he committed the crime for which he had been condemned to die.

Cashman, a twenty-eight-year-old Irish seaman recently discharged from the royal navy, had been tried and convicted of breaking into Beckwith's shop and, with other rioters, of stealing arms which he meant to use in an insurrection. He had protested his innocence at the trial, but later, while in prison awaiting execution, had confessed to his two cellmates that he had taken part in the riot and had been inside the gunshop, though not with any insurrectionary purpose and while befuddled by large quantities of gin and rum.

.

If not innocent, Cashman was at least the victim of a larger crime than the one he had committed, or so it appeared to the hundreds of Londoners who came to watch—and condemn—the execution. They knew a good deal about him, for in the several months since his trial and sentencing his case had become something of a *cause célèbre* in the radical press, and even those with scant sympathy for him hoped that he might "become an object of royal clemency" and have his sentence commuted. The injustice of the young sailor's general circumstances was beyond dispute. He had served for a number of years, bravely and in peril of his life, in the royal navy yet on his discharge in 1815 had been unable to collect his arrears in pay and prize money—in all some two hundred pounds, a very considerable sum—despite his good record and evident valor. (He had been wounded nine times, with three severe head wounds.) Complicating his problem was that some of his papers had been lost when a schooner he was serving in was seized, and his head wounds may have left him less than wholly competent to handle his affairs.

Still, competent or not, Cashman had been badly treated by the Admiralty. According to one newspaper account, "he wrote to the Lords of the Admiralty for assistance; they told him he must appear before them; he did so and was sent to the Transport Board; there they told him they would write to the Surgeons; and he went to the Surgeons, they told him to go about his business."[1] He had been to the Admiralty Board, in fact, on the morning of the day he broke into the gunshop. Clearly he had done what he did that day at least partly from a justifiable sense of frustration and anger.

Cashman had been left fatherless as a young child. His father, also a seaman, had been killed while serving aboard the frigate *Diana*, and his mother had struggled to raise six children on what little she could earn from fishing. When that failed, she had been obliged to beg. She had looked forward to the pound a month Cashman promised to send her from his wages, but because he hadn't been paid, she had had to do without. While in prison Cashman had made a

.

will, leaving his prize money, if and when it was paid to his executors, to his mother.

The spectators who began to collect in front of the gun-smith's shop at five o'clock that morning thought it outrageous that the "gallant tar" John Cashman should have to suffer death. They remarked to one another about "the awful example about to be made," and shook their heads disapprovingly at the workmen who drew the wheeled platform with its gibbet from the prison yard to Skinner Street.[2] There were a good many of the very poor in the crowd, but also some of "decent appearance," and hour by hour the number of spectators grew until by midmorning it "exceeded all calculation, extending in every direction as far as the eye could reach." It was a discontented crowd, and the city officials, fearing a disturbance, had taken the precaution of placing a large guard of constables armed with staves in front of the prison yard, to block it off, and stationing others along the route the prisoner would take on his way to the execution site. The Special Constables of each of the City wards were present, and in Newgate itself sixty militiamen waited in reserve. Even the firemen were on alert, ready to be called in to control the crowd if needed. The officials feared that an attempt might be made to rescue Cashman, and had prepared themselves for the eventuality. Several parties of soldiers were in readiness, out of sight of the crowd, to ride in at a prearranged signal and disrupt any rescue effort.

Cashman's expression was resolute when he left the prison and got into the waiting cart that was to carry him to Skinner Street. He wore his sailor's uniform of blue jacket and white trousers, and added to it a black silk handkerchief tied around his neck. He showed, one observer thought, "not the slightest appearance of fear," and bantered with the people who, in defiance of the constables, rushed up to the cart to shake his hand.

"Good bye, Bishop," he was heard to call out to one of the turnkeys standing nearby. "God bless you, my hearty." To the crowd he added, "This is not for cowardice—I am not brought to this for any robbery—I am going to die; but

·

I shall not shrink. If I was at my quarters, I would not be killed in the smoke; I'd be in the fire. I have done nothing against my king and country, but fought for them."

Reluctantly the press of people gave way as the cart began to move, escorted by coaches carrying the sheriffs who were to officiate at the execution and two clerics who were to minister to the victim in his last moments of life. The procession moved slowly along, with Cashman acknowledging the shouts of the onlookers by nodding and shouting back to them. His punishment was unjust, he proclaimed. He had done nothing but what he had been driven to do. The government had robbed him, pure and simple. "I always fought for my king and country, and this is my end," he repeated loudly again and again, each time rousing the crowd to renewed expressions of fury at the death that awaited him and at the government that had condemned him. When the sheriffs passed they were greeted by hisses and groans. People rushed forward as if to attack them, but were kept back behind the barriers by the wall of constables with their staves.

As the procession approached Skinner Street the dialogue between the prisoner and his thousands of supporters became a frenzied chorus of shouts and acclamations.

"Huzza! my boys, I'll die like a man!" Cashman yelled as he reached the scaffold. The crowd answered him, he shouted back, seeming, as an eyewitness wrote, "to enter into the spirit of the spectators," so that they were one. Cashman was a luckless criminal, but he was at the same time a symbol of popular grievances, a focus for the deepgoing anger and defiance of those who had come to see him die. He was at once hero and sacrificial victim, rabble-rouser and martyr. In his brief moment of ghoulish notoriety, he incarnated everything his supporters resented about their government and the society that kept it in power.

"Hurra, my hearties in the cause!" he cried. "Success! Cheer up!" He mounted the scaffold, still talking, addressing the sea of faces spread out below him and repeating his story of hardship.

"Don't bother me—it's no use," he was heard to say to

.

the clergyman who tried to calm him and make him repentant. "I want no mercy but from God!"

The rope was put around his neck, making the crowd groan and gasp. But when the executioner tried to put a nightcap over Cashman's head and face, he rejected it, saying he wanted to "see till the last." He turned to look at Beckwith's gunshop, and cursed it angrily. "I'll be with you there," he called out, meaning that his unquiet spirit would haunt the premises, and no doubt making poor Beckwith, who had begged to have Cashman executed somewhere other than at his door, shiver in dread.

The executioner had left the scaffold, and stood ready to trip the board from beneath the prisoner's feet.

"I am the last of seven of them that fought for my king and country!" Cashman was shouting. "I could not get my own, and that has brought me here." He was still shouting, swearing freely, telling the hangman to "let go the jib-boom" and urging the spectators to give him three cheers at the last, when his words were suddenly choked off. His body swung crazily in midair, his animated features frozen in a grimace. His struggle was brief, but horrifying enough to silence the crowd completely. They watched, stunned, as the nightcap was put over the dead man's face and his body was cut down and laid in a plain coffin. Only then, after their hero had been borne off toward Newgate, did they recover themselves enough to renew their protest.

Cries of "Murder! Murder! Shame! Shame!" came from all sides, and again people rushed forward in an effort to break through the wooden barriers. The constables stood firm and prevented this, but could not prevent the hissing, milling thousands from thronging Skinner Street for the remainder of the day, threatening revenge and bemoaning the loss of the defiant Cashman.

His fate disturbed them, not merely because his case was pitiable or because his bravado in the face of death quickened their own defiance of authority. He was a sailor, one of thousands who had served in the valorous defense of Britain and had helped to defeat the French. Yet like a great many other

.

sailors, and even more soldiers, Cashman had foundered badly after being turned adrift in civilian life.

Over a quarter of a million men had been dismissed from the army and navy within months of Waterloo, with no pensions or other provisions to ease their way back into the society they had left years earlier. Some managed to find work, or to return to their farms or occupations, but a conspicuous number could not. These drifted through the towns and along the highways, trying to sell things or doing the humblest and most humiliating sorts of odd jobs. The sight of one of Wellington's intrepid fighting men, his uniform in tatters, cleaning gutters or shoveling snow—or worse, lying drunk and dirty by the roadside—evoked a sense of shame and repugnance in the citizens who passed him by, averting their eyes. Britons were outraged that soldiers and sailors should be brought so low. Their plight was just one more symptom that things were going terribly awry, that sweeping changes in the social order could not be deferred much longer.

Demands for change were becoming increasingly sharp and strident. In the Midlands, where the end of the war had meant a drop in government orders and consequent large-scale unemployment, workers massed in protest. Bread riots broke out in dozens of towns where work suddenly became scarce. The relief rolls in Birmingham swelled to include one out of every five citizens, and in Lancashire the poor were lucky to get one meal a day, and that only a little water and salt and oatmeal. Food shortages were made worse when farm laborers, incensed by high prices and low wages, refused in some places to gather in the harvest, leading to further unrest in urban areas and to lawlessness on an unprecedented scale. The Corn Laws, whose passage had elicited dangerous mob violence in the capital in the spring of 1815, continued in effect, keeping grain prices high; this plus the export of grain abroad, which seemed to the laboring poor nothing short of an act of betrayal by the government, made them bitterly resentful.

"Down to hell with the devil and all his brood, the ministers, men of Parliament fellows!" Coleridge had overheard

.

this and similar sentiments among the working people of London following the assassination of Perceval in 1812. Such feelings were tame compared with the attitudes prevalent in 1815 and 1816, when without a wartime emergency to create cohesion the enmity of the lower classes toward the privileged was becoming increasingly uncontained.

A large segment of Britain's populace was becoming resolutely, ungovernably opposed to the prevailing order. Hungry, impoverished, thanklessly employed—if employed at all—they were weary of their deprivation and angry at those they held responsible for it. They blamed the members of Lord Liverpool's government, and of Parliament, for enriching themselves while heartlessly taxing the poor. They blamed them too for increasing the national debt to such an extent that the interest payments alone were staggeringly high, and taxes had to be increased to enable the Treasury to meet them. They blamed the Regent for his extravagance—made more unendurable by his dissipated private life—and the Regent's sycophantic courtiers for their greed and worthlessness. They blamed, in short, an economic order which, however it may have suited eighteenth-century society, was gravely out of joint with the present.

Yet it was not this strong sense of blame, or even the unruly destructiveness it engendered, that made the disaffected seem so dangerous to the rest of society: it was that in their desperation they had seized hold of a vision. They saw the old order collapsing, sinking under its own corrupt weight. And in its place they saw, however vague its outlines, a vision of reform.

This vision took shape in meetings large and small, in taverns and trades' clubs and in the open air. Anywhere working people gathered they talked of reform, organizing themselves into impromptu debating societies and listening to one another and to visiting speakers with eager, if argumentative, attention.

Samuel Bamford, a weaver from Middleton in Lancashire who came to London and moved in radical circles, described the public gatherings of working people he observed there. "They would generally be found in a large room," he wrote, "an elevated seat being placed for the chairman. On first opening the door, the place seemed dimmed by a suffocating vapor of tobacco, curling from the cups of long pipes, and issuing from the mouths of the smokers, in clouds of abominable odor, like nothing in the world more than one of the unclean fogs of their streets." Everyone spoke at once, Bamford recalled, and the din and confusion were terrible. Eventually the chairman would call the meeting to order, and then would introduce a speaker.

"Hear, hear, hear," would follow, "with clapping of hands and knocking of knuckles on the tables till the half-pints danced." Then the speaker would deliver his oration, and afterward someone would propose a resolution in favor of parliamentary reform. Someone else would make a seconding speech, another would propose an amendment, and then there would be further debate. At this point, Bamford noted, there would often be an argument, begun by some choleric individual with strong opinions; factions would form, with six men defending one point of view and a dozen another. "The vociferation and gesticulation would become loud and confounding," he wrote, until interrupted by the arrival of newcomers or some other disturbance.[3]

The liveliness and confusion of these meetings, and the factionalism they revealed, did not dilute their central focus, which was to promote fundamental electoral and governmental change. On this the advocates of reform reached a general consensus: they wanted annual Parliaments, and they wanted the Members of the House of Commons to be elected by all, or at least a majority, of male citizens. A Commons so constituted, they were certain, would be sympathetic to the mass of the people and not merely to the wealthy few. Old laws would be changed, and new ones enacted that would put an end to unemployment and burdensome taxation, while lowering the debt and controlling the extravagance of the Regent and his courtiers.

This, broadly speaking, was the radicals' program. (Though some on the far left advocated more extreme changes, they were a tiny minority.) The doctrine was spread through local political clubs—national political organizations were illegal—such as the Hampden Clubs founded by the peripatetic reformer John Cartwright in 1812 and the Union societies of the Midlands, founded in 1816. It was spread, and persuasively articulated, in William Cobbett's *Political Register,* which in the fall of 1816 reached the huge circulation of nearly fifty thousand.[4] And it was spread at the vast open-air meetings where hundreds and sometimes thousands would gather to listen, spellbound, to the perorations of speakers denouncing corruption and arousing hopes for change.

With their tavern debates and their pointed journalism, their impassioned spokesmen, above all their sheer numbers the radicals made the Tories anxious. The very word "radical" inspired terror. It was a new word, whose precise meaning was unclear—Walter Scott wrote that people took it to mean "any fellow in a ragged jacket"—but whose connotations were unmistakable. To those who feared them the radicals were bandits, English Jacobins, devils let loose upon the unsuspecting, law-abiding, respectable populace. They were republicans who carried their principles to excess; their leaders were irresponsible, their followers murderous. ("Is there one among them with whom you would trust yourself in the dark?" asked the Whig Lord Grey in 1819.)

In a much-quoted passage the writer Harriet Martineau, who was a young girl during the Regency, recalled later "how great was the panic which could exist without any evidence at all: how prodigious were the radical forces which were always heard of, but never seen . . . how country gentlemen, well-armed, scoured the fields and lanes, and met on heaths to fight the enemy who never came: how, even in the midst of towns, young ladies carried heavy planks and ironing-boards, to barricade windows in preparation for sieges from thousands of rebels whose footfall was long listened for throughout the darkness of the night."[5]

Young ladies armed with ironing boards and country gentlemen hunting for radicals among the hedgerows must have presented a ludicrous spectacle, yet their terror was real. Memories of the Luddites, with their secret armies and sudden midnight raids, their ferocious masked hammermen

.

smashing frames and burning workshops, were still vivid, and people whispered that there were caches of Luddite arms hidden underground, awaiting some imminent bloody day of reckoning. Many Luddites and former Luddites espoused the radical cause, and it was feared their tradition of destructive protest would become general among the radicals.

To the serious-minded, radicalism was the political dimension of the deadly canker pervading society; radicalism combined moral benightedness with godless effrontery, and it was the sacred duty of pious men to oppose it. Pitt Clubs, taking their name from the conservative war leader William Pitt, who had guided Britain through the earlier years of the Napoleonic Wars, sprang up to counteract "atheistical philosophy, Jacobinism and diabolism" wherever they appeared, and to defend conservative principles. Club members took the view that the radicals were the dupes of hotheaded demagogues and irresponsible, if not treasonous, journalists. There were no true grounds for popular agitation, the conservatives argued; traditional values and England's traditional political order were sound, but the confusion and excitement of the times had temporarily thrown people's judgment into disarray.

And they perceived an even greater danger: the danger that the consensual foundation of government, cemented by deference to authority, might break down. Most of the English were patriots, but they no longer expressed their patriotism through unquestioning subservience to the king and his deputies. The time-honored balance between self-interest and the interest of the crown, or the realm, was being altered. Men might gladly risk their lives in England's defense, as John Cashman had, but they would not cooperate with the government in policies which, in their eyes, prolonged their postwar miseries. Their needs, their cause, loomed as an overriding imperative, compelling their paramount loyalty. It seemed possible, in the fall of 1816, that the radical cause might attract so many people to its banners that they would rise up en masse and overwhelm the forces of order.

The crowd that gathered in an open area called Spa Fields outside London on November 15 was large and unruly. Some said ten thousand were present, others said twenty. The purpose of the meeting was to draw up a petition to be carried to the Regent, on behalf of the people of London, by the radical M.P. Francis Burdett and Henry Hunt, the radicals' most colorful spokesman. The crowd cheered loudly when "Orator" Hunt made his appearance in the window of a public house and prepared to address them.

Hunt, whose magnificent, elegantly dressed tall figure and white top hat were familiar to working-class audiences, smiled and doffed his hat in response to the cheering. He was not a working man himself, but a country gentleman, yet his dedication to reform was sincere and visceral. He devoted his boundless energy and mighty lungs to the cause, along with a commanding presence and a charisma that led people to wear his portrait in lockets hung around their necks and to write songs and poems in his honor. Hunt was vain and egotistical, with more of the braggart than the politician about him, but his effectiveness as a speaker was unmatched.

"His voice was bellowing," wrote Samuel Bamford, "his face swollen and flushed; his griped hand beat as if it were to pulverize; and his whole manner gave token of a painful energy, struggling for utterance." His eyes gave away his frenzy. While he was speaking they "seemed to distend and protrude; and if he worked himself furious, as he sometimes would, they became blood-streaked, and almost started from their sockets."[6]

Hunt began his harangue, and soon worked himself up to a fury. His theme was the overtaxation of the poor, the root cause of all distress. It was taxation that threw men out of work, he shouted, banging his fist. It was taxation that kept corrupt officials in power and enfeebled the laboring poor. His words were as familiar as the man himself, yet the crowd was roused as if they were hearing his message for the first time.

"Hunt and Liberty!" they cried, waving homemade banners and punctuating the oration with applause. Hunt himself held aloft a huge flag in green, red and white, emblazoned with the slogans "Bread to feed the Hungry," "Truth to crush the Oppressors," and "Justice to punish Crimes."

.

The afternoon wore on, and at length, the oration con-cluded, some resolutions were moved and voted on by accla-mation. They called for universal male suffrage, annual Parliaments and voting by ballot. Hunt agreed to deliver the petitions, and then he and the thousands went their sepa-rate ways.

The November 15 meeting had been remarkably orderly, but when a second gathering occurred on December 2 a darker and more embattled mood prevailed. Orator Hunt brought disappointing news. He had failed to deliver the petition (Burdett had decided not to join him in attempting to deliver it), and had been disillusioned by his meeting with the amiable but unhelpful Home Secretary Lord Sidmouth. But before he could give the crowd his news, Hunt was upstaged by a small knot of ultraradicals, members of the Society of Spencean Philanthropists, who exhorted the crowd from atop a cart.

The Spenceans, as they were known, had come together in 1814 to promote the land-reform scheme of the late Thomas Spence, an obscure Newcastle schoolmaster. Spence's uto-pian scheme called for the equal division of land among rich and poor, but his followers added to this their own bloody plans for a revolution. They dreamed of seizing the capital, slaughtering the ministers and setting up their own govern-ment, counting on crowd support to achieve this and espe-cially on the support of the many soldiers and sailors in London.

There were only a handful of Spenceans at Spa Fields on December 2. One of these, a young doctor named Watson, decided that the moment for revolution had arrived. Ha-ranguing the crowd, and addressing himself particularly to the soldiers and sailors, Watson succeeded in unleashing a tide of anger.

"If they will not give us what we want," he cried, "shall we not take it?"

"Yes," came the shouted reply.

"Are you willing to take it?"

"Yes!"

"Will you go and take it?"

·

"Yes!" The cries of assent grew louder and louder, emboldening the young doctor and involving more and more people. Among those responding was John Cashman, who had been brought to the meeting by another sailor, both of them full of drink. When Watson spoke of "giving us what we want," Cashman's befuddled thoughts immediately turned to the Admiralty, which had refused him his pay, and to his mother and brother, and to his own months of discouragement and hardship. When Watson shouted, "If I jump down amongst you, will you come and take it?" Cashman was more than ready to follow him, as were many others.

Watson leaped into the crowd and set off for the Tower. A relatively small number of the thousands who had come to hear Hunt followed Watson, and still fewer stayed with him for long. The splinter group divided itself into still smaller remnants as it went along, losing the original impetus to follow Watson and being diverted in other directions. Cashman, bleary with drink and full of anger, stayed with Watson and, with others, broke into Beckwith's gunshop. Whether he realized that Watson meant to assault the Tower is unknown. Before long a force of constables captured him, along with his companions, and he was taken into custody. (Watson evaded capture, went into hiding, and eventually escaped to America.) Cashman was tried and sentenced to death. A little over three months later he was executed.

So great was the public outcry following the execution that the authorities made no effort to prevent Cashman's friends from giving him an honorable public funeral.[7] A wake was held, with the body laid out in an elm coffin garlanded with ribbons and flowers. Wax tapers were kept burning beside the coffin, illuminating a plate with the inscription "Mr. John Cashman died the 12th of March, 1817, aged 28." Cashman's friends were too poor to pay the cost of the wake and burial, but donations made by those attending the wake were found to be more than ample to cover the expense.

A great many people came to pay their respects to the "gallant tar," and stayed on to hear his friends tell stories of his exploits at sea. For five days and nights the mourners continued to stream in, until on March 17 the undertaker

.

arrived to escort the body to the grave. "A vast multitude of persons of every description, especially sailors," walked in the funeral procession to Stepney Churchyard where Cashman was interred. Fearing a riot, the aldermen ordered several constables to be present, but the crowd was hushed and sorrowful as the body was laid to rest, and the day passed without incident.

.

Rumor had it that the Princess of Wales was deeply in debt. She had been wandering through Europe since the summer of 1814, "receiving royal honors everywhere," behaving in her customary reckless, devil-may-care way and enjoying herself thoroughly. As the Regent's despised wife she had been shut out from the splendid life of the court; freed from her husband's constraining hand, she created her own splendid court in exile, decking herself in diamonds and silks and her servants in velvet liveries embroidered in silver and gold.

She had spent lavishly for three years and more, and when the money the English government allotted her ran out she had begun to borrow. Heedless of her mounting debts, she continued to spend and overspend, keeping up a costly establishment of eighty servants, a stable of forty-eight horses—many of them fine Arabians—and a ship with captain and crew. Her trip to the Holy Land in 1816 was a gaudy and expensive spectacle, complete with donkeys and camels and Arab hordes, and her imposing residence on the shores of Lake Como, the Villa d'Este, was said to have cost thirty thousand pounds. By early 1818 Caroline was "in very distressed circumstances," and was reduced to trying to collect money from the estate of her late brother the Duke of Brunswick.[1] Like many another Regency spendthrift, she was seriously down on her luck.

The princess's debts were nothing, however, compared with her disrepute.

She seemed determined to make a laughingstock of herself—and by association, of her husband and his country. Everywhere she went, in Germany, Switzerland, Italy and the Middle East, she drew crowds by dressing in gowns so sheer they were indecent and so girlish they were ridiculous on her coarse and lumpy figure. She paraded herself through the streets like a circus performer, making people stare with amazement and then burst out laughing. In the evenings she went to balls or suppers or to the opera, astounding the genteel company with her scanty costumes and brash bad manners. A mad energy possessed her; she danced on and on, long past the hour when she ought to have made a dignified departure, and seemed to delight in offending her aristocratic hosts.

Lady Bessborough, who was staying in Genoa while Caroline was there, described a ball she attended. "I cannot tell you how sorry and ashamed I felt as an Englishwoman. The first thing I saw in the room was a short, very fat, elderly woman, with an extremely red face (owing, I suppose, to the heat), in a girl's white frock looking dress." The peculiarity of this apparition was underscored by her obscenely low décolletage and by the maidenly wreath of light pink roses she wore on her head. Her hair and bushy eyebrows were dyed midnight black, "which gave her a fierce look," Lady Bessborough thought, and her vigorous dancing and general air of animal high spirits were somehow alarming and upsetting. "I was staring at her from the oddity of her appearance, when suddenly she nodded and smiled at me," the account continued. "Not recollecting her, I was convinced she was mad." Realizing at length who the extraordinary personage was, Lady Bessborough was forced to acknowledge her, but found the encounter a painful one.[2] Not only was the princess much "fatter and redder" than she had been, and outlandish in her dyed black hair, but she was the object of whispers and titters and mocking couplets from the other guests. Caroline provoked disrespect, and took a perverse pleasure in provoking it. The spectacle was grotesque.

The princess's political gestures were provocative as well. She visited Bonaparte's brother-in-law Murat in Naples (and seduced him, it was said), and later went to see the former emperor's living quarters on Elba.

"Napoleon, I salute you!" she exclaimed on seeing his portrait there. "I always had and have now the greatest esteem for you!" She followed this disloyal outburst by requesting a "precious memento" of her hero, much to the disgust of the English informers who watched her every move. It was outrageous that she should insult her husband this way, they wrote in the detailed reports they sent back to England. She was intolerable—but less intolerable abroad, they knew, than at home where her irritating presence would only serve to embarrass the Regent and the government.

By 1818 Caroline had in fact settled down to a relatively quiet and happily domestic life with her handsome Italian Chamberlain Bartolommeo Bergami—or Pergami, as he preferred to style himself. They lived very much as man and wife in the villa she bought for him on the Adriatic coast, the Villa Cassielli, with a staff of Italian servants—among them Pergami's mother and sister and brother—and with Pergami's little daughter. (His wife was nowhere in evidence.) Leaving aside the inconvenient fact that theirs was an adulterous liaison, something the English informers who spied on them dwelt on in tiresome detail, the princess and Pergami were quite content together and for once Caroline's obstreperous, passionate nature found an equilibrium.

But she had her debts to contend with, and the sad misfortune of her daughter's death (which no one at the English court had bothered to inform her of in a personal message), not to mention the constant presence of her husband's agents. With Princess Charlotte dead, Caroline knew, she was expendable. Her husband loathed her, but could not divorce her without exposing himself to damaging scandal, something he could not risk given the current rebellious temper of his subjects. She feared that in his desperation he might try to have her killed, and set two servants to keep watch outside her apartments at night to prevent assassins from breaking in. Even so she worried, convinced that her enemies had tried to poison her and might try again.

The Regent, meanwhile, was far too preoccupied with his worsening health and his shattered nerves to plot his wife's assassination. He would of course have been exceedingly glad to learn that she was dead, but he was much too fastidious to order her killed, even though his advisers were hounding him about marrying again and begetting an heir to the throne. He had suffered for several years from a "weakness of his lower limbs" accompanied by "strong dropsical symptoms."[3] At times he was so ill he stayed in bed for days, and when well enough to get up he could not walk, and had to be pushed from room to room in a wheeled chair. He lost weight—though he always managed to put it on again eventually—and had to have his tailors alter his trousers to fit his thinning legs.

"I have been, though without any very serious or actual occasion or call for alarm, still very much and very truly indisposed for the last ten days," he wrote in a letter to his mother in December, 1817. "I do not know under what denomination to class the attack, or by what name regularly to define and call it, for it seems to me to have been a sort of mishmash, Solomongrundy, Olla podrida kind of a business in itself that is quite anomalous." His rheumatism had been bothering him, he had a cold, he was bilious, and no doubt he was taxing his constitution to the limit by eating stupendous meals and drinking quantities of cherry brandy. "In short all this potpourri," he told the queen, "has rendered me both bodily as well as mentally very unfit and indeed quite unable to take up a pen until this day, when I begin to feel myself entering I hope into a convalescent state."[4]

.

The letter was written only a few weeks after Charlotte's death, while her father was grieving over her loss and meditating on death itself, which always unnerved him. Not too long before this he had survived an attempt on his life, when someone had shot at him as he rode in his coach toward Carlton House. His subjects were enjoined to pray for his preservation "from the base and barbarous assaults of a lawless multitude" every Sunday, "from the secret designs of treason and from the madness of the people," and if this were not reminder enough of his mortality, his gout and other afflictions surely were. He worried over his aged mother, who from time to time seemed to lie at death's door and who was dosing herself, rather violently and excessively, her servants thought, with foxglove. His father the king was perennially dying—and perennially recovering—but could not live forever. Sooner or later he would go to his grave, and his son would become George IV—if his ailments didn't carry him off first.

Along with these morbid preoccupations the Regent was nursing a wider grievance. He was unappreciated. His valuable personal qualities—his empathy, his deep and sincere appreciation of art and music, his refined courtesy and generosity—were discounted by a public that despised and ridiculed him. Beyond this, his valuable contributions to the nation were ignored. Had he not brought England through the terrible war? Had it not been his firm, unfailing leadership that held the realm steady through political and social crises? He imagined that he had commanded troops in Spain, that he had been at Waterloo in charge of a division. Yet these services, like all his others, were thankless. An ungrateful Parliament voted the huge sum of 640,000 pounds to build a palace for Wellington, yet voted their leader nothing.

"I am a different animal a different being from any other in the whole creation," he once wrote to Maria Fitzherbert. And so he was. But by 1818 it had become evident to him that no one knew this, or understood it, and it seemed that no one ever would. He no longer made much effort to accommodate to the world that scorned his talents and failed to understand his unique nature. He retreated behind a facade

.

of regal amiability and patronizing graciousness, keeping his distance from nearly everyone and guarding to himself the secrets of his heart.

He retreated in the physical sense to Brighton, to the inner recesses of the Marine Pavilion. Here amid the celestial feelings of his Chinese fantasy world he soothed his wounded feelings and indulged his senses and his imagination. He anointed his gigantic body in jasmine oil and milk of roses and dusted it with perfumed almond powder. He softened his face with cold cream, and flattered its rotund contours with false curls. He soaked in his white marble bath, sixteen feet long and filled with salt water, then dressed for dinner in his boudoir, with its elegant floor-to-ceiling draperies of fluted blue silk. At night he lay under four paper-thin swanskin blankets, his head resting on satin bolsters. And in the morning he woke late, and did not get out of bed until the middle of the afternoon.

The town of Brighton was no longer the Regent's private municipality, part fashionable resort and part seedy demimonde. It had grown. Middle-class tourists now came by the hundreds from London by coach each day to gape at the Pavilion—whose strikingly original architecture drew universal comment, if not universal admiration—and stayed on to bathe in the sea and promenade along the Steine, mingling with their social superiors. They hoped to catch a glimpse of the Prince Regent, but he disappointed them. He "never stirs out of his parlor," a Brighton hostess wrote, "and no one sees him."

His one daily outing was to visit Lady Hertford in the late afternoon, but as she had a house on the Pavilion grounds, at the end of a covered walkway, this hardly counted as an excursion. Lady Hertford was as reclusive as the Regent, never allowing herself to be seen in any but artificial light if she could possibly help it and indulging her pleasures within the seclusion of the Pavilion. Like the prince she was opulently fat, with an overripe heaviness that lent itself to satire. She was a woman of strong convictions, an ardent Protestant and an ardent Tory, but unlike Maria Fitzherbert, who was generally liked and who still lived in Brighton dur-

·

ing the season, Lady Hertford won no hearts but that of the Regent, and was roundly hated and slandered by the Whigs.

Among the Regent's chief delights was exquisitely prepared food. The feasting at the Pavilion began at six o'clock, when the host and his select party of guests sat down to table, and not infrequently went on until ten. There was music in the background all this time, and polite conversation, but the principal entertainment was the food itself, each course handed around the table in the Russian style and accompanied by an appropriate wine. The entrées were truly magnificent: ham in Madeira sauce, sweetbreads Provençal, lark pasties and woodcock fillets, pheasant with truffles, every sort of meat and fish and game in delicate sauces and garnished with vegetables and succulent side dishes. At one memorable banquet, with the Grand Duke Nicholas and five ambassadors present, the guests were presented with three dozen main dishes, followed by almost as many side dishes, followed in turn by grape pudding and cream rolls, apricot cake and chocolate and apple soufflé.

Beyond all this there were eight great pastry creations, each a visual work of art as well as a culinary triumph. The "Indian Pavilion" was a tall, turreted structure sculpted in white almond paste, with a roof of orange icing and balconies, arches and miniature fanlights outlined in spun sugar colored yellow and rose. The Gothic Tower was a fantasy of columns, arches and towers executed in chocolate, with a palm tree beside it colored pistachio green. It sat atop a three-layered cake that blended almond, apricot, chocolate and a great deal of granulated sugar.

The myriad flavors of the banquet, the wines and liqueurs, the aromas of perfume and scented oil, the insistent music of the wind band, above all the richly ornate interior of the Banqueting Hall with its high domed ceiling and dramatic focal point of lotus leaves, winged silver dragon and shimmering, cascading chandelier must have been almost overpowering. Certainly they were meant to satisfy the Regent's craving for a sensory nirvana, without cares or sorrows and without memories. He sought relief from the worries that pressed in on him, worries about his health, his finances, his need for an heir, and his governmental responsibilities in a time of unprecedented political turmoil.

Lord Liverpool and his ministers had responded to the violent unrest of the postwar years with a series of restrictive acts making it more difficult for angry dissidents to assemble and giving wider powers to local magistrates to use force against them if they did. Though a good many people objected to the un-English denial of civil liberties these laws brought into being, the need for strong measures seemed obvious. There was sedition everywhere, or so the newspapers claimed. Conspirators were at work throughout the kingdom, especially in the manufacturing districts. In Manchester disaster was narrowly averted when a "diabolical conspiracy" to take over the city was discovered and the plotters apprehended. Their plan had been to discharge a number of rockets into the factories on the outskirts of the city, setting them ablaze. The constables and local militia, attracted to the scene of the destruction, were to have left the inner city undefended, whereupon the conspirators planned to lead a mob to seize the banks, the barracks and the prison. According to the Manchester police, the plotters had hoped to seize Nottingham, Birmingham and Derby by the same strategy, and then to march on London.

A few months after this a former Luddite, Jeremiah Brandreth, raised a small army on the Derby border. He called on all those faithful to the radical cause to join him, and to enlarge his contingent still further he forced a number of farm laborers to come with him at gunpoint one night, promising that every man who joined him would have bread and a hundred guineas once they all reached Nottingham. Brandreth was a desperate unemployed weaver, possessed by the deluded certainty that he could succeed where the Luddites of 1811 had failed. He nearly made it to Nottingham, but a few miles from the town a troop of dragoons appeared in the distance, and his army of would-be rebels dispersed. Brandreth was caught and executed, and many of his followers were deported to Australia.

Brandreth's revolt and the Manchester conspiracy were

·

only the best publicized of many incidents which seemed, to the authorities, to call for harsh and even repressive countermeasures. Secret committees of both Houses of Parliament issued reports detailing many plots to overthrow the government, to destroy the established social order, obliterate property rights and seize privately held wealth. The country, it appeared, was not only awash in dissent, it was on the verge of revolution. To combat the danger, the officials employed spies and agents provocateurs, and increased the numbers of soldiers ready to rush to the assistance of the local constables should any demonstration get out of hand. In the immediate postwar years there were more than twenty-five thousand soldiers stationed in England, most of them in the Midlands and the North. And they were a different breed from the stouthearted veterans of Wellington's army: they were professional military men, a number of them foreigners, representing a military establishment which, if it offered protection to the citizenry, was faintly menacing as well.

A standing army in England! The idea was as startling as it was appalling. The England of sturdy common sense and peaceableness, of unpaid Justices of the Peace and an overriding sense of law and order—had it vanished for good? Or was it merely that, as the Evangelicals said, Satan had loosed the forces of darkness in his frustration over the prosperity of the saints?

As disorder widened, the march of Evangelical religion increased. "Tract mania" gripped society. Millions of tracts were distributed, and millions more sent abroad into the mission field. "Never did we, until these days, hear of millions of Tracts, Moral and Religious," Cobbett wrote, astonished at the flood tide of pamphlet evangelism. In the past, sermons had sufficed, but now every village had its tract-mongers, hawking their cheap wares and making religion a fad. (Cobbett, whose *Political Register* had soared in circulation when he reduced its cost to two pence, could hardly fault the Evangelicals for using the same tactic. But fault them he did.) Salvation was on everyone's mind. Byron's friend Thomas Moore wrote to a friend in 1818 warning him not to speak of religion or morality, "the mania on these subjects being

.

223

so universal and congenital that he who thinks of curing it is as mad as his patients."

Devotional books were on every table, though some people, mindful, they said, of the brevity of human life, renounced all reading but Bible reading, and prided themselves on the narrowing of their literary horizons. A much larger number broadened their reading to include Evangelical books along with the others they eagerly devoured. "Improving" novels took their places alongside *The Demon of Sicily*, *Midnight Weddings* and *The Romance of the Forest* on ladies' bookshelves, as did Hannah More's *Practical Piety*, a perennial favorite, and Mrs. Gore's *Manners of the Day*.

Another novel in the Evangelical mode which brought its author, Mary Sherwood, great success was *The Fairchild Family*, a book for children. Mrs. Sherwood, an exceedingly prolific writer of hundreds of tracts and pamphlets as well as books, published her novel in 1817 and almost at once it became a classic. It is a simple and straightforward story of good rewarded and evil punished. The main characters are children, the main action the mischief they cause. Prompted by Satan, the children misbehave—not very seriously, and with no harm done to anyone else. Then they are systematically and cruelly punished, so that the devil in them will be subdued. "All children," Mrs. Sherwood states emphatically, "are by nature evil." If parents fail to chastise them severely enough, God will assuredly chastise them in hell. The mischief-makers are horsewhipped, locked in the attic, deprived of food and comfort. As an object lesson they are taken to see the body of a criminal hanging in chains, and admonished to note well the terrible fate that awaits children who grow up harboring dark emotions: they turn into murderers.

Morality tales flooded popular culture under Evangelical influence. Moralistic "biographies" of atheists and radicals were concocted that told how the men died anguished by self-torture—or underwent dramatic deathbed conversions. Evidence of divine retribution was sought everywhere. The old king's illness, the Regent's weakness and ineffectuality, Princess Charlotte's death were all seen as punishment for

.

sin. Some said Bonaparte was bound to escape from St. Helena before long, and predicted that when he did he would enslave wayward England and make her people lament their errors.

Yet godliness, the Evangelicals believed, was surely on the increase. "Brighter day seems to dawn upon us," wrote the Committee of the Merchant Seamen's Auxiliary Bible Society in its Annual Report. The times were "pregnant with wonderful events," none more wonderful than the conversions of so many formerly worldly-minded men and women to the ways of faith. "Life how short, eternity how long!" believers proclaimed, and nonbelievers envied them their capacity to look beyond the turmoil of daily events and glimpse unending serenity.

The outward and visible signs of England's expanding piety were the churches the government undertook to build in the capital. The Church Building Act set aside the imponderably large sum of a million pounds to pay for more than two hundred new churches, which rose heavenward at a rapid rate. Most were of brick, Gothic rather than classical in style, utilitarian structures with capacious interiors fitted out with identical inexpensive baptismal fonts and altar furnishings. They were meant to represent tradition and stability, to restore in parishioners a sense of godliness and sober deference to their superiors. They were meant to help keep society intact, and in this endeavor the Evangelicals and the Prime Minister and his cabinet were of one mind.

But where the government was content to hold back anarchy, the Evangelicals were determined to reform and renovate the world—despite Satan's increasing mischief. The Society for the Suppression of Vice continued to do its purifying work, hounding those who broke the sabbath, inveighing against dancing, marching or holding boat races on the Lord's Day, prosecuting printers who sold risqué books and shopkeepers who sold obscene snuffboxes and bringing to justice the authors and publishers of "infidel" literature. Amusements were a particular target of their scrutiny. Shows and fairs tended to corrupt morals, they insisted, while games of chance led easily to serious gambling and graver sins. The

.

Society prosecuted tavern owners and brothel keepers, though they could not suppress the demand for drink and sexual companionship that kept them in business. Still, in keeping up their campaign of moral influence the Evangelicals succeeded in driving the demand underground, and, gradually, in changing the face of Regency England.

Society would never be completely cleansed, but its surface appearance was becoming altered. Open license was slowly starting to disappear. Though furtive vice would remain, it would carry the stigma of furtiveness. The prickings of a pervasive moral conscience were widely felt, even by those who had no particular religious leanings and whose worldly habits were deeply ingrained. The way people talked, the way they dressed, their very ways of thinking were being altered. Serious-mindedness was ceasing to be a peripheral social current; it was becoming the mainstream.

The first week of May, in England, was known as "holy week." It was then that the Evangelical Societies held their annual meetings, gathering together to conduct business, set policy and praise God for their advancement during the previous twelve months. The Societies themselves increased in number year by year, providing hospitals for the infirm, refuges and asylums for the mad, the unfortunate and the morally depraved, especially prostitutes. The list was a very long one: The Forlorn Female's Fund of Mercy, The Scripture Admonition Society, The Societies for the Blind and for the Deaf and Dumb Children of the Poor, The City of London Truss Society for the Relief of the Ruptured Poor Throughout the Kingdom. Some organizations, such as The Society of Young Ladies to Sell Clothes at Reduced Prices, or The Society for Returning Young Women to their Friends in the Country, were very specific in their aims; others, such as The Vice Society, combated Satan on as many fronts as their funds and their members' energies permitted.

But the work of social purification was not limited to these formal organizations. It went on in drawing rooms, parlors, ballrooms—anywhere genteel society gathered. The tone of polite conversation was changing. People who pronounced the words "legs" or "breast" or "torso," or indeed any word

·

which alluded to physicality (and by association, to sexuality) were shunned. If a young lady had the misfortune to allude to a gentleman's "trousers" instead of his "inexpressibles" she was condemned as brazen in the extreme. In some circles, formal manners were breaking down but among the serious-minded they were becoming more formal than ever. Young women were chaperoned, and expected to be addressed at all times by their surnames and not their Christian names. They dressed soberly, and avoided places where temptation lurked. Not for them the flirtation of the assembly room or theater, or the pleasure gardens of Vauxhall, where the "squealing and squalling" of less guarded young ladies could be heard coming from the erotic Dark Walk.

Family prayers, common since the 1790s, were now the norm. The entire household, patriarch first, then wife, children and other relations, then servants in order of their rank, filed into the room and knelt down facing the wall. The head of the family—or a clergyman in noble households—read prayers, with the servants giving the responses as in church. Sometimes this ritual began the day, sometimes it came before the midday meal. But its regularity never varied, and it gave a distinctive flavor—wholesome and uplifting, or stiff and sanctimonious, depending on the family—to family life. In the evenings parents and children gathered once again, to listen to readings from bowdlerized classics.

Servants discovered that it was increasingly difficult to get a place in many households unless they shared their employers' strongly expressed moral sensibilities. "As housemaid, a steady respectable young woman," one advertisement in the *Morning Chronicle* began, "twenty-seven years of age, of serious character." "As nursemaid, a young person from the country, with evangelical principles," went another. Once hired, they were watched to make certain they attended religious services and did not waver in their highmindedness. The scrutiny was mutual, to be sure. Godly servants required godliness in their masters and mistresses, and servants sometimes left their posts when their employers' behavior was objectionable.

The evolution of morals, and the shift in outlook that accompanied it, were unmistakable. Social commentators pointed to dozens of changes, from greater temperance in drinking habits to more churchgoing among Cambridge undergraduates.[5] Stricter morality meant less promiscuity and therefore, some thought, less venereal disease. The transformation was apparent in the House of Commons where, as Wilberforce remarked, only a few years earlier there had been "not a Member of the House that was publicly considered to be a religious man," while now religion was widely "professed and respected" there.[6]

But the change went beyond the mere professing of religion and showing it respect; it reached deeper into the social temperament. Evangelical hopes were leavening the whole of British culture. People were gradually becoming caught up in a conviction of their own efficacy in refashioning their world. Their moral energy, they believed, could work wonders, provided it was directed toward the accomplishment of specific tasks. Serious-mindedness went with hardheadedness, and hard work relentlessly pursued. Grim though the effort might be, a better future could be wrung into existence. The knowledge was at hand, diffused among a wide and increasingly literate public. The technology was at hand as well. When these were combined with sincere aspiration and earnestness of purpose, no obstacle could stand for long in the path of betterment.

In 1818 the high priestess of the Evangelicals, Hannah More, was at work on yet another of her edifying books, *Moral Sketches of Prevailing Opinions and Manners.* She was seventy-four now, and world-famous. Her books continued to outsell even the most popular novels, and admirers came to see her at the rate of ten or twelve a day from as far away as America.[7] Her health was often poor, but she boasted of having outlived several doctors—and of having written nearly a dozen books after her sixtieth birthday. The clergy had ceased to persecute her; instead they paid her polite visits and solicited her views. She read a great deal, wrote long letters denouncing the teaching of science and mathematics to the poor (who ought to be content with basic reading and writing and moral instruction) and often gathered children around her.

"Many a child is brought to me in my room for a little reward of a treat," she told a friend in a letter. "Since I began this scrawl, a sharp little girl was brought for this purpose. She repeated a short poem extremely well."

"Now I must examine what you know of the Bible," Hannah told the child. "Who was Abraham?"

After some hesitation, the answer came. "I think he was an Exeter man!"[8]

Though some thought her bigoted and insufferable, "Holy Hannah" reigned serenely on, her sweetness and simplicity radiating from her books. She was convinced that moral reform was advancing, that virtue was fast outpacing vice.

No greater proof of this could be offered, she thought, than the hospitality the Regent extended toward her spiritual co-worker Wilberforce at Brighton. That the vice-ridden prince should seek the company of the saintly reformer Wilberforce, and not once but many times, seemed remarkably clear evidence that sin was in retreat. (It was certainly evidence that exquisite tact and good breeding could bridge almost any ideological gap.) The two men did not discuss morality, presumably, or Wilberforce's proposal to make adultery a criminal offense. Their one recorded conversation was about a ball both had attended as young men decades earlier.

"The prince came up to me," Wilberforce wrote in his diary, "and reminded me of my singing at the Duchess of Devonshire's ball in 1782, of the particular song, and of our then first knowing each other."

"We are both I trust much altered since, sir," the reformer remarked.

"Yes, the time which has gone by must have made a great alteration in us."

"Something better than that, too, I trust, sir." Wilberforce's allusion to his conversion was not lost on the prince, but he let it pass.

"He then asked me to dine with him the next day," Wilber-

.

force wrote, "assuring me that I should hear nothing in his house to give me pain."[9]

At first the reformer declined the invitation, but eventually he accepted. And in fact nothing painful or offensive was said in Wilberforce's presence at the Pavilion, though after he had gone, and the Regent was alone with his trusted intimates, the easing of tensions must have been almost palpable. Still, the gesture had been made, and this, to More, was the significant thing.

"The Prince Regent has done himself great credit by the respect, I had almost said reverence, with which he has behaved to Mr. Wilberforce at Brighton," she noted. "He went frequently, and was on the whole much pleased." To be sure, the reformer was not given any direct opportunity to convert the prince to a better life. But his presence counted for a great deal, More was certain, in elevating the moral tone and preparing the ground for a substantial spiritual harvest. "It is pleasing to see," she wrote, immensely gratified, "how consistency in religion ultimately beats down all hostility."

17

*A*fter Byron left England in
April of 1816 he spent some time at Geneva, toured the Swiss
Alps and northern Italy and finally settled in Venice. The
watery old city with its picturesque canals and crumbling
pink palaces eloquent of faded grandeur suited him. "Venice
and I agree very well," he wrote. "In the mornings I study
Armenian—and in the evenings I go out sometimes—and
indulge in coition always."[1]

The worldly and tolerant Venetian mores allowed Byron
to indulge his passions to the full. Venetian society did not
condemn married women for infidelity, as long as they limited themselves to one lover (with two or three lovers they
were thought to be "a little wild"). Moreover, Byron judged,
Venetian women "kissed better than those of any other nation," and were generally much to his taste.[2] For once he
was among people who were his equals in debauchery; he

.

did not feel ostracized or self-conscious, and the cozily libidinous atmosphere renewed his zest for writing. During his Venetian sojourn Byron produced the fourth canto of *Childe Harold's Pilgrimage,* the tragedy *Manfred,* all of one narrative poem, *Beppo,* and part of another, *Don Juan.* He also composed his memoirs and wrote dozens of letters to the friends and associates he had left behind in England describing his amatory intrigues.

Byron was clearly in his element, and was often buoyant and sanguine. He boasted of being not "the misanthropical and gloomy gentleman" he was reputed to be "but a facetious companion . . . and as loquacious and laughing as if I were a much cleverer fellow."[3] Yet below the surface gaiety he remained, like his creation Childe Harold, "the wandering outlaw of his own dark mind," quixotic and mercurial and at the mercy of his morbid reflections. "I am so changeable, being everything by turns and nothing long—I am such a strange mélange of good and evil, that it would be difficult to describe me." He would have blown his brains out more than once, he confessed, had he not realized what pleasure it would afford his mother-in-law. He was by turns jokey, misanthropic, high-spirited and depressed—and always the dedicated voluptuary, "half mad . . . between metaphysics, mountains, lakes, love unextinguishable, thoughts unutterable, and the nightmare of my own delinquencies."[4]

As for his delinquencies, they had produced, early in 1817, a bastard daughter, Allegra. The poet had cast off the child's nineteen-year-old mother, Claire Clairmont, long before her delivery but he did take some responsibility for Allegra. Deep fatherly affection was beyond him, however, and his somewhat exotic household was no place for a child. Ultimately Allegra was placed in a convent, where sadly she sickened and died in 1822.

Heartlessness was not in Byron's nature, yet he could be extremely callous, and his years in Venice, his friends thought, coarsened him both physically and emotionally. He was only in his late twenties, but his looks had altered. The pale, beautifully poetic young man had grown fat and a little gray. His head had lost its noble contours, and his remarkable eyes were dulled and often ringed with dark circles. Women still sometimes fainted when he entered a room, but whether from lovestruck admiration or shock and disgust was impossible to judge.

The rupture between Byron's two selves—the jovial, warmhearted, fun-loving adventurer and the tormented, joyless pleasure-seeker—was finally complete. He had become Childe Harold, the errant prodigal lost in Sin's labyrinth and terminally afflicted with ennui. As a younger man he had seemed poised between good and evil, redemption and damnation. In Venice he had lost his balance, and gone hurtling down into the abyss. In truth, of course, Byron had not so much lost his balance as made his choice. He could not stay poised between his two selves forever, the strain was too great. Besides, pleasure was pleasure; though it left a sour aftertaste he liked dissolute living, he enjoyed the "world of harlotry" he discovered in Venice. He opted, consciously and without reservations, for the darker path.

Yet having chosen it he cut himself off from the majority of his English contemporaries. Even his friends were scandalized by the letters he wrote them, letters which told them stories of his seductions, of the half-murderous, half-farcical combats between his rival mistresses, of sordid escapades and nightlong drinking bouts that left him ill and depressed. What was worse, they knew he intended the letters "for the edification of all and sundry, heedless of the women's reputations." It was all too much: the calculated profligacy, the denial of all moral restraint. "This is really too gross," Tom Moore declared after reading one of Byron's missives.[5] Byron had put himself outside the pale.

His poetry too had reached a moral nadir, or so it seemed to his publisher, John Murray, and to the writers whose opinions Murray solicited. They judged it strange and vaguely horrifying in its freedom, offensive to be sure, but more harmful in its celebration of meaninglessness than in its license. "He seems," Moore wrote in his journal, "by living so long out of London, to have forgotten that standard of decorum to which everyone must refer his words at least, who hopes to be either listened to or read by the world."[6]

.

Byron stood to lose what remained of his diminished readership. He was adrift, for the time being at least, in his own sordid universe.

Byron had succumbed to the strain of his divided self. Others succumbed to the strain of the times, to the relentless pressures of rapid change, the confusions of social upheaval and endless financial crisis.

Lady Melbourne, certainly one of the toughest women of her generation, became addicted to opium and wasted away, her health broken and her mind dimmed, until she died in the spring of 1818. Others too turned to opium, or to numbing quantities of alcohol, or to the (fortunately harmless) laughing gas that the chemist Humphry Davy dispensed to the fashionable in his Albemarle Street laboratory. Several prominent politicians—and a great many more obscure persons—shot themselves or swallowed poison or threw themselves into the Thames. It seemed as if the tempo of self-destruction was quickening, and people wondered whether the harsh winters or the unhealthy river air might be affecting Londoners' brains. How else, they mused, could one explain the numbers of young ladies who tried to drown themselves in the Serpentine or in the fountain at Trafalgar Square? Or the official in the Stamp Office who, driven to distraction by his debts, was suddenly seized by a "momentary frenzy" and threw himself out of an attic window?

The threat of personal catastrophe hung like an opaque London fog over the waning years of the Regency, colliding with the bright vision of improvement to which the Evangelicals and radicals firmly clung. From the continent came word that Field Marshal von Blücher, idol of the war years, was possessed by the bizarre hallucination that he was pregnant, and that his child's father was a Frenchman.[7] Wellington's heretofore unsullied integrity was tarnished somewhat by libelous newspaper reports accusing him of adultery. All around the mighty were falling. Some, like Byron, escaped into exile abroad, among them the onetime dictator of male fashion Beau Brummell and the renowned courtesan Henriette Wilson. Others were trapped by their debts before they could escape.

.

Bankruptcies multiplied. "Few objects, domestic or foreign, remaining to excite political interests," a contemporary
newspaper declared, "the public feelings were nearly concen-
trated upon private and personal distress." The papers were
full of descriptions of "substantial family residences" vacated
by their debt-ridden owners and put up for auction. The
furnishings too were sold to satisfy the creditors, everything
from four-poster beds to "drawing room suites of fashionable
furniture," cut-glass dessert plates, Grecian lamps, pier
glasses, Turkey carpets, pianofortes and patent mangles. One
diarist sighed over what she called "this declining age, when
too many worthy members of the community seem to have
an alacrity in sinking."[8]

The worthiest members of all, the royal family, were the
most conspicuously enmired in debt. The Regent's brothers,
the royal dukes, were notorious spendthrifts, notoriously unrepentant. The Regent himself owed perhaps half a million
pounds, roundly estimated, and was blithely enlarging that
total by spending seventy-five thousand pounds a year on
jewels and plate and upholstery. His wife, whose financial
straits had until recently been more pressing than his own,
managed to evade ruin only by signing over her magnificent
villa to her Roman banker.

Nearly as sordid as the plight of the many bankrupts was
that of the once-prosperous lady or gentleman of fashion
whose income had been severely reduced. They tried to keep
up appearances, while scrimping on servants' wages, pawn-
ing jewels and furnishings, even economizing on food.

"Last night's ball at Lady Hyde Parker's was a bad concern," one irritated guest complained. "Her ladyship is getting out of date, and, I fear, out at elbows; for she gave us
no supper! At three o'clock we were all squeezed into one
room to scramble for a few sandwiches, etc., which were
very soon devoured, and, unlike the Hydra's head, were not
succeeded by others."

Lady Parker's guests were greatly put out, and began to
say so in loud tones.

" 'If for this,' said one of the party, who had not succeeded
in picking up even a few crumbs, but held aloft an empty

235

plate, 'if for this we are asked to turn night into day, I, for one, decline, and return to the natural order of things.' " There was general assent to this sentiment, and Lady Parker was disgraced by the whole fiasco.[9]

In the uncertain postwar years prosperity could vanish overnight. One socially prominent family, the Chinnerys, seemed very comfortably situated. Chinnery had a post in the government, his wife was an ornament to society, their daughter had enjoyed the distinction of entertaining the Regent at one of his musical evenings. Then, suddenly, Chinnery defaulted on his debts, to the amount of fifty or sixty thousand pounds. All comfort ended, shame replaced respectability. The musical daughter became dangerously ill, and died. Her mother wrung her hands; her father, finding the thought of suicide distasteful, took ship for America.

The Chinnerys' friends shook their heads and fairly gloated over the debacle. "I foresaw how it would end," they told one another. "Their style of living was quite inconsistent with the amount of his official income." "So much pride and pretention!"[10] So it went, as disaster succeeded disaster and fortunes rose and fell.

Money itself partook of the general instability. Small notes were in short supply, and all notes, small or large, were suspect, as counterfeiters were at work in every city printing false ones. In Birmingham, forged bank notes in large denominations were for sale for five shillings, and the forgers were known to be turning a brisk trade. The radical press exposed case after case in which government informers, eager to prove their usefulness to their employers, planted counterfeit money on innocent men and then turned in their victims to the authorities—and were rewarded when they were convicted.[11]

People sometimes wrote messages or other ephemera on bank notes. One that came to Walter Scott's notice was a guinea note, "pretty dirty and greasy," with a barely decipherable verse on its back:

> Farewell my note! and wheresoe'er ye wend
> Shun gaudy scenes to be the poor man's friend.

•

Ye've left a poor one, go to one as poor,
And drive despair and hunger from his door.[12]

If prosperity was fleeting, beauty was even more so. By 1818 the belles of the early Regency were fading, their freshness dulled by anxiety, worry lines marring the perfection of their mouths and eyes. A story was told of Lady Jersey who once exclaimed, when catching a glimpse of herself in a mirror, that "it were better to go to hell at once than live to be old and ugly!"[13] She was not yet old and ugly, but her good looks had lost much of their luster. Along with many other former beauties, some of them still in their twenties, her youthful radiance had given way to a middle-aged afterglow. "I'm wearing away, like snow-wreaths in a thaw," went the words of a popular song of the day. The song captured the mood of transience, the melancholy realization that the glory of a lovely face and a statuesque body was a momentary glory at best.

The once-splendid balls and assemblies where the beauties had reigned supreme had lost some of their gaiety and glamour. The lines of carriages waiting to deliver their occupants to the doors of the great houses had become grotesquely long. People hurled stones and bottles at the carriage windows, frightening the partygoers. Once they arrived, they were alarmed still further by the enormous crowds of guests filling the suffocatingly hot rooms. Lady Shelley recorded her impressions of a soirée at Gloucester House in the spring of 1818. "At the entrance we were nearly squeezed to death, and people cried out in alarm," she wrote. "The Duke of Wellington, who was standing halfway up the stairs, called out to the ladies below that there was not the slightest danger; but the pressure was so great that many of them fainted." More than sixteen hundred people had been invited to a house barely capable of holding six hundred. The resulting crush nearly led to fatal injuries.[14]

Denying their mounting sense of loss and disillusionment, the fashionable turned, as Byron did, to more and more frenzied pleasure-seeking. They took their pleasure wherever they could find it: at Carlton House, which they referred

.

to as "Nero's Hotel," at Crockford's, the favorite gambling club where government ministers joined in the illegal and ruinous games of faro and *jeu d'enfer;* at the opera, where the costliest courtesans were to be found, and enjoyed; and at the theater, where the entertainment was at times spoiled by the spectacle of people being trampled in the overcrowded pit. They gorged themselves on food, taking emetics before they dined so that they could eat more. They drank themselves to the point of stupefaction, night after night, quaffing bottle after bottle of port and sherry and hock as if in the grip of a perpetual thirst. There were four- and five-bottle men, and even a few phenomenal six-bottle men—so called because of their remarkable capacity for drink. They held their liquor, after a fashion at least (they were bleary-eyed and incoherent, "fit for nothing but bed"), but they did not escape its long-term effects. Gout, cirrhosis of the liver, diseased kidneys were common; like the Regent, the multibottle men were forever taking pills and patent medicines to relieve their stupendous hangovers.

The widespread drunkenness of the time must have blighted its opulence and graciousness. Men sodden with wine swayed stupidly on the brocaded sofas, were sick on the costly carpets, picked fights with one another like stableboys, crashing into furniture and breaking vases and lamps. Many an elegant evening ended in ugly scenes, or in embarrassed silence as servants carried the unconscious host or guests upstairs to bed. Men who, as one diarist put it, "lived indulgently in table gratifications," were not always fastidious about their persons; at least one aristocrat, the excessively convivial Duke of Norfolk, slept in his evening clothes and rarely washed.[15]

The unwashed duke was at one extreme among the pleasure-seekers; the dandies were at the other.

Dandyism, in the early years of the century, had been a faddish form of individualism. Its foremost proponent, George Brummell, attracted the fascinated attention of his social superiors by the elegant simplicity of his dress and the cleanliness of his linen. Compared with his restrained toilette, the belaced and beribboned costumes of the aristocracy seemed gaudy and foolish. Brummell's style was an anti-style, a denial of ostentation and self-congratulation. His originality and disdainful self-confidence had the effect of making others doubt their taste, with the result that when Brummell dressed in the morning, a roomful of titled admirers came to watch.

Brummell had left England in 1816, and the dandies of the postwar years, though they inherited his disdain for other people's dress and his hauteur, departed from his taste. Instead of impeccable restraint they affected bizarre extremes in dress, extremes by which they called attention to themselves in ways their predecessor had not. When they paraded in St. James's and Piccadilly in their perfectly cut, exaggeratedly narrow-waisted coats and tight trousers, their precisely tied, starched white neckcloths and their chicken-skin gloves, people turned to stare at them—as they were meant to. Their style was at once effeminate—so contemporaries said—and militaristic; their languor suggested decadence, but their habitual superiority was not unlike that of archly elitist officers snubbing those of inferior rank. The dandy "uniform" was similar in outline to a military uniform, with its hugely padded shoulders and puffed-out torso, made still more extreme by tight corseting. A pantomime presented at the Drury Lane Theatre in April of 1818 summed up the postwar dandy's appearance:

> France gave his step its trip, his tongue its phrase,
> The head its peruke, and his waist its stays . . .
> On the roug'd cheek the fresh-dyed whisker spread,
> The thousandth way of dressing a calf's head . . .
> The neckcloth next, where starch and whalebone vie
> To make the slave a walking pillory . . .
> What straps, ropes, steel, the aching ribs compress,
> To make the Dandy—beautifully less.[16]

Eccentric narcissism was the hallmark of the dandies. They reputedly spent hours tying their cravats, making a fine art of adjusting the creases and folds with mathematical precision. A satirist wrote a mock-scholarly treatise called *Neckclothitania* on the dozens of stylish ties: the "Oriental Tie"

·

(white, made of a very stiff and rigid cloth), the "Mathematical Tie" (a triangle, whose height from neck to chin determined the sharpness of its angles), the "Napoleon Tie" (violet, with "a very pretty appearance, giving the wearer a languishingly amorous look"), the "Mail Coach Tie" (a tie with a single knot, hidden in the folds of a starchless length of shawl, favored by stagecoachmen and guards), and so on through a long catalog of variations.[17]

One dandy was known for his elaborately groomed whiskers, another for his gloves, which were fitted and refitted until they clung to his pale white hands like a second skin. Still another was renowned for his perfumed baths, and for the huge gold dressing case he took with him everywhere he went, carried by two grunting and puffing servants.[18] One of the vainest and haughtiest of the dandies, Colonel Kelly of the 1st Foot Guards, prided himself on his highly varnished boots, polished with a special blacking of which only his valet knew the secret. Kelly, so the story went, was burned to death in attempting to save his boots during a fire—whereupon the other dandies fought among themselves to obtain the services of the invaluable valet.[19]

The postwar dandies were caricatures of narcissism, symptomatic of a society in the throes of self-definition. As distinctive as their costumes was their rudeness, their "art of cutting people." "The highest triumph of the English dandy," commented a visitor to London, Prince Pückler-Muskau, "is to appear with the most wooden manners . . . and to contrive even his civilities so that they are as near as may be to affronts." He assaulted decorum, was pointedly impolite to women, and treated even his best friends like strangers "if they ceased to have the stamp of fashion."[20]

Rudeness was by no means confined to the dandies, of course. Social critics complained that "courtesy was out of fashion," and pointed to numerous examples of uncouth manners. Young women were going about unchaperoned, calling their own coaches and behaving with impertinent independence. People were calling one another by their first names, heedless of titles or social standing. (Princess Charlotte had called Wellington "Arthur," a familiarity that infuriated him.) Gentlemen were forgetting themselves and jumping on furniture or climbing the walls of drawing rooms like monkeys, just for the fun of it. But the dandies carried the cult of rudeness to its farthest extreme, taking up a defensive posture toward everyone who was not of their circle and making enemies of the outsiders.

Behind their odious manners was a preoccupation with their own identity, a need to define who they were and who they were not. In an age of settled values and easy social interchange this would not have been necessary. But after 1815 fashionable society was awash with newcomers: wealthy tradesmen, city merchants, manufacturers. To the entrenched inner circle, such people were usurpers and opportunists; they had to be kept at bay or else the whole precariously erected social hierarchy would collapse.

There was no way the newcomers could be kept out on grounds of income, for they were in many cases far wealthier than their social betters. (Six thousand pounds a year sufficed to support a fashionable household, it was said; a great corn merchant could command three hundred thousand.) Nor was the lack of a title sufficient grounds for exclusion, for many among the elite had modest titles or none. No, the only way to prevent the glut of mediocrity was to erect artificial barriers, and this the arbiters of society did with a vengeance.

They scrutinized their guest lists and struck off any unworthy names that had crept in. They stopped going to Kensington Gardens—where the middle classes promenaded—and kept to themselves in Hyde Park, never going near the area frequented by ordinary Londoners. The men exercised particular vigilance in admitting new members to their clubs, which often had dozens of applicants for every vacancy, while the women kept watch over the lists of people to be admitted to subscription balls—especially those held at Almack's.

Almack's, "the seventh heaven of the fashionable world," had come to be synonymous with exclusivity. Those admitted to its rather plain assembly rooms counted themselves singularly fortunate; those unlucky enough to be shut out sneered at the "lady patronesses" who ruled there and secretly nursed their wounds. "Select" society went to Almack's, everyone

.

else stayed home. Yet there was something brittle and unnatural about the "little dancing and gossiping world" that met at Almack's, under the censorious eye of the lady patronesses. It was full of preening self-congratulation, and offered little real pleasure or comfort. The dance floor was inferior, the anterooms unadorned, the refreshments unappetizing, one visitor commented. And besides, despite all the snobbery, the company was full of nobodies.[21]

Preoccupied as they were with their own frantic efforts to preserve and, if possible, advance their status the fashionables paid scant attention to the death of the old queen in November of 1818. She had been quite ill for six months, and her death had been anticipated, but hardly anyone had bothered to order mourning clothes, and the shops were full of bolts of cloth in bright colors, with hardly any somber black stuff to be had. In London people wore as much white as they did black, and appeared to be ignoring the fact that a feeble old woman who had reigned over them for half a century and more was gone. At court things were different. There, out of deference to the Regent, everyone was in black crape and bombazine, and even the guards at St. James's were draped in long crape scarves and wore black sashes and large black cockades in their hats.

The Regent, who had been at his mother's bedside holding her hand when she died, took her death greatly to heart. He announced that he intended "to wear the longest mourning that ever son did for a mother having lost one who was his guide and counsellor in all his varied distresses and difficulties," but in fact he limited the official mourning period to only six weeks, a surprisingly short term.[22]

The queen left a million pounds' worth of jewelry and her valuable wardrobe to her long-suffering daughters, who had nursed her and humored her bad temper for decades. She left very little ready money, however, having given a good deal of her income to the Regent to subsidize his renovations to the Marine Pavilion and most of the rest to her numerous charities. There was not enough cash, in fact, to pay her debts or to cover the cost of her funeral, or to arrange for annuities for her servants. Her sons, the always impecu-

.

nious royal dukes, received little or nothing from their mother's estate, but rather than offend the Regent by complaining, they held their tongues and waited for their father to die.

The king was eighty years old now, ancient and spectral with his long white hair and beard and his bent back. His condition was much as usual. He ate his breakfast at eight, his dinner at one, and his supper—which, when in a tranquil state, he chose himself, usually ordering mutton or beef— in the early evening. His page and one of his doctors were always at hand, but there were no crises to demand their attention. Hour by hour they watched their afflicted master, his sightless eyes fixed on an imaginary guest, delivering lectures or talking about the past. "His Majesty's habits have not, in consequence of infirmity, or old age, undergone material change," the *Morning Chronicle* reported. His health was good, and he was "perfectly happy." There was every reason to think he would live to be two hundred.

Under the circumstances, there was no reason to tell him of the queen's death. He would not have understood it, and besides he had the queen with him often in his imagination, exhorting him by her own pious example to deepen his religious faith and commending him and his errant mind to God.

.

18

*W*hen the doctor at London
Hospital saw the wounds and bruises on the body of six-
year-old John Hawley, he told the coroner that he was in
no doubt about how the boy died. There was a large and
ugly bruise on his forehead, and another on his knee, and
a deep gash running down one leg and foot that had become
septic and caused death. The boy had evidently received no
medical treatment, though his condition had been grave and
the look of him most pitiable.

At the inquest the facts came out. John Hawley was a
climbing boy, an apprentice to a chimneysweep named
Moles. He lived with Moles and his wife in Spitalfields, in
the heart of London's most wretched slum. The climbing
boys of Spitalfields, and there were many of them, were rou-
tinely beaten and abused but Moles's mistreatment of his

·

apprentice was exceptionally brutal, and had drawn the attention of concerned neighbors, three of whom testified at the inquest.

One of the neighbors, George Rolt, told the court how as he was walking down the street he heard a child "screaming violently, crying out murder, and begging for mercy." The screams were so alarming, and went on for so long, that Rolt went to the door of the lodging where the commotion was going on and kicked on it until a man came out.

"Why are you beating that child so cruelly?" Rolt asked the man, who answered that it was no business of his. He had flogged the boy, he said, and would flog him again. A woman came out of the house then, holding a leather strap. She was covered in sweat, and had evidently been exerting herself to her utmost. She told Rolt that both she and her husband had been punishing the child, one holding him while the other wielded the strap. Moles swore at Rolt then and slammed the door in his face, but Rolt, not content to let the matter rest, made inquiries and found out that the child had eventually been sent to the hospital.

Rolt visited him there, he testified, and found him "in a shocking state," swollen and cut and miserable. He was only five or six at that time, small and emaciated, caked with soot and grime so thick that no amount of scrubbing could remove it. He told his visitor that his master and mistress had beaten him for failing to go up a narrow chimney, "which he had not power to do, being very lame."

The court heard more testimony to the same effect, about how other people had heard little John Hawley screaming and shrieking as he was being beaten, how they had seen him coming out of the Moleses' house, and were in no doubt whose apprentice he was, how Moles had been accustomed to beat his apprentice with a large brush to force him up the narrow flues of burning chimneys. One woman told of watching Moles mistreat the boy, complaining to him about it ("I told him he was not the child's father to use him so cruelly"), and then seeing Moles "pull the child, who was some distance up the chimney, down again by the legs."

.

"The poor creature's head was struck with great force against the hearth-stone," she added, "and he appeared in the most deplorable state."

The jury listened to the witnesses, and then without hesitation returned a verdict of Wilful Murder against the chimney sweep and his wife.[1]

By one contemporary estimate there were a thousand climbing boys in London in 1819, and hundreds more in smaller cities and towns and rural areas. The majority were subjected to abuse, for, quite understandably, they did not climb the flues willingly and had to be slapped and pinched and bullied into doing their work. They were thrust, arms upraised and frequently naked (for clothes could be a dangerous hindrance) up into the passage, and then urged higher by the pain of pins stuck into the soles of their feet. Usually the chimneys were on fire; the boys were expected to locate the burning material clogging the airflow in the maze of connected passageways and put the fire out. Often they were burned. Always they gasped for air, for the fire consumed a good deal of the available oxygen and made the labyrinth of tunnels suffocating. The blackness, the eye-burning smoke, the rough walls that scraped knees and elbows raw, above all the fear of being trapped in a tunnel so narrow that it was impossible to go either forward or backward: all these combined to terrify and intimidate the little boys. After a year or so of steady work they developed huge hard callouses on their sore limbs, which made the ascent somewhat less painful—though no less frightening—but with the passage of time came a worse hazard. "Sooty warts" grew on their unwashed bodies, cancerous growths that were nearly always fatal.

Even under the best conditions, when the master was kind and provided nourishing food and washed his boys now and then, there remained the dangerously harmful nature of the work itself, and for this there was no remedy. Chimneys were becoming narrower. Many a sweep advertised "small boys for small flues," and put his climbing boys to work at younger and younger ages. Four-year-olds were sent up when five- and six-year-olds were too large. Or, occasionally,

·

climbing girls were used. In 1817 the chimneys of Windsor Castle were tended by two sooty little girls named Morgan.[2]

The plight of the climbing boys (and girls) had moved humane people to pity for decades. In 1788 Parliament had passed an act whose provisions were meant to protect the children from the worst abuses. No child was to be apprenticed to a master chimneysweep before the age of eight; masters were limited to six apprentices (to prevent them from taking on dozens, and forcing them to live cheek by jowl in overcrowded cellars); masters were obliged to wash their boys at least once a week and to send them to church on Sundays; and finally, masters were forbidden to send their boys up any chimney actually on fire, or to beat them if they refused to work. The act, had it been observed, would have gone a long way toward improving the lot of the children. But it was ignored, for the most part, and meanwhile the chimneys grew ever narrower and the climbing boys ever younger.

A Society for Superseding Climbing Boys was formed to tackle the problem in 1803, and in highly practical fashion, offered a reward to the inventor who could devise a chimney-sweeping machine. Almost immediately one was invented, by a Mr. Smart, who over the next fourteen years put his machine to work on chimneys of every sort all over England. It worked perfectly well, so he and the Society believed, on ninety-nine chimneys out of a hundred.[3] Yet when a bill was proposed in Parliament in 1817 to prohibit the use of climbing boys, it was defeated, despite the influential backing of Wilberforce. The bill passed the Commons in 1818, but not the Lords; the same thing happened in 1819. Cynics believed that the Lords' opposition was purely selfish. Of those few chimneys Smart's machine could not manage to sweep, most were in the mansions of the very rich; what were the needs of a few dirty children compared to the need for smoke-less chimneys in a great house?

Whatever the actual reasoning of the peers, the climbing boys went on at their work—and incidents like the tragic death of John Hawley went on being reported in the newspapers, along with accounts of overturned coaches and petty

·

thefts and people accidentally run over in the street by cavalry. In actuality a good many people benefited from the continued existence of climbing boys. Poor parents with too many mouths to feed welcomed the opportunity of disposing of their children as apprentices, at as early an age as possible, and the master sweeps took them younger than any other masters. Parish officers with hundreds of discarded children to look after were eager to turn them over to whoever would take them, and the chimneysweeps took them in great numbers. It was a convenient and much-needed solution to a serious problem—the problem of too many unwanted children.

Every day children were "laid in the streets" of London. Some were illegitimate, the offspring of upper-class people who considered them an inconvenience or of teen-age prostitutes who could not provide for them. Some were orphans, some were foundlings whose parentage would always remain a mystery. Infants were rescued from the river, where they had been left to drown. Babies were born to women dying in the workhouse and orphaned within hours of their birth. Now and then a servant would alight from a coach carrying a bundle in his arms, and deliver the bundle to the churchwarden of a poor parish, along with an anonymous gift of money. The bundle proved to be an infant, and the money a sort of dowry, or conscience money, from the anonymous parent or relative.

Older children were abandoned as well: children whose fathers went off to sea or whose mothers disappeared to try to make a new life; children with simple minds or crooked backs who would never be able to support themselves, and were a liability to their impoverished parents; vagrants and runaways; child apprentices turned out to fend for themselves when their masters went bankrupt.

The burden of looking out for these children fell primarily on the overworked, unpaid officers of the London parishes whose responsibility it was to disburse poor relief. Well-intentioned though they were, the churchwardens and overseers were overwhelmed by the sheer numbers of boys and

·

girls brought to them. Foundling hospitals, orphan asylums and charity schools accommodated some of the children, but the majority were put out to work.

And work they did, for long wearying hours on end, six and sometimes seven days a week. They climbed chimney flues and scrubbed floors, swept stables and ran errands. Boys were apprenticed to watermen, who frequently sold them to the navy, or to poor street tailors and cobblers who gave them piecework to do. Some spun catgut, retching from the stink and reeking of it even after the work was done. Others sold milk in the streets, or made buttons, or collected stray animals to be torn to pieces at sporting events. The girls, who were looked on as weaker and less desirable as workers, generally fared worse than the boys. They were taken on in homes where the mistresses set them to scraping pots in the scullery or cleaning out the hearths. Or they were apprenticed to dressmakers or ribbon-weavers, or put to work sewing trimmings for hats.[4] One evil had ended. An act of Parliament passed in 1816 put a stop to the practice of sending homeless children by the cartload to work fifteen- and sixteen-hour days in the industrial factories of the North.

Only the hardiest of these children survived. Living chiefly on bread and water, with an occasional bit of meat or boiled greens, dressed in thin and ragged clothes, shivering with cold, habitually mistreated and always pitifully overworked, they eked out a grim life. For many, the constant fatigue and neglect led to despair, listlessness and illness. A great many of them, a contemporary wrote, "died of wounds and want of looking after and hunger and cold together"—only to be replaced immediately by others in a bleak and sorrowful cycle.

For those who escaped the cycle, either by running away or through luck or sheer determination to survive, there was the life of the criminal underworld.

Poor children lived perpetually on the outskirts of that shadowy domain. The taverns they went to in their fleeting hours of recreation had their share of criminal patrons, boast-

·

ing of their robberies and swindles and displaying their loot. The pawnbrokers they turned to in hard times to lend them a penny or two on an old coat were on good terms with all the thieves and pickpockets in the neighborhood. There were gin shops and brothels in every street, full of disreputable characters; no child could walk half a block without encountering streetwalkers and dangerous-looking toughs and drunken seamen spoiling for a fight.

An apprentice who ran away from his master was ripe for recruitment into the criminal life. He usually crept away secretly in the middle of the night, avoiding the risk of unlatching a downstairs door and going out instead by way of the trapdoor in the attic. Once on the roof, he made his way to shelter, either in the nearest empty house or underneath a market stall or in a field. Chances were good that he would not find himself alone there, for gangs of boys took refuge in such places. The hardened boys would try to tempt the newcomer into joining them, and if he resisted they threatened to beat him—or worse, to tell his master where he was. Fearing his master's brutal punishment, more often than not the boy gave in.

Gangs of young boys roved the streets, pilfering whatever was left lying unguarded. They tagged along behind coal carts, and when the coal was being delivered, pretended to help carry it into the house; while inside they helped themselves to the silver spoons. They went into shops and, while one engaged the shop clerk in haggling over a price, the others robbed him of a dozen other things and then ran off.[5] They stole meat from the butcher and turnips from the grocer. They even took the oats from the horses' feed bags when their owners' backs were turned.

There was a ready market for everything they took, from old shoes to pocket watches to candlesticks. The proprietors of "green stalls," who sold odds and ends in the streets, encouraged urchins to steal by promising to buy from them. Chandlers' shops were another source of profit to the thieves, as well as to thieving servants. "There is scarcely what is called a chandler's shop in any part of the metropolis . . .

·

but buys old bottles and linen or anything that a servant girl when she goes there to purchase things can take with her." So went the report of the Upper Marshal of the City to a committee of Parliament.[6]

There were parliamentary inquiries into the policing of the capital, and its vast population of wayward children, in the immediate postwar years. What these inquiries revealed was that crime among children of twelve or thirteen and younger had become institutionalized. Left on their own through abandonment or bad luck, traumatized by mistreatment in charity schools or as apprentices, the boys and girls found their way by the hundreds to "flash houses" which offered them security and acceptance—albeit under grotesque circumstances. The flash houses were, in effect, crime schools with vast dormitories. The children who flourished there were only too happy to exchange the cold charity of the parish churchwarden for the warm companionship of pickpockets and prostitutes their own age. New arrivals quickly learned their disreputable trades, and kept the flash houses running from the profits of their robberies and illicit assignations.

For the boys the life of the flash house was far better than the alternatives. There was constant excitement, the ever-present risk of being caught and sent to prison and the everyday rough-and-tumble of comradeship with the other boys. There were adults to contend with too, of course. Many flash houses were owned and operated by women, who left deputies in charge of the children. Yet the children set the tone. It was no life for the sensitive or the timid; among the boys, boxing was a necessary skill, often practiced. There was honor of a sort among the thieves, however, and loyalty, and a sense of belonging. The boys yearned for the day when they would be old enough to live on their own, to own their own cutter and sail her upriver to Richmond on sunny afternoons. They glimpsed a future, and that helped to sustain them through the bad times when the law caught up with them. Boys caught stealing could be sentenced to death, but were usually given a beating and then released.

.

Afterward they found their way back to the flash house again.

Girls suffered a much more sordid experience. When very young they were sent out to beg. Later, by the time they were eleven or twelve, they were beginning to walk the streets, accompanied and encouraged, in the beginning, by the procuresses to whom they turned over the few shillings they earned. Reports made to Parliament indicated that the procuresses habituated little girls to prostitution by keeping them drunk most of the time and in a state of slavelike dependency. Later still, flash house girls of twelve and thirteen joined the boys they lived with in gangs of twenty or thirty and terrorized their neighborhoods.

The number of prostitutes in London had doubled during the war years. As the Regency drew to a close, there were by one low estimate thirty thousand women and girls earning their living in brothels and on the streets. Most of these were barely women at all. The average age of convicted prostitutes in the London Female Penitentiary was sixteen.[7] What the social reformers referred to as "female depravity" was clearly on the rise. Brothels were far more common than churches, despite the Church Building Act. Officials counted some 362 houses of ill repute in three London parishes alone, a good many specializing in offering their patrons extremely young girls.

"The number of abandoned children, from the age of twelve to fourteen years, living in a state of prostitution, who are brought daily before the magistrate for petty crimes, are increased to an alarming degree within these few years," reported the Provisional Committee of the Guardian Society in 1815. There were hundreds of procuresses and madams scouring the alleys and doorways every day for destitute children needing shelter. A high proportion of them found that shelter in brothels.

One who did was Harriet Lester, a pretty, well-mannered young girl who came to Hannah More's attention. Harriet had thrown herself into a canal, and had been saved from drowning and taken to a hospital. When More found her she was living in "a street of very bad fame," caught in the snare of the streetwalker's life.[8] There was a tragic look about her, More thought. She had a sad face, and when she told the reformer her story it proved to be sad as well.

Her father, she said, had been a prisoner in the King's Bench prison. While there he had sold Harriet, then barely out of childhood, to a fellow prisoner. Harriet had gone to live with this man as his mistress—her father having ceased to have any place in her life, presumably—and had suffered when he neglected her and was unfaithful to her. Her depression deepened, and before very long she tried to kill herself. After her rescue she had gotten by on what little she could earn from prostitution. Though More continued to have doubts about Harriet's ability to lead a normal life ("We are by no means sure of Harriet going on well," she commented, "and shall not be surprised if she leaves us in a moment"), she did live to reach adulthood. Some years after her suicide attempt More still had hopes for her, deeply scarred though she was by her past.

Children were oppressed in another way in this era, one that, on the face of it, seemed likely to be beneficial. They were crammed uncomfortably full of knowledge at the age of two and three and four, made into infant prodigies able to regurgitate facts and recite long poems and reel off long passages in Latin and Greek. Not a few children were reading at age three, mastering the ancient classics at five and six, tutoring other children at seven and eight. One little girl memorized all of Shakespeare; children in devout families were able to quote vast portions of the Bible.

Perhaps the best known of the Regency prodigies was John Stuart Mill, who as a three-year-old learned the Greek alphabet and memorized long lists of Greek words together with their English equivalents. By the time he was eight young Mill had read all of Herodotus and a good deal of Plato, along with a half-dozen other Greek authors. Beyond this he had worked his way through at least fifty volumes of history and theology in English—works that would have made demanding reading for a scholar of mature years.

.

Mill's early and rapid progress in learning was accomplished under the relentless scrutiny of his father, whom he described in his *Autobiography* as "constitutionally irritable," "deficient in tenderness," and "one of the most impatient of men." The older Mill was a stern disciplinarian. Other forward children were driven on to achieve feats of learning by the fear of painful punishments. Disapproving parents whipped their children with rods or struck their elbows repeatedly against their desks. Lessons were memorized under torturous conditions. The novelist Mary Sherwood described how as a child of five she had been strapped into an iron collar attached to a wooden backboard. "It was the fashion then," she wrote. "I generally did all my lessons standing in stocks, with this same collar round my neck; it was put on in the morning, and seldom taken off till late in the evening; and it was Latin which I had to study."[9] Translating fifty lines of Vergil was her morning's task, and a grueling one for a young child. Still, in later life she "often times thanked God and her beloved mother for the discipline to which she was subjected, which was very much to the good."

The pressure to which highly intelligent children were subjected was not always to the good, as the life of little Thomas Malkin showed. His genius was apparent at the age of eighteen months, when he learned his alphabet.[10] At two he could read and at three he could write; at four he was sending his mother dignified letters informing her of the titles on his current reading list—including a Latin grammar and a work on mental improvement—and summarizing his lessons. Geography, biology, literature and Greek all came within the boy's compass by the age of five. He balked at poetry, bursting into tears when his father urged him to try his hand, but he did undertake other imaginative writing.

There was no doubt Thomas had a remarkable intellect. He outshone his younger brother Benjamin in every arena except mathematics (Benjamin, at four years old, was good at algebra but wrote only halting Latin, and his English lacked polish), and except for a preternatural seriousness, showed almost infinite promise. But the strain was too much

·

for him. He died at the age of seven, and unkind people accused his father of killing him with overwork. The elder Malkin, being a man of reason, defended himself against these accusations by having his son's body exhumed and his head dissected; he was gratified to be able to tell his accusers that there were no signs of brain disease.

Still another precocious child was Thomas Cooper, whose story had a much happier ending than that of Thomas Malkin. Cooper, whose widowed mother struggled to support herself and her son by making boxes out of pasteboard and selling them from door to door, was left to develop his intellect on his own. "I learned to read almost without instruction," he wrote in his autobiography, "and at three years old I used to be set on a stool, in Dame Brown's school, to teach one Master Bodley, who was seven years old, his letters."[11] By the age of five Cooper was a show pupil, able to read the Bible, with all its difficult Hebrew names, "like the parson in the church," and wondrously good at spelling even the longest and most intricate words.

His future was uncertain, however, for when he was six years old his mother, deeply in debt, was finding it harder and harder to sell her boxes. With her son by her side, holding on to her apron, she took to the road one day, hoping for better luck in another district.

"We were halfway towards Lea," Cooper recalled, "when we were met by Cammidge, a master chimney-sweeper, and his two apprentices bending under huge soot bags." The master sweep tried to entice Cooper's mother to sell him into apprenticeship, and offered her two golden guineas for him. She was desperate for the money; at that moment it must have seemed that only a miracle could save her and her son from the workhouse. But after a brief hesitation she shook her head at the man and looked at her son, who remembered long afterward the tears in her eyes.

"Oh, mammy, mammy!" he remembered saying, "do not let the grimy man take me away!"

"No, my dear bairn, he shall not," she answered.

The master sweep, who was not accustomed to having his offers rejected, swore at Cooper's mother as the pair

.

walked on, shouting in his rage "that she was a fool, and he was sure to have me, sooner or later!"

They kept walking, and eventually came to Lea, where she sold her boxes and in time paid her debts and set up a thriving business. Cooper escaped the fate of John Hawley and the thousands of other climbing boys like him. But the image of the enraged master sweep and his two little drudges was to haunt him for the rest of his life.

19

"*I*nhabitants of Manchester!"
"The eyes of all England, nay, of all Europe, are fixed upon
you!" Orator Hunt's call to the citizens of Manchester announcing the forthcoming political meeting to be held at
St. Peter's Fields on August 16, 1819, made the meeting's
importance plain. "Every friend of real reform and of rational
liberty," he wrote, "is tremblingly alive to the result of your
meeting on Monday next."[1]

It was to be the climax of a summer of reform agitation.
Mass meetings and political demonstrations had been held
all over the country. Hunt and others like him had addressed
very large crowds, brought together, as always, to show their
support for parliamentary reform. "Hunt and Liberty" was
the radicals' omnibus slogan; they chanted it, they carried
it aloft on banners and scrawled it on walls and fences, along
with their ubiquitous symbol: a pike with a sharp blade

.

shaped like that of a medieval battle-ax. The pikes were everywhere, it seemed, and they worked with greater effect on the imaginations of the men and women who feared the radicals than any slogan could.

The drilling on the hillsides had gone on all summer too. Bands of reformers, many of whom had served in the militia during the war years, marched and drilled in good order by the hundreds, striding, wheeling and parading as one man to the accompaniment of fifes and drums and bugles. They practiced their marching in order to be able to turn out smartly when they arrived at the open-air meetings, they said, but those who distrusted them thought otherwise. They were planning, one police-office manifesto claimed, "to overthrow the constitution of the country, under the pretext of a radical reform of Parliament." In other words, they were plotting treason, and violent revolution.

Nothing could be further from the truth, the radicals insisted. They believed in the constitution and in the rule of law. But the constitution was being undermined by corruption, it needed reform. And if the government would not carry out this reform on its own, the people must prevail upon the government to do so, through their representatives. Birmingham reformers had elected Sir Charles Wolseley, a well-born radical, to serve as the city's "Legislatorial Attorney and Representative" in July. It was now proposed that Manchester—which, like Birmingham, had no parliamentary representation—should elect Hunt to serve in this capacity. Yet, as Hunt himself never tired of pointing out, whatever action was taken must be taken in complete peaceableness on the reformers' part. "Our enemies," he cautioned, "will seek every opportunity by the means of their sanguinary agents to excite a riot, that they may have a pretense for spilling our blood." To forestall this, the demonstrators must avoid unruliness at all costs. They must not breach the peace, or bring to the meeting any weapon other than "that of a self-approving conscience."

Hunt hoped for an orderly demonstration, yet the Manchester magistrates feared that violence might prove unavoidable. Workers were embattled, locked in conflict with

·

employers over rates of pay and working hours. Bitter strikes by weavers and spinners the previous year had left grievances and hatreds that still rankled, and for the average poor laborer, political reform was bound up with such immediate and urgent issues as the price of bread and the firm refusal of mill owners to agree to a minimum wage. Gathered in their tens of thousands, these angry men and women were bound to be a danger to order, so much dry tinder waiting for Orator Hunt—"that coarse and noisy person," as *The Times* described him—to ignite them. Determined to be prepared in case the crowd rioted, the magistrates called in a very large constabulary force backed up by between a thousand and two thousand soldiers, both infantry and cavalry, and two cannon.

When the people began to pour into the open space in front of the hustings on the morning of August 16 they knew—they must have known—that there might be a confrontation of some sort. For days there had been a rumor among them "that if the country people went with their caps of liberty, and their banners, and music, the soldiers would be brought to them." The magistrates, as if in warning of what the day would bring, posted notices urging peace-loving citizens to stay inside their houses and to keep their children and servants indoors.[2] As they made their way along the narrow streets leading to the open area the demonstrators must have seen the soldiers, or heard their horses; the Manchester Yeomanry and troops of the 15th Hussars were concealed in locations surrounding the fields but their presence could not have been kept secret, and word of it must have gone out through the crowd. In any case there was tension and excitement in the air, and the electricity of massed bodies pressing together into an area too small for them, under an exceptionally hot sun.

It was so hot, in fact, that some of the many women present began to feel sick and faint. The wife of Samuel Bamford, the Middleton weaver, was in the thick of the crowd with several of her friends, when the heat and dust and the surging bodies began to affect her. "We were surrounded by men who were strangers," she wrote, "we were almost suffocated, and to me the heat was quite sickening." She was afraid that she would faint, and asked the men around her to give way and let her out. At first they didn't move, but as she grew worse she managed to persuade some of the men to make a pathway for her.

"Make way, she's sick, she's sick, let her go out," the cry went along, and the crowd parted. Mrs. Bamford eventually got clear of the demonstrators and after pausing to recover a little she walked up a hill from which she could look down on the crowd and watch the meeting.

It was an impressive sight. At least sixty thousand people— some said eighty, some even more—were packed in around the hustings and spreading outward from it, spilling into the surrounding streets and lanes. They were dressed in plain country attire, wearing hats and carrying walking sticks. Most were men, but there were many women and some children as well; girls in white dresses, dancing and singing to the music of the bands, had preceded some contingents. Individual groups could be clearly distinguished within the larger mass: the Rochdale Union, the Lees and Saddleworth Union, the Royton Union, and so on, each group demarcated by the huge silk banners its members held aloft. "Universal Suffrage," "Annual Parliaments," "No Corn Laws," the banners spelled out the words in red and white and green. One black banner read "Equal Representation or Death." A red one, carried by the Female Reformers of Royton, was inscribed "Let us die like men, and not be sold like slaves." The Female Reformers had turned out by the hundreds, and one of their representatives shared the hustings with Orator Hunt.

Hunt had begun to address the crowd, which had settled down to await his words after singing the national anthem. He quickly warmed to his subject, his booming voice audible to many, if not all, in the sea of faces. He thundered on as he always did, energetically and vociferously, his flushed face nearly purple in the heat, his fist banging down again and again to punctuate his impassioned phrases. Liberty, representation, the people, taxes, corruption, the suffrage: the rhet-

.

oric of popular sovereignty poured out of him, and the crowd, now silent, straining to hear, now urging him on with noisy approval, followed his every word.

The magistrates, looking on from a house adjoining the field, thought it prudent to arrest Hunt and the other leaders before excitement turned into mayhem. Warrants for their arrest were given but the deputy constable who received them, Joseph Nadin, was dubious about being able to serve them. It was a logistical problem. Although there were several hundred constables lined up to form a cordon between the hustings and the crowd, Nadin thought it would be impossible to get through to where Hunt and his companions were "without force," and his constables alone lacked that force.[3] Moreover, only a few nights earlier he and his men had skirmished with a hostile mob in a street brawl, and had come away bruised and injured. They were not about to take on a vast assembly of sixty thousand and more.

There was no help for it, the Yeomanry would have to be called in.

They appeared suddenly, coming into view around the corner of a building and clattering into formation. Mrs. Bamford saw them from the window of a house she had gone into. She was alarmed, but heard others say that "the soldiers were only come to keep order, they would not meddle with the people." Another man, a newspaper reporter who stood quite near the hustings, was told by the people standing beside him that the soldiers belonged to the Manchester Yeomanry.[4] It was a bad moment; the demonstrators who, according to Nadin, had linked arms to protect Hunt must have grasped each other more tightly, tensing to resist an assault.

The horsemen of the Yeomanry tensed themselves as well on their skittish mounts. Neither men nor horses had ever been in battle, they were newly recruited and untried. The men would do their duty, but they were bound to be clumsy at it; they sweated under their hot uniforms and struggled to control their horses.

"Do not be alarmed, stand firm," Hunt shouted, "in a most emphatic manner." Taking off his white hat, he said,

.

"Let us give them three cheers." The crowd responded at once with three loud, lusty cheers—a deafening sound, and to the soldiers, most likely, a challenging one. They began to cheer back, drawing their swords and waving them around and around in the air above their heads. Women were hissing and hooting at the horsemen, some people thought they saw bricks and stones thrown at them. The horses shied, and then the bugle sounded.

"I heard the bugle sound," the reporter wrote later. "I saw the cavalry charge forward sword in hand upon the multitude, I felt on the instant, as if my heart had leaped from its seat. The woeful cry of dismay sent forth on all sides, the awful rush of so vast a living mass, the piercing shrieks of the women, the deep moanings and execrations of the men, the confusion—horrid confusion, are indescribable." He was carried forward toward danger in a wave of bodies, helpless and in fear of his life. He dove under a carriage; seconds later, he said, "the cavalry were around me, trampling down and cutting at all who could not get out of their way."[5]

Charging on toward the hustings, maddened by the dense thicket of bodies that blocked their progress, the soldiers lost sight of their purpose—which was to facilitate the arrest of Hunt and the others—and acted automatically to protect themselves. They were swordsmen; they laid about them with their swords, flat on when they could remember to, but often edge on, slicing through the obstinate unmoving bodies and hewing at the men who were waving sticks at them and throwing stones at them out of the rising dust. They struck at the women too, not that they wanted to hurt them but because, once engaged in what seemed a desperate combat, they could hardly stop themselves. Fear made them brutal, and their mindless brutality fed on itself, shutting down reason and carrying them on to further destruction. When they reached the hustings they cut down the banners that decorated it and the poles from which the banners had been suspended. Everything was torn, defaced, shattered. Nothing must stand in their way.

From where he was watching the Chief Magistrate, William Hulton, saw the charge and saw the riders swallowed up in the morass. They were being cut off, they needed help to defend themselves. "Disperse the crowd!" he told the commander of the Cheshire Yeomanry and the 15th Hussars. These troops rode in then, as if into battle, their buglers sounding the charge and the men, seeing their comrades in danger, hardening themselves to do their fearful work. These were experienced troops, expert at the cavalryman's art of fine saberwork, able to judge their strokes to within half an inch and able, under battle conditions, to control their plunging mounts.

But these were not battle conditions. There were no battle lines, only a vast open field choked with panic-stricken civilians rushing in all directions, colliding with one another and shrieking inhumanly. Many lay prostrate. The horses stumbled over them, as did the fleeing men and women. No one knew where safety lay.

"They are killing them in front!" people shouted. "They cannot get away!" "Break! break!"

Some ran in circles, or were driven by one oncoming rush of cavalry into the path of another. Some crouched where they were, dazed and breathless, until the horsemen ran over them and trampled them. The wounded staggered to safety when they could. Mrs. Bamford saw "a man pass without a hat, and wiping the blood off his head with his hand, and it ran down his arm in a great stream." A little while later a number of men came into the house where she had taken shelter, "carrying the body of a decent, middle-aged woman, who had been killed." Her faintness returned as the screaming and shouting grew louder; she could not bear to hear the dreadful cries, or to watch "all the dreadful work" through the window. The tears were streaming down her cheeks, and indeed everyone in the house with her was crying, so piteous was the slaughter.

It was all over very quickly. In scarcely a quarter of an hour the cavalry were regrouping and the men were attending to their horses, easing their girths and adjusting their accouterments. The sun beat down on the open field, littered with hundreds of wounded. Here and there knots of consta-

.

bles were gathered in conversation, while from neighboring houses men came out to gather in those who had been injured. The hustings with its drooping banners and broken flagstaves was deserted and ignored. Torn and bloody clothing was everywhere—shoes, hats, women's bonnets and shawls.

"Several mounds of human beings still remained where they had fallen, crushed down and smothered," recalled Samuel Bamford, whose account of the bloody affray at St. Peter's Fields was suffused with his resentment toward the military and civil authorities and his intense compassion for those who suffered. "Some of these still groaning—others with staring eyes, were gasping for breath, and others would never breathe more. All was silent save those low sounds, and the occasional snorting and pawing of steeds." It was a "hideous and abhorrent" sight, a violation of all that was peaceable in England. The wounding and trampling of women and children were to Bamford beyond explanation. It was a massacre, as pitiless as the routing of an enemy army. It was Waterloo fought all over again.

Within days of the event people were referring to "Peterloo," and lamenting the "Peterloo Massacre." A poem in the radical *Manchester Observer* expressed the sentiments of most of the English:

> Sad sixteenth of August! accursed be the day;
> When thy field, oh, St. Peter! was crimson'd with gore;
> When blue-mantled bullies, in hostile array,
> Struck down to the earth the defenceless and poor.
>
> Yes, yes! It was valour to gash the unarmed,
> To bear down the aged—the cripple—the child;
> It was manly to vanquish the female, alarmed,
> To mangle her bosom was gentle and mild.[6]

Printshops sold graphic representations of the event, panoramic scenes with bloodthirsty horsemen pursuing their terrified victims in a melodramatic caricature of the real tragedy. People rushed to buy a published report of the massacre, advertised as containing "a full, true, and faithful account of the inhuman murders, woundings, and other monstrous cruelties exercised by infernals (miscalled soldiers) upon an unarmed and distressed people . . . when they were broken in upon by bands of armed ruffians, who murdered many, and cut and maimed hundreds more in a horrid manner."

At least eleven people died on August 16, and well over four hundred—some estimates say six hundred—were injured.[7] No doubt a good many of the injured died soon afterward, in an era when wounds frequently became fatally infected. Yet the loss of life, whether one considered it great or small, was only one aspect of the appalling incident at Manchester. The rights of Englishmen had been ruthlessly violated, and under circumstances which even the chief legal authority in the land thought to be ambiguous. The Lord Chancellor, Lord Eldon, confessed that the matter seemed murky to him. "Can any man doubt," he wrote, "that these meetings are overt acts of conspirators, to instigate to such specific acts of treason or some of them? I can't doubt it." Yet conspirators or not, they had the right to assemble— even when their assembly was declared unlawful. "An unlawful assembly, as such merely, I apprehend can't be dispersed; and what constitutes riot enough to justify dispersion is no easy matter to determine where there is not actual violence begun on the part of those assembled."[8]

There had been no "actual violence" on the part of the Manchester demonstrators—or so most people thought. "The bloodhounds of Manchester" had moved in to do their killing work with no justification. The slain of Peterloo had suffered and died needlessly.

"Ah! Ah! For shame! For shame!" someone remembered the demonstrators shouting to the soldiers as they were ridden down. In the aftermath of Peterloo, most of England echoed their cry.

20

*T*he Peterloo disaster was still fresh in memory when the Regent came to London to open Parliament late in November of 1819. Prints and written accounts of the event were still for sale, Hunt and his colleagues were awaiting trial, and the government, which had had to withstand high minority votes on a number of important bills in the previous session, expected more sound and fury to come. The Prime Minister, Lord Liverpool, remarked that the Commons was pervaded by an "evil temper and disposition." Others referred to an "abominable revolutionary spirit" that infected people's judgment and threatened to make them even more ungovernable than usual.[1]

The Whigs had gained in the last elections, held in the previous year, and the independent Members of the Commons were proving to be intractable. Though the addition of Wellington to the cabinet had strengthened its appeal,

·

the heavy-handed attitude of most of the ministers when it came to suppressing unrest, coupled with their unresponsiveness to the widespread hunger and joblessness and real distress among working people, made Liverpool's Tory government highly unpopular.

The Regent was, if anything, even more unpopular. When it became known that he had written a letter commending the decision of the Manchester officials forcibly to disperse the crowd in St. Peter's Fields, and that he had applauded the "forbearance" of the military the public outcry was loud and prolonged. He was hissed and booed, his elegant yellow carriage was dirtied and dented when people pelted it with stones and eggs. He endured these insults with his own long-suffering forbearance, consoling himself afterward during long evenings of intoxication. His gout had kept him in a purgatory of agony for much of the past year, forcing his attention away from public affairs and making him thankful for days when the pain lessened enough for him to attempt to ride.[2] As for his unpopularity, he had long since resigned himself to being misunderstood and despised by the majority of his subjects, and though he felt injured by their hostility, he rarely showed it, at least in public.

His natural dignity was intact now as he rode to open Parliament, wearing a military cocked hat and looking out with affable princeliness at the immense crowd that had gathered in Green Park to watch the procession.[3] The crowd was surly; missiles flew past the windows of the coach and there was a chorus of catcalls and insults. A great deal of "tumult and disorder" was expected, as London crowds had been turning riotous of late, but the Regent arrived safely at his destination and went in to join the Lords and to await the arrival of the Commons.

He stood calmly, nodding and smiling to friends, with Wellington at his side. He whispered to the duke, under his breath, that his carriage had been struck repeatedly and that the people had insulted him, but Wellington, who privately thought him repugnant, was unsympathetic. (He told friends later that he didn't believe a word the Regent said to him.) With Wellington carrying his sword and another

.

of the Lords his crown, he took his place and delivered his address, "performing," one observer thought, "remarkably well." His voice was distinct and carried well, and he read his speech with more force and energy than many expected.[4]

His strong performance did him credit, for the medical bulletins from Windsor were making him very nervous. His father the king had suffered a relapse. He was "much affected and chilled," the doctors said, his bowels were working erratically. There was "cause of alarm," as Frederick, Duke of York and the king's official custodian, confided to his brother. Anything, even a chill, might kill the feeble old man now, the duke said. He was eighty-one. He had lost many of his teeth, and those that remained were in such a state that he could hardly chew his meat, and had to be content with soft foods and a little wine. "His Majesty," Frederick wrote, "is greatly emaciated within the last twelve months and though his general health bears no appearance as yet of decay yet the frame is so much weaker that we can no longer look forward with any confidence to his being preserved to us for any length of time."[5] In short, the king was dying, and any relapse might be fatal.

The Regent would soon be king. It was in the air; in any number of ways, the country was gearing up for it.

The Regent himself gave warning that his kingship was imminent by submitting to Lord Liverpool a plan for the enlargement of Buckingham House to serve as his royal palace. The "necessities of the crown" demanded a fitting residence, he pointed out. "The sovereign and representative is left without a becoming residence for the conduct of the affairs of the state or the ceremonials connected with it." Carlton House, gorgeous as it was, was hardly palatial, but Buckingham House could be made suitable, provided enough was spent on it. To spend hundreds of thousands of pounds on a royal residence was far from being politically expedient, and the Regent knew it. Not only was there the stark contrast between his lavish expenditure and his people's penury to contend with, but beyond this, he had already spent a fortune—indeed, the equivalent of many fortunes—on his Ma-

.

rine Pavilion, and the more money he spent, the more ridicule the unique monument received.

"The Pavilion at Brighton," wrote William Hazlitt, "is like a collection of stone pumpkins and pepper-boxes. It seems as if the genius of architecture had at once the dropsy and the megrims. Anything more fantastical, with a greater dearth of invention, was never seen." Cobbett remarked that the Pavilion looked like a box with five turnips sitting on top of it, while Walter Scott said simply that if the structure were to go up in flames, "it will rid me of a great eyesore."[6]

The renovation of Buckingham House would have to wait, but another and much more delicate matter associated with the new king's imminent accession could not be forestalled so easily. Princess Caroline, though out of his sight for five years and more, was rarely out of her husband's mind. He wanted to divorce her, but the cabinet advised him not to. A formal separation, ratified by an act of Parliament, would be the best solution to an all but insoluble problem, they said. Yet the Regent had been toying with the idea of marrying again, and was considering several eligible princesses, among them an Esterhazy and the daughter of Victor Emmanuel, King of Sardinia. Caroline, besides being an annoyance and an ever-present threat to his peace of mind, stood in the way of his remarriage.

Earlier in 1819 a compromise had seemed possible, for Caroline, who claimed that all she wanted was "to pass the remainder of her life quietly," had then been willing to give up her right to be queen and to agree to a formal separation in return for a lifetime annuity. But her husband had refused to agree to this, and now, in November, Caroline had apparently abandoned her compromising attitude and was on her way to England. She had come as far as Marseilles, and was waiting for her Whig advisers to tell her when to cross the Channel. Meanwhile her presence in France, and her probable return to London once her father-in-law died, if not before, were the talk of Paris.[7]

When Parliament adjourned at the end of December the government had gained its principal objectives. New laws were on the books providing, from the ministers' point of view, safeguards against further havoc from the radicals. They prohibited the sort of drilling that had gone on in Manchester in the weeks leading up to Peterloo, they allowed town magistrates to seize arms, they greatly restricted the right of citizens to hold public meetings and they taxed newspapers and granted wide latitude in the punishment of libel— in effect, gagging the press. Beyond this, the army was strengthened by the addition of ten thousand troops. If, as seemed likely, there was soon to be a change of reigns, with all the confusion and discontent that might entail, the authorities would be ready.

The winter was exceptionally cold. The horses slipped on the icy streets, and there was frost on the iron railings in front of the great houses. Men wrapped their scarves more tightly around their high collars and bent their heads against the wind; women abandoned their fashionable pelisses in favor of warm wool cloaks and fur muffs. The chill gusts blew over carriages and wrecked the stalls of street vendors, and along the coaching roads the rain churned deep pits in the pockmarked highways.

At Windsor, the cold wind off the North Terrace blew along the staircase and into the king's bleak apartments. Screens were put up to block out at least some of the drafts, and the royal doctors ordered that the king's vests be lined with flannel to warm his emaciated chest. But the rooms and passages remained icy, and the blind old patient was seen to shiver and to draw his violet dressing gown tightly around him as he stumbled from bedroom to sitting room and back again. No one suggested moving him to warmer quarters, even though Windsor was notorious for being, in the late queen's words, "the coldest house, rooms and passages that ever existed." He was at home there after all, amid his few familiar pieces of furniture and the antique harpsichord that had belonged to Queen Anne. He often sat at the instrument, his thin white hands stretched out over the keys groping for his favorite Handel melodies, his singing voice still as strong and firm as the rest of him was frail.[8]

He was still, in his shadowy way, king and father to a

.

people who had outgrown him. His hoary presence haunted the ministerial chambers and haunted, too, the luxurious salons of aristocrats whose great-grandfathers, had they been alive, would have remembered him as monarch. Shut away from the world as he was, and had been for nearly a decade, he continued to provide a measure of security. He, and not his wastrel son, still held the title of king. It was as if he bore in his skeletal body the restraining spirit of the old century, with its slower pace and smaller human compass. When he died, the last ties to that older, safer world would be broken. People had begun to look back toward a past that was just out of reach, to speak of a time, a generation earlier, "when England was itself," before what they called "the rancor and venom of the present days." The elderly king was a relic of that past which, as it receded, took on a verdant, sunlit glow.

In late December the king suffered another relapse, and by the last week of January, despite the agitated assurances of his physicians that he might live for another several months, those closest to him knew that he was very near death. Unaware as he was of anything or anyone around him he was spared the shock of his fourth son's death. Edward, Duke of Kent, who only six months earlier had ensured the continuity of the dynasty into another generation with the birth of his daughter Victoria, caught cold and died on January 23 after the briefest of illnesses. The duke had been robust and exceptionally healthy, and his sudden demise startled his brothers. The Regent, who had been unwell for several weeks, got worse, and because of his own indisposition, was not at his father's bedside in his last days.

On the evening of January 29 Frederick was in attendance in the small bedroom at Windsor, along with the doctors and several servants. The king was lying limp on his narrow bed, his long white hair spread out on the bolster. For the past week he had been living on nothing but milk, and his life was ebbing rapidly. Suddenly he raised his arms, asking to be lifted up. The doctors were reluctant to allow this, but he seemed insistent. When he was raised up a little he thanked his attendants, and then asked that they wet his

·

271

parched lips with a sponge.⁹ The duke heard him say, "with perfect presence of mind," "Do not wet my lips but when I open my mouth," adding later, "I thank you, it does me good."

They were his last words, and his son swore that in that final quarter of an hour he showed a flicker of lucidity. Soon afterward he appeared to fall asleep. When the doctors listened for his breath, they knew that he was gone.

When word reached the Regent that his father was dead at last he was, as always in times of crisis, beside himself with nervous distress. He got out of his sickbed to read the bulletin from Windsor, then collapsed back into bed, calling for brandy and for his doctor, as his heart began to pound wildly and his breath to come in anxious gasps. His father, "the poor dear king," as he called him, was dead. His old enemy, arch-censor of his youthful pleasures, was gone. He wept, gulping his brandy and holding his hand to his chest. Some time later, having recovered enough to hold a pen, he wrote his brother a brief letter of condolence.

He managed to get through the next day, gathering his brothers and sisters around him in his bedroom at Carlton House—now called Carlton Palace—to support him through his first official duties as king. The ministers and Privy Councillors met to sign the proclamation declaring him King George IV. Then he swore them in to their offices and mustered up enough strength to make a short speech. The following day the ceremonial proclamation took place, with the marching of the guardsmen, the firing of guns and the endless massing of crowds whose huzzas and cheers created a terrible din. Ill or not, the new king insisted that his palace be thrown open to the people, and the gates were opened to permit "every person of respectable exterior" to enter and write his or her name in a book in the grand hall.¹⁰ A few persons, it was noted, took "improper advantage" of their sovereign's hospitality, but only a few.

But after two days of unprecedented "hurry and agitation," he could stand no more. He fell seriously ill with pleurisy.

For the next several days, as his brothers and sisters hovered around him and his ministers conferred throughout sleepless nights, the king's health deteriorated so rapidly that his doctors believed he was dying. They bled him, taking 130 ounces of blood, after which he was "much worse, alarmingly worse."[11] They bled him again. He was "in imminent danger," and people speculated that there might be a triple royal funeral soon, for the old king, the new king and his brother Edward, whose body lay in state, all but forgotten in the larger scheme of things.

By some miracle—and he had performed such miracles before—the king's enervated, much-abused constitution rallied, and by February 5 he was noticeably better. Rumors of his death were stilled. He had no sooner begun to show signs of improvement, however, when fresh anxieties plagued him.

"Long live the queen! Protect the queen!" the people cried when the king was proclaimed. They had no more forgotten Caroline than her husband had, and now that he was on the throne they wanted her to be beside him. The king's Whig enemies lost no time in stirring up this public feeling on Caroline's behalf by alluding to the "curious and delicate emergency" of her status and printing two letters she had written late in December.

"During the five years of my long absence from my dear old England," Caroline wrote, "I can assure you it has been the first real happy moment I felt, having received such satisfactory information respecting the feelings of the people of England towards me." Her advisers had assured her that whatever the attitude of her husband and his ministers, the hearts of her subjects were with her, and for this she was grateful. "My traducers and enemies in England have again held secret inquisition in Milan, through the means of spies and many old servants," she said, yet she continued to trust "in the generosity of the great nation to protect me from the hands of my enemies."[12]

Her forthright letter was calculated to exacerbate a dilemma that was already doing grave political damage. The findings of the Milan Commission, which the king believed to be utterly damning in proving Caroline's treasonous adul-

·

tery, were judged by his ministers to be inconclusive. When he demanded that they support him in his desire for a divorce, they balked, and the impasse provoked a crisis.

It made no difference to the king that his advisers were both shrewd and reasonable in their assessment of the situation. They urged him to accept a formal separation, with a provision allowing Caroline an income so long as she remained abroad, but stating clearly that if she returned to England, her allowance would be cut off. Parliament meanwhile was drawing up new measures to provide for her financial support, as her old income as Princess of Wales ceased with George III's death. It was urgent that some agreement be reached soon, yet the king would not listen to reason. No one could persuade him that a divorce would offer his wife (and his political enemies) the opportunity to bring out in open court every embarrassing detail of his own immoral past, surrounding a great many prominent people with scandal; no one could tell him, for he refused to listen, that the publicity of a trial would do untold damage to his esteem as king and to his realm. He was obsessed with ridding himself of Caroline, and in his weakened state his obsession "took a wonderful hold of his mind."[13]

The first Sunday of the new reign was at hand, and the king suddenly realized on Saturday night that because of his illness no thought had been given to changing the liturgy that would be read throughout the kingdom the following morning. He was frantic. Unless he did something to stop them, his subjects would pray next day "for their most excellent majesties, the king and queen." Invoking the blessings of the Deity on a creature too horrid to deserve the name of wife seemed to him a fearful enormity. "He immediately ordered up all the prayerbooks in the house of old and new dates, and spent the evening in very serious agitation on this subject."[14] He found no way around the enormity that night, but before another Sunday passed an order went out that the queen was not to be prayed for by name.

But this did nothing to alleviate the larger question, and the longer the ministers held to their opinion, the more angry and frustrated the king became. "He is furious," one official wrote, "and says they have deceived him; that they led him on to hope that they would concur in the measure, and that now they leave him in the lurch."[15] "The cabinet offer all but a divorce; the king will have a divorce or nothing." Politicking went on behind the scenes, the king wanted new ministers who would do his bidding. He was unhappy over other things besides the queen: the ministers' proposals with regard to the Civil List were completely inadequate. He needed much more income than they thought he did. There were his renovations at Buckingham House, the upkeep and refurbishing of his other residences, his superb art collection (which, to protect it from possible attack by a hostile mob, he had recently insured), his wardrobe and his stables and his household. There was his future coronation to think of, and the rich new crown covered in diamonds he was discussing with his jewelers, which would cost upwards of a hundred thousand pounds.[16]

In his frustration and anxiety the king again jeopardized his health. His usually huge appetite dwindled, until he was living on dry toast washed down with a little claret and water. His agitation was "extreme and alarming," and he displayed a regal stubbornness that made his advisers despair.

The first weeks of the new reign passed and Londoners, wearing crape-draped hats and black cockades, wondered how long the mourning would continue. They scanned the newspapers, looking for more letters from the queen and for announcements about the king's illness and the disposition of his father's corpse. There were eulogies of George III, and anecdotes of his life, and reports—which most people read with skepticism—about the "weeping fondness" his subjects felt for him. There were a good many jibes in the obituaries. "He had the elements of some excellent things in him; but they seemed twisted and cut short." "His tastes and habits were those of private life, and had he not had the misfortune of being a king, he would have made a very respectable country gentleman, a little obstinate or so in parish matters, but upon the whole good-natured and useful."[17] The theaters and other places of amusement were closed, and were to remain so until after the funeral. There was little to do but

·

gossip, and speculate about the coronation, and wait for the great public ritual of the king's funeral to be over.

People began to pour into Windsor several days in advance of the solemnities, which were to be held February 16. The town was crowded and so were the outlying towns of Staines, Egham and Slough.[18] There was not enough accommodation, either for the people or their horses; many people ate and slept and waited in their carriages, while the horses were turned out into the fields to graze.

On the morning of the funeral day the castle gates were opened and the crowd rushed in, hoping to secure good vantage points from which to watch the procession into St. George's Chapel. The day was chilly and foggy, and by evening, when the first of the cavalry of the honor guard came into view, the temperature had dropped and people shivered and huddled together, their legs stiff from staying in one spot all day. The Life Guards and the Oxford Blues stretched themselves out into two lines extending from the castle entrance to the lower court and on up the High Street. The entire lower court was filled with people, packed in so tightly that some of the horsemen swung women and children up onto their saddles to make more room.

At eight o'clock the 3rd Regiment of Guards took up positions along the procession route, carrying flambeaux whose fitful light threw into relief the towers and crenellated battlements of the medieval castle. The guns had been firing most of the day, at five-minute intervals, and the bells in the castle belfry had not ceased to ring since morning. They ceased now, as from the state apartments came the sound of music, the "Dead March" from Handel's oratorio *Saul*, "reverberating as from a distance through the castle walls." Shortly afterward trumpeters standing in the park below the walls took up the same dirgelike melody, which echoed eerily through the night mist.

A little after nine o'clock the first members of the procession appeared, knights and pages marching to the beat of kettle drums, then following these a hundred or more members of the royal household, then the justices, the peers, and churchmen in order, and behind them the royal crown of

.

Hanover and the imperial crown of the United Kingdom carried on velvet cushions. The coffin, covered with a sheet of fine cloth and a purple velvet pall, and under a purple velvet canopy, came next, carried by ten Yeomen of the Guard supported by sixteen peers. Behind the coffin walked Prince Frederick, his features marked, some thought, by "deep and unaffected sorrow," the train of his long black cloak borne by two peers. His brothers followed him, and behind them came councillors and the late king's personal attendants and equerries. Last of all marched the Gentlemen Pensioners with their axes carried backward as a mark of respect to the dead.

"As the procession moved round the edge of the castle walks, the dismal and monotonous sounds of trumpets from the park below had a very solemn effect," wrote one who attended the funeral, and the rich singing of the choir inside the chapel, the "seriousness and suffering" of the mourners and the hush that passed through the crowd as the coffin passed by, with each man taking off his hat and bowing his head, left a deep impression on all who witnessed it.

One mourner was missing. George IV was ill again, his ongoing quarrel with his ministers having weakened his health. His physicians urged him not to expose himself to the damp night air of Windsor, and he consented. Another mourner too was missing, but she had plans to pay her respects to the late king in person before long. A swift courier had brought Caroline word that she was now Queen of England, and she had made up her mind to come home as soon as she could and claim her throne.

·

Afterword

Caroline did come home, in June of 1820, but did not succeed in claiming her throne. At her husband's insistence a Bill of Pains and Penalties was introduced in the House of Lords accusing her of adultery and denying her the title of queen and the status of the king's wife. Had the bill passed, Caroline would in effect have become a divorced woman—though without a formal trial. But it did not pass. Instead, after more than three months of speechifying in the Lords, gossip-mongering in drawing rooms and uproar in the London streets, the bill was abandoned for lack of sufficient support.

George IV was crowned in July of the following year, in a magnificent ceremony to which his wife was denied admission. Ill and worn down by the strain of her long and ultimately futile struggle for recognition, Caroline died some three weeks later after suffering excruciating abdominal pains and overdosing herself with too much opium and castor oil. The king was free at last, yet he did not remarry, and so when he died in 1830 the throne passed to his oldest surviving brother William, who became King William IV.

Notes

Chapter 1

1. Stanley Ayling, *George the Third* (London, 1972), 181.
2. *Morning Post*, October 23, 1810.
3. Richard G. Glover, *Britain at Bay: Defence Against Bonaparte 1803–1814* (London, 1973), 38, thinks the Duke of York has been underrated as a general. For details of the inquiry into his alleged corruption, see Joseph Farington, *The Farington Diary*, ed. James Greig, 8 vols. (London, 1922–1928), V, 110, 112–14, 122–23, 126–29 and *passim*.
4. *Autobiography of Miss Cornelia Knight, Lady Companion to the Princess Charlotte of Wales*, 2nd ed., 2 vols. (London, 1861), I, 173.
5. *The Later Correspondence of George III*, ed. Arthur Aspinall, 5 vols. (Cambridge, 1962–70), V, 639.
6. King George was in fact suffering from porphyria, though both the term and the disease were unknown to medicine in his time. Among its symptoms are severe abdominal pain, uncontrolled loquacity and an appearance of madness. See I. Macal-

.

pine and R. Hunter, *George III and the Mad-Business* (London, 1969) and Ayling, *op. cit.*, 329–45 and *passim*. According to Macalpine and Hunter, whose findings are generally accepted, three of George III's children—George, Prince of Wales, Frederick and Augustus—inherited the disease in a milder form. They conjecture that Prince Edward almost certainly was afflicted and possibly Princess Sophia as well.

7. Knight, *Autobiography*, I, 174ff.
8. Ayling, *op. cit.*, 222.
9. *Later Correspondence of George III*, V, 639 note.

Chapter 2

1. *An American in Regency England*, ed. Christopher Hibbert (London, 1968).
2. *The Letters of Private Wheeler, 1809–1828*, ed. B. H. Liddell Hart (London, 1951), 35.

Chapter 3

1. *Later Correspondence of George III*, V, 639 note.
2. *Diary and Letters of Madame D'Arblay, 1778–1840*, ed. Charlotte Barrett, 7 vols. (London, 1843–46), VI, 333–34.
3. *Farington Diary*, V, 287.
4. *Lord Granville Leveson Gower, Private Correspondence, 1781–1821*, ed. Castalia, Countess Granville, 2 vols. (London, 1916), II, 349–50.
5. *Correspondence of George, Prince of Wales, 1770–1812*, ed. Arthur Aspinall, 8 vols. (London and New York, 1963–71), IV, 55.
6. *Ibid.*, IV, 61–62.
7. *The Bath Archives: A Further Selection from the Diaries and Letters of Sir George Jackson, K.C.M., from 1809 to 1816*, ed. Lady Jackson, 2 vols. (London, 1873), I, 227.
8. *Farington Diary*, VII, 22.
9. *Bath Archives*, I, 216–17.
10. *Ibid.*, I, 248.

Chapter 4

1. *Bath Archives*, I, 247–73 describes the Regent's ball and the excitement leading up to it.

2. *Ibid.*, I, 268
3. Simond, 149; *Bath Archives*, I, 270–71.
4. Simond, 148–49.
5. *Farington Diary*, VII, 8–9.
6. Lewis Melville, *Brighton: Its History, Its Follies and Its Fashions* (London, 1909), 80.
7. *Morning Herald*, August 21, 1788.
8. Melville, *Brighton*, 109.

Chapter 5

1. F. O. Darvall, *Popular Disturbances and Public Order in Regency England* (Oxford, 1934), gives the most detailed and straightforward exposition of the Luddite phenomenon. E. P. Thompson, *The Making of the English Working Class*, 2nd ed. (London, 1968), makes a case for the political dimension of Luddism and undermines some of Darvall's arguments as well as those of J. L. and Barbara Hammond in their classic study *The Town Labourer* (New York, 1932).
2. Quoted in Peter Quennell, *Byron, The Years of Fame* (London, 1935), 65.
3. *Byron's Letters and Journals*, ed. Leslie A. Marchand, 12 vols. (Boston and London, 1973–82), II, 167.
4. Thompson, 582.
5. Malcolm I. Thomis, *The Luddites: Machine Breaking in Regency England* (Newton Abbot, 1970), 118.
6. Thompson, 714.
7. *Granville Leveson Gower Private Correspondence*, II, 415–16.
8. *Ibid.*, II, 426.
9. *Ibid.*, II, 429.
10. *Bath Archives*, I, 373–75.
11. *Letters of Samuel Taylor Coleridge*, ed. Ernest Hartley Coleridge, 2 vols. (Boston and New York, 1895), II, 597–98.

Chapter 6

1. *Childe Harold's Pilgrimage*, Canto I, 1. 46–54.
2. *The Journal of Thomas Moore, 1818–1841*, ed. Peter Quennell, rev. ed. (New York, 1964), xiii.
3. Leslie Marchand, *Byron: A Biography*, 2 vols. (New York, 1957), I, 291.

4. *Byron's Letters and Journals*, I, 234; II, 163.
5. Simond, 14–15.
6. Elizabeth Jenkins, *Lady Caroline Lamb* (London, 1932), 113.
7. Quennell, 69.
8. Marchand, I, 333.
9. Quennell, 127; Marchand, I, 333.
10. *Lady Bessborough and Her Family Circle*, ed. The Earl of Bessborough (London, 1940), 206.
11. *Byron's Letters and Journals*, II, 170–71.
12. Quennell, 237–38.
13. *Byron's Letters and Journals*, II, 177.
14. Quennell, 149.
15. *Don Juan*, Canto I, 1. 175–76.
16. *Byron's Letters and Journals*, II, 244.
17. *Ibid.*, II, 198.
18. *Ibid.*, II, 218.

Chapter 7

1. Hannah More, *Practical Piety*, in *The Christian Library*, Vol. I (London, 1835), 55.
2. *Letters of Hannah More*, ed. R. Brimley Johnson (London, 1925), 163–73 describe the Evangelical activities at Cheddar.
3. *Granville Leveson Gower Private Correspondence*, I, 214–15.
4. *Letters of Hannah More*, 178.
5. *Ibid.*
6. *Ibid.*, 175–79, 191 and *passim*.
7. William Wilberforce, *Practical View of the Religious System of Professed Christians Contrasted with Real Christianity*, quoted in F. K. Brown, *Fathers of the Victorians* (Cambridge, 1961), 120.
8. Muriel Jaeger, *Before Victoria* (London, 1956), 109.
9. More, *Practical Christianity*, 53–54.
10. *Granville Leveson Gower Private Correspondence*, I, 60.

Chapter 8

1. *Bath Archives*, II, 146–47.
2. This account of events in London in the first week of July, 1813 is drawn in part from the *Morning Chronicle* and *Manchester Gazette*.

3. *The Diary of Frances, Lady Shelley*, ed. Richard Edgcumbe, 2 vols. (New York, 1912–13), I, 48.
4. *Farington Diary*, VII, 158, 200, 181.
5. *Ibid.*, VII, 153.
6. *The Life of Thomas Cooper, Written by Himself*, 2nd ed. (London, 1872), 1.
7. The poem was printed in the *Manchester Gazette* in the first week of July, 1813, attributed to "some seditious Anti-Warrite." The second and seventh words of the second line were patriotically omitted, but my conjectures are probably those that would have occurred to contemporary readers.
8. *Byron's Letters and Journals*, II, 81; *The Letters of Sir Walter Scott*, ed. H.J.C. Grierson, 12 vols. (London, 1932–37), II, 406; *Morning Chronicle*, first week of July, 1813; *Bath Archives*, I, 280–81.
9. *The Letters of King George IV*, ed. Arthur Aspinall, 3 vols. (Cambridge, 1938), I, 299–300.
10. *Ibid.*, I, 270.
11. *Scott Letters*, III, 241.
12. Sophia Edgcumbe, Countess Brownlow, *Eve of Victorianism; Reminiscences of the Years 1802 to 1834* (London, 1940), 12–13.
13. *Farington Diary*, VII, 89.
14. *Bath Archives*, II, 409.
15. *Farington Diary*, VII, 161.
16. *Letters of George IV*, I, 407.

Chapter 9

1. The service is described in *Farington Diary*, VII, 264.
2. *Brownlow Memoirs*, 56.
3. Harold Nicolson, *The Congress of Vienna: A Study in Allied Unity, 1812–1822* (New York, 1946), 108.
4. *Shelley Diary*, I, 55.
5. *Ibid.*, I, 59.
6. *Ibid.*, I, 59–60.
7. *Ibid.*, I, 60, 62.
8. *Farington Diary*, VII, 26.
9. *Ibid.*, VII, 33.
10. *Ibid.*
11. *Ibid.*, VII, 203.

Notes

Chapter 10

1. Cited in Brown, 1.
2. John W. Osborne, *The Silent Revolution: The Industrial Revolution in England as a Source of Cultural Change* (New York, 1970), 45.
3. *Farington Diary,* VII, 262–63.
4. *Granville Leveson Gower Private Correspondence,* II, 419.
5. *Scott Letters,* III, 61–62.

Chapter 11

1. *Farington Diary,* VII, 170.
2. *The Croker Papers, The Correspondence and Diaries of the late Right Honourable John Wilson Croker,* ed. Louis J. Jennings, 2 vols. (New York, 1884), I, 51.
3. *Farington Diary,* VII, 283; *The Reminiscences and Recollections of Captain Gronow* (London, 1964), 76.
4. *Gronow Memoirs,* 79, 81.
5. *Ibid.,* 101.
6. *Ibid.,* 108.
7. M. Dorothy George, *Hogarth to Cruikshank: Social Change in Graphic Satire* (London, 1967), 211.
8. *Letters of Hannah More,* 190.
9. *Granville Leveson Gower Private Correspondence,* II, 387.
10. *Ibid.,* II, 386.

Chapter 12

1. This account of the March 1815 riots is taken in part from the *Morning Chronicle,* March 7–10.
2. Arthur Bryant, *The Great Duke* (London, 1971), 19.
3. Elizabeth Longford, *Wellington: The Years of the Sword* (London, 1969), 206–07.
4. *Letters of George IV,* II, 43–44.
5. Christopher Hibbert, *George IV,* 2 vols. (London, 1972–73), II, 79.

Chapter 13

1. In addition to the accounts of contemporaries, this chapter is based in part on John Keegan's admirable account of Waterloo in *The Face of Battle* (New York, 1976), 117ff.

2. *Correspondence of Charlotte Grenville, Lady Williams Wynn,* ed. Rachel Leighton (London, 1920), 191–92.
3. *Lady Bessborough and Her Family Circle,* 242–43.
4. *Scott Letters,* IV, 78–83.

Chapter 14

1. *The Times,* May 1–6, chronicles the wedding and events leading up to it.
2. *Letters of George IV,* II, 632.
3. Hannah More, *Strictures on the Modern System of Female Education* (London, 1799), I, 142–43.
4. *Granville Leveson Gower Private Correspondence,* II, 381.
5. I Cor. 14:34; I Tim. 2:9–15.
6. Marchand, I, 411.
7. *Byron's Letters and Journals,* IV, 231.
8. *Scott Letters,* III, 2–3; *Byron's Letters and Journals,* II, 132.

Chapter 15

1. *Black Dwarf,* March 19, 1817.
2. This account of the execution of John Cashman is drawn from the *Courier,* March 12, 1817, reprinted in the *Weekly Political Register,* March 15, 1817, cols. 334–45.
3. Samuel Bamford, *Passages in the Life of a Radical and Early Days,* ed. Henry Dunckley (London, 1905), 25–26.
4. Cobbett himself claimed a circulation of forty-four thousand for the November 30, 1816 edition of the *Register.*
5. Quoted in R. J. White, *Life in Regency England* (London and New York, 1963), 95.
6. Bamford, 19.
7. *Morning Chronicle,* March 17, 1817.

Chapter 16

1. *Farington Diary,* VIII, 170.
2. *Granville Leveson Gower Private Correspondence,* II, 535.
3. *Grenville Letters,* 193.
4. *Letters of George IV,* II, 223.
5. *Farington Diary,* VII, 190–91.
6. *Ibid.*

7. John E. Jordan, *DeQuincey to Wordsworth: A Biography of a Relationship* (Berkeley and Los Angeles, 1962), 252.
8. *Letters of Hannah More,* 202–3.
9. Quoted in Brown, 60.

Chapter 17

1. *Byron's Letters and Journals,* V, 162.
2. *Ibid.,* V, 155.
3. *Ibid.,* V, 186.
4. *Ibid.,* V, 165.
5. *Thomas Moore Journal,* 25.
6. *Ibid.,* 18–19.
7. *Shelley Diary,* II, 33.
8. Cited in *Gronow Memoirs,* 14.
9. *Bath Archives,* I, 244–45.
10. *Ibid.,* I, 344, 350 and *passim.*
11. Thompson, 488, cites instances documented in the *Black Dwarf* and *Duckett's Dispatch.*
12. *Scott Letters,* III, 263 note.
13. *Farington Diary,* VIII, 93.
14. *Shelley Diary,* II, 12.
15. *Farington Diary,* I, 233 note.
16. Quoted in George, *Hogarth to Cruikshank,* 164.
17. Lewis S. Benjamin, *Beau Brummell: His Life and Letters* (London, 1924), 52–54.
18. *Gronow Memoirs,* 198.
19. *Ibid.,* 127.
20. George, *Hogarth to Cruikshank,* 164.
21. *Ibid.,* 163.
22. *Grenville Letters,* 221.

Chapter 18

1. Testimony given at the inquest is printed in *The Times,* May 10, 1816.
2. Hammond, II, 13.
3. *Ibid.,* 18–19.
4. George, 232–33.
5. *Ibid.,* 395.
6. *Ibid.*
7. Brown, 23–25 discusses prostitution in Regency England in some detail.

8. *Letters of Hannah More*, 14.
9. *The Life and Times of Mrs. Sherwood 1775–1851*, ed. F. J. Harvey Darton (London, 1910), 34–35.
10. Thomas Malkin's story is told in Jaeger, 114–15.
11. *Life of Thomas Cooper*, 5, 7, 9–10.

Chapter 19

1. Hunt's announcement is printed in Robert Walmsley, *Peterloo: The Case Reopened* (Manchester, 1969), 115.
2. Bamford, 166; Walmsley, 24.
3. Walmsley, 176.
4. Walmsley, 182–83 gives this reporter's account of the events of August 16.
5. *Ibid.*, 183.
6. *Manchester Observer*, September 18, 1819.
7. For estimates of the dead and wounded see Walmsley, 30 and Asa Briggs, *The Age of Improvement*, rev. ed. (London, 1979), 210.
8. Walmsley, 247.

Chapter 20

1. *Letters of George IV*, II, 301, 290.
2. *Ibid.*, II, 291. Though the Regent's biographers have assumed that he could not ride in the later years of the Regency, there are intermittent references to his doing so, admittedly with increasing difficulty.
3. The Regent's opening of Parliament is described in *Shelley Diary*, II, 85–86.
4. *Shelley Diary*, II, 85.
5. *Letters of George IV*, II, 298–99.
6. Melville, *Brighton*, 45–46.
7. *Croker Papers*, I, 137.
8. *Letters of George IV*, II, 298–99.
9. *The Jerningham Letters*, ed. Egerton Castle, 2 vols. (London, 1896), II, 157, 159.
10. *Examiner*, February 6, 1820.
11. *Croker Papers*, I, 143–44.

12. *Examiner,* February 6, 1820.
13. *Croker Papers,* I, 145.
14. *Ibid.*
15. *Ibid.,* I, 146–47.
16. *Letters of George IV,* II, 323–24.
17. *Examiner,* February 6, 1820.
18. This account of George III's funeral is drawn from the *Examiner,* February 20, 1820 and *Croker Papers,* I, 148.

·

Suggestions for Further Reading

*T*he source materials available to the researcher on England in the early nineteenth century are far too numerous to be listed individually here. Collections of letters, diaries and memoirs, journals, autobiographies, government records and personal papers, literary works and contemporary journalism exist in vast abundance, while the number of interpretative books and articles by historical specialists is very large and expanding rapidly. One scholar has estimated that some three thousand books and articles on the reign of George III have been published in the last fifteen years alone.

Some idea of the extent of this material can be gained from Lucy M. Brown and Ian R. Christie, *Bibliography of British History 1789–1851* (Oxford and New York: Oxford University Press, 1977), and an overview of recent trends in historical interpretation from Robert A. Smith, "Reinter-

.

preting the Reign of George III," in *Recent Views of British History*, ed. Richard Schlatter (New Brunswick, New Jersey: Rutgers University Press, 1983), pp. 197–253. Chapter eight of *The Oxford Illustrated History of Britain*, ed. Kenneth O. Morgan (Oxford and New York: Oxford University Press, 1984), written by Christopher Harvie and entitled "Revolution and the Rule of Law (1789–1851)," is a solid and up-to-date brief survey of the entire later Hanoverian and early Victorian era.

The following short list of books, which includes no contemporary sources, only secondary studies, is intended to provide a starting point for deeper reading and to supplement, where possible, the themes explored in the foregoing chapters. The titles have been chosen for their readability and availability to the general reader.

Ayling, Stanley. *George the Third.* London: Collins, 1972.

Briggs, Asa. *The Age of Improvement.* London: Longman, 1959, rev. 1979.

Brooke, John. *King George III.* London: Constable, 1972.

Brown, F. K. *Fathers of the Victorians.* Cambridge: Cambridge University Press, 1961.

Bryant, Arthur. *The Age of Elegance 1812–1822.* New York: Harper, 1950.

Burton, Elizabeth. *The Georgians at Home, 1714–1830.* London: Longman, 1967.

Cecil, David. *Melbourne.* London: Constable, 1939, 1954; rev. 1965.

Christie, I. R. *Wars and Revolutions: Britain 1760–1815.* Cambridge: Harvard University Press, 1982.

Cole, G.D.H., and R. Postgate. *The Common People 1746–1946.* 4th ed. London: Methuen, 1963.

Darvall, F. O. *Popular Disturbances and Public Order in Regency England.* Oxford: Oxford University Press, 1934.

Dinkel, John. *The Royal Pavilion, Brighton.* New York: The Vendome Press, 1983.

Emsley, Clive. *British Society and the French Wars, 1793–1815.* London: Macmillan, 1979.

George, M. Dorothy. *Hogarth to Cruikshank: Social Change in Graphic Satire.* London: Allen Lane, 1967.

————. *London Life in the Eighteenth Century.* London: K. Paul, Trench, Trubner, 1925; New York: Harper & Row, 1965.

Glover, Richard G. *Britain at Bay: Defence Against Bonaparte 1803–1814.* London: George Allen & Unwin, 1973.

Halévy, E. *History of the English People in the Nineteenth Century.* Vol. I: *England in 1815.* Vol. II: *The Liberal Awakening (1815–1830).* 6 vols. 2nd rev. ed. London: E. Benn, 1949–52.

Hay, D., P. Linebough and E. P. Thompson. *Albion's Fatal Tree: Crime and Society in Eighteenth-Century England.* London: Allen Lane, 1975; New York: Pantheon, 1975.

Hibbert, Christopher. *George IV.* Vol. I: *Prince of Wales 1762–1811.* London: Longman, 1972. Vol. II: *Regent and King 1811–1830.* London: Allen Lane, 1973.

Hilton, B. *Corn, Cash and Commerce.* Oxford: Oxford University Press, 1977.

Himmelfarb, Gertrude. *The Idea of Poverty: England in the Early Industrial Age.* New York: Knopf, 1983.

Jaeger, Muriel. *Before Victoria.* London: Chatto & Windus, 1956.

Jenkins, Elizabeth. *Lady Caroline Lamb.* London: Victor Gollancz, 1932.

Landes, D. *The Unbound Prometheus: Technological Change and Industrial Development in Western Europe from 1750 to the Present.* Cambridge: Cambridge University Press, 1969.

Longford, Elizabeth. *Wellington.* Vol. I: *The Years of the Sword.* Vol. II: *Pillar of State.* London: Weidenfeld & Nicolson, 1969, 1972.

Marchand, Leslie. *Byron: A Biography.* 2 vols. New York: Knopf, 1957.

Nicolson, Harold. *The Congress of Vienna: A Study in Allied Unity, 1812–1822.* New York: Harcourt, Brace, 1946.

Osborne, John W. *The Silent Revolution: The Industrial Revolution in England as a Source of Cultural Change.* New York: Scribner's, 1970.

Owen, J. B. *The Eighteenth Century, 1714–1815.* London: Nelson, 1974.

Peacock, Alfred J. *Bread or Blood: A Study of the Agrarian Riots in East Anglia in 1816.* London: Gollancz, 1965.

Plumb, J. H. *England in the Eighteenth Century.* London: Penguin, 1950.

―――――. *The First Four Georges.* London: Botsford, 1956.

Porter, R. *English Society in the Eighteenth Century.* London: Allen Lane, 1982.

Rudé, George. *Hanoverian London 1714–1808.* London: Secker & Warburg, 1971.

Stevenson, J. *Popular Disturbances in England 1700–1870.* London: Longmans, 1979.

Thomis, Malcolm I. *The Luddites: Machine Breaking in Regency England.* Newton Abbot, England: David & Charles, 1970.

Thompson, E. P. *The Making of the English Working Class.* London: Gollancz, 1963; New York: Pantheon, 1964.

Trevelyan, George Macaulay. *British History in the Nineteenth Century and After, 1782–1919.* New York: David McKay; London: Longman, 1922; new ed., 1937.

Walmsley, Robert. *Peterloo: The Case Reopened.* Manchester: Manchester University Press, 1969.

Watson, J. Steven. *The Reign of George III 1760–1815.* Oxford: Clarendon Press, 1960.

White, R. J. *The Age of George III.* London: Heinemann, 1968.

―――――. *Life in Regency England.* London: B. T. Botsford; New York: Putnam's, 1963.

―――――. *Waterloo to Peterloo.* London: Heinemann, 1957.

Williams, R. *Culture and Society, 1780–1850.* New York: Columbia University Press, 1958, 1966.

Woodward, E. L. *The Age of Reform, 1815–1870.* Oxford: Clarendon Press, 1938; second ed., 1962.

·

Index

About the Author

The London *Times Literary Supplement* has called Carolly Erickson "one of the most accomplished and successful historical biographers writing in English." As one of America's foremost young historians, Carolly Erickson, a Ph.D. in medieval history, has taught at Barnard College, Brooklyn College, Mills College, and California State University at Northridge. In 1970, she left teaching to write full time—and since then has written extensively for both scholarly and general audiences. Her Tudor biographies, *Bloody Mary, Great Harry, The First Elizabeth,* and *Mistress Anne,* have been popular commercial successes as well as having been widely and enthusiastically reviewed. *Our Tempestuous Day* is her eighth book. Carolly Erickson lives in Albany, California, and is currently at work on a new biography about Bonnie Prince Charlie.